Campaign Communication
and Political Marketing

By the same author

In English

Political Communication in a New Era
(Co-edited with Gadi Wolfsfeld), Routledge, London, 2003

Communication and Political Marketing
John Libbey, London, 1995

In French

La communication politique de la Présidentielle de 2007
L'Harmattan, Paris, 2009

Communication et marketing de l'homme politique
third edition, Litec/LexisNexis, Paris, 2007

Chronique de'un «non» annoncé: La communication politique et l'Europe
L'Harmattan, Paris, 2007

La communication politique française après le tournant de 2002
L'Harmattan, Paris, 2004

Média et malentendus, cinéma et communication politique
EDILIG, collection Médiathèque, Paris 1986

La censure cinématographique
Litec, now Litec/LexisNexis, Paris, 1982

De mai 68 aux films X, cinema politique et société
Dujarric, Paris, 1978

In Spanish

Marketing político y comunicación
second edition, Planeta/Paidos, Barcelona/Buenos Aires/Mexico, 2009

Campaign Communication and Political Marketing

Philippe J. Maarek

WILEY-BLACKWELL

A John Wiley & Sons, Ltd., Publication

This edition first published 2011
© 2011 Philippe J. Maarek

Blackwell Publishing was acquired by John Wiley & Sons in February 2007. Blackwell's publishing program
has been merged with Wiley's global Scientific, Technical, and Medical business to form Wiley-Blackwell.

Registered Office
John Wiley & Sons Ltd, The Atrium, Southern Gate, Chichester, West Sussex, PO19 8SQ, United Kingdom

Editorial Offices
350 Main Street, Malden, MA 02148-5020, USA
9600 Garsington Road, Oxford, OX4 2DQ, UK
The Atrium, Southern Gate, Chichester, West Sussex, PO19 8SQ, UK

For details of our global editorial offices, for customer services, and for information about how
to apply for permission to reuse the copyright material in this book please see our website at
www.wiley.com/wiley-blackwell.

The right of Philippe J. Maarek to be identified as the author of this work has been asserted in accordance
with the UK Copyright, Designs and Patents Act 1988.

Library of Congress Cataloging-in-Publication Data

Maarek, Philippe J.
  Campaign communication and political marketing / Philippe J. Maarek.
    p.   cm.
  Includes bibliographical references and index.
  ISBN 978-1-4443-3234-6 (hardback) – ISBN 978-1-4443-3235-3 (paperback)
1. Political campaigns – United States.   2. Communication in politics – United States.
3. Marketing – Political aspects.   4. United States – Politics and government.   I. Title.
  JK2281.M33 2011
  324.7′30973–dc22

                                             2011001825

A catalogue record for this book is available from the British Library.

This book is published in the following electronic formats: ePDFs 9781444340686; ePub 9781444340693

Set in 10.5/13pt Minion by SPi Publisher Services, Pondicherry, India
Printed in Malaysia by Ho Printing (M) Sdn Bhd

1   2011

To my wife and children,
so patient when I leave them for the computer keyboard

To my mother,
an example of work and dedication

And in memory of my father,
my smiling hero, my role model

Contents

Detailed contents   ix
List of Figures   xv
List of Tables   xvi

Introduction   1

Part I   The rise of modern political communication   5

1   Birth and rise of political marketing in the United States   7

Part II   The foundations of modern political marketing   31

2   Political marketing: a global approach   33

3   The means of analysis and information   72

Part III   Political marketing tools   91

4   The traditional tools   93

5   Audiovisual tools   113

6   Direct marketing methods   140

7   The growing importance of the Internet   158

Part IV   The actual running of election campaigns   177

8   Structure and organization of the campaign   179

9   The particularities of local campaigns   220

Conclusion: how to use this book ...   232

Appendix 1: Memorandum of Understanding between the Bush
and Kerry Campaigns for the 2004 Televised Debates (extract)   ˙ 237

Appendix 2: Internet "Final Rules" decided by the Federal Elections
Commission, March 27, 2006   244

Bibliography   248
Index   256

Detailed contents

List of Figures   xv
List of Tables   xvi

Introduction   1

Part I   The rise of modern political communication   5

1   Birth and rise of political marketing in the United States   7
  1.1   The grounds for development of modern political marketing
     in the United States   7
    1.1.1   The particular nature of the electoral system   8
    1.1.2   The tradition of elections for all public offices   9
    1.1.3   The early development of modern media
       in the United States   10
  1.2   The main stages in the evolution of political marketing
     in the United States   11
    1.2.1   Infancy: 1952–1960   11
       1.2.1.1   1952: Instant success for Eisenhower and Nixon   11
       1.2.1.2   1956: triumph of the political commercial   13
       1.2.1.3   1960, or the birth of the decisive debate   13
    1.2.2   Adolescence: 1964–1976   14
       1.2.2.1   1964: the first stumbling block: the "Daisy spot"   14
       1.2.2.2   1968, or the invention of the close-up   15
       1.2.2.3   1972: alliance of text and image   16
       1.2.2.4   1976: televised political communication
         comes of age   16
    1.2.3   Adulthood: political communication and campaigning
       in the United States since the 1980s   17

1.2.3.1   A recurrent simplification of campaign themes   17

1.2.3.2   Television domination and its new "trends"   18

1.2.3.3   Rising campaign costs and the increased need
          for fundraising   20

1.2.3.4   Legal loopholes and increasing aggressiveness
          of campaigns   21

1.2.3.5   Early integration of the Internet and new media
          in campaigns   25

1.2.3.6   The recent increase of personalization of campaigns:
          "storytelling" in modern campaigns   26

Part II   The foundations of modern political marketing   **31**

2   Political marketing: a global approach   33
    2.1   The foundations of political marketing   33
          2.1.1   The originality of political marketing   33
                  2.1.1.1   From commercial marketing to political
                            marketing   33
                  2.1.1.2   Political marketing, advertising, propaganda,
                            information and communication   35
          2.1.2   General rules of conduct in political marketing 37
                  2.1.2.1   Coherence   37
                  2.1.2.2   Systematic re-examination of earlier campaigns 37
                  2.1.2.3   Minimal differentiation   38
                  2.1.2.4   Maximum security   38
    2.2   Main stages of the political marketing process   39
          2.2.1   Planning a campaign strategy   40
                  2.2.1.1   The basis of the strategy   40
                  2.2.1.2   Determining the strategy   42
          2.2.2   Devising tactics and implementing them:
                  "the campaign plan"   55
                  2.2.2.1   Charting the campaign timetable   55
                  2.2.2.2   The media plan   59
3   The means of analysis and information   72
    3.1   The general operative framework for informational
          and analytical tools   73
          3.1.1   The operational chronology of informational
                  and analytical tools   73
          3.1.2   The kind of information expected   74
                  3.1.2.1   Aid in establishing targets   75
                  3.1.2.2   Aid in setting objectives   75
    3.2   The different types of informational and analytical tools 76
          3.2.1   Past election results   76
          3.2.2   Opinion polls   77

3.2.2.1	The different types of surveys	78
3.2.2.2	Problems caused by opinion surveys	79
3.2.2.3	Consequences of the existence and use of opinion surveys	84
3.2.3	Other types of information and analysis tools	87

Part III   Political marketing tools   **91**

4   The traditional tools   93
  4.1   Interactive tools   93
    4.1.1   Actual direct contacts with the voters   94
      4.1.1.1   Special relationships with main contributors   94
      4.1.1.2   Canvassing, grassroots campaigning and other forms of direct contact with communication recipients   94
    4.1.2   Substitutes for direct contacts   96
      4.1.2.1   Direct contact substitutes with a narrow target   96
      4.1.2.2   Substitutes for direct contacts with a wide target   100
  4.2   Unidirectional tools   101
    4.2.1   The press and printed matter   101
      4.2.1.1   The non-partisan press   101
      4.2.1.2   The partisan press and printed matter   104
    4.2.2   Posters and billboard advertising   107
      4.2.2.1   Characteristics of billboard advertising   107
      4.2.2.2   Different kinds of poster advertising   108
    4.2.3   Miscellaneous advertising accessories   110

5   Audiovisual tools   113
  5.1   The complexity of practice of the audiovisual means by political communication   114
    5.1.1   The difficulties of using audiovisual means   114
      5.1.1.1   Delayed effects of audiovisual media   115
      5.1.1.2   Problems generated by the non-verbal element of audiovisual communication   116
    5.1.2   Media training arising from the difficulties of using the audiovisual media   118
      5.1.2.1   Formal training   119
      5.1.2.2   Training in substance   122
  5.2   Principal applications of audiovisual means to political communication   123
    5.2.1   The problem of access to audiovisual media   124
    5.2.2   Televised debates   125
      5.2.2.1   Negotiating the technical conditions of televised debates   125

	5.2.2.2	Broadcast control	127
5.2.3	Televised newscasts		128
	5.2.3.1	Intervention in the form of newscast participation	128
	5.2.3.2	Difficulty of steering issues	129
5.2.4	Political commercials		130
	5.2.4.1	Advantages of political commercials	130
	5.2.4.2	The dangers of political commercials	131
5.2.5	Non-directly political television programs		132
	5.2.5.1	Participation in indirect political broadcasts	133
	5.2.5.2	Audiovisual exhibition representing the "private life" of politicians	133
	5.2.5.3	Participation in pure entertainment programs	134

6   Direct marketing methods   140

6.1   Direct marketing rediscovers traditional media   141

    6.1.1   Direct mail, or mailings: re-establishing a direct link   141

        6.1.1.1   Direct marketing: a well-suited tool
                  for political communication   142

        6.1.1.2   The different uses of direct mail   144

        6.1.1.3   The disadvantages of direct mail   145

    6.1.2   Direct marketing by telephone, or phone marketing:
            re-discovering bidirectionality   148

        6.1.2.1   The advantages of phone marketing   148

        6.1.2.2   The drawbacks of phone marketing   149

6.2   The use of audiovisual media for direct marketing   152

    6.2.1   Direct marketing by television or radio   152

    6.2.2   Videos   153

        6.2.2.1   Circulating videos inside campaign
                  organizations or political parties   153

        6.2.2.2   Videos intended for election meetings and rallies   154

7   The growing importance of the Internet   158

7.1   The multiple aspects of the Internet   159

    7.1.1   Web 1.0: improved targeting and versatility   161

        7.1.1.1   Consulting a web site   161

        7.1.1.2   Posting messages   162

        7.1.1.3   Interactivity among recipients   162

    7.1.2   Web 2.0: from interactivity to "social" media   162

        7.1.2.1   Becoming a provider of online information   162

        7.1.2.2   From online video sharing to becoming
                  a web broadcaster   163

    7.1.3   The Internet as a virtual conduit for other media   164

7.2   The main kinds of Internet use for political communication   165

7.2.1 Institutional uses of the Internet: from the official
party web site to political *spam* 165
7.2.2 Using the Internet during election campaigns 166
7.2.2.1 Campaign web sites 166
7.2.2.2 Other kinds of Internet use for a campaign
by the candidates 168
7.2.3 Lobbies and "marginal" political parties
on the Internet 170

Part IV The actual running of election campaigns 177

8 Structure and organization of the campaign 179
8.1 The campaign set up 181
8.1.1 The appointment of the two key position holders 181
8.1.1.1 The campaign manager 182
8.1.1.2 The field co-ordinator 183
8.1.2 Choosing the management style 184
8.1.2.1 Horizontal task division 184
8.1.2.2 Vertical task division 184
8.2 Establishing campaign headquarters 187
8.2.1 The location of campaign organization premises 187
8.2.1.1 The location of central headquarters 188
8.2.1.2 Decentralized campaign premises 188
8.2.2 Equipment 189
8.3 The problem of finance 190
8.3.1 The cost and financing of political campaigning 190
8.3.2 Fundraising 191
8.3.3 Financial management 192
8.3.3.1 "Smoothing" the income 192
8.3.3.2 Keeping expenses under control 193
8.3.3.3 Complying with the law 195
8.4 The staff 196
8.4.1 The central campaign organization staff 197
8.4.1.1 Staff directly involved in communication activities 197
8.4.1.2 Personnel assigned to routine tasks 203
8.4.2 Outside consultants 208
8.4.2.1 The utility of outside consultants 208
8.4.2.2 The drawbacks of working with
outside consultants 210
8.4.3 The field organization 211
8.4.3.1 Field personnel and their role in political
communication 212
8.4.3.2 Underutilization of field personnel in current
political marketing 213

9   The particularities of local campaigns   220
    9.1   The coexistence of local and national campaigns   220
          9.1.1   Introducing a national dimension in local campaigns   221
                  9.1.1.1   Increasing preeminence of the national dimension
                            in local elections   221
                  9.1.1.2   Co-ordinating the two kinds of campaigns   222
          9.1.2   The need to maintain a local dimension   224
                  9.1.2.1   Precinct analysis: taking into account the
                            particularities of the constituency in relation
                            to the national context of the election   225
                  9.1.2.2   Specific analytical tools for local elections   226
    9.2   The preferred communication means of local campaigns   227
          9.2.1   Direct contact with the local population: personal
                  campaigning   227
                  9.2.1.1   Canvassing   227
                  9.2.1.2   The distribution of locally-targeted leaflets
                            and other printed material   229
                  9.2.1.3   Office hours   229
          9.2.2   Mediated contact with the local population   229

Conclusion: how to use this book ...   232

Appendix 1: Memorandum of Understanding between the Bush
and Kerry Campaigns for the 2004 Televised Debates (extract)   237
    Memorandum of understanding   237
      5.   Rules Applicable to All Debates   237
      6.   Additional Rules Applicable to September 30 and
           October 13 Debates   239
      9.   Staging   240

Appendix 2: Internet "Final Rules" decided by the Federal
    Elections Commission, March 27, 2006   244
    Internet Final Rules   244
    Background   244
    Final Rules   245

Bibliography   248
Index   256

Figures

Figure 2.1   Commercial marketing, symbolic value and practical value   34
Figure 2.2   Commercial and political marketing: two parallel strategies   36
Figure 2.3   The main steps of the political marketing process   39
Figure 2.4   The role of opinion relays in the communication process   43
Figure 2.5   Segmenting the population   44
Figure 2.6   Targeting the communication recipient by political affinity   46
Figure 2.7   The forces hindering the choice of campaign themes   52
Figure 2.8   The different stages of a political communication campaign   56
Figure 2.9   Coding and decoding: from candidate to recipient   60
Figure 2.10   Feedback and the communication process   61
Figure 3.1   The different operative stages of informational
              and analytical tools   74
Figure 3.2   Diversion of political communication by opinion surveys   86
Figure 4.1   Dual media publicity (or second degree political
              communication)   100
Figure 6.1   The traditional fundraising circuit   147
Figure 6.2   The "diversion" of the fundraising circuit caused
              by direct mail   147
Figure 6.3   Political opinions and responsiveness to direct marketing   156
Figure 7.1   The exponential growth in the number of Internet websites   159
Figure 7.2   The Internet: a versatile medium   160
Figure 8.1   Horizontal task division in a campaign organization   185
Figure 8.2   Vertical task division in a campaign organization   186
Figure 8.3   Combined division of tasks in a campaign organization   187
Figure 8.4   The media department of a campaign organization   200

Tables

Table 1.1 Presidential debates in the United States   19
Table 1.2 Geographical penetration of the Internet, 2000–2008   24
Table 2.1 The distribution of media according to target types   63
Table 2.2 The two criteria of a communication's complexity
           and its intended speed   64

Introduction

The worlds of politics and the media seem, in recent years, to be tangled in an increasingly complex relationship. Politicians are taken to task for indulging themselves in media exposure of their personal life in an ultimate effort to please some of their communication advisors, with an eye solely on their personal interests to serve a new kind of modernized populism. Italian Prime Minister and media mogul Silvio Berlusconi epitomizes such behavior and Barack Obama's naked torso in the Hawaiian waves, or Nicolas Sarkozy's public exposure of his tumultuous private life, seem normal today while they would have looked improper only a few decades ago. As for the media, dominated as it is in our society by almighty television, it now appears unwieldy in the very manner it appropriates politics itself, by inflicting on it an involuntary and uncontrolled input. Finally, the influence of the new uses of "new media," particularly the Internet, now further complicates political communication.

This phenomenon is unmistakable as much as from within as from without: confronted with unverified information (from Romania to Iraq, as well as in our own inner cities), or an exacerbated political show, the average citizen confusedly understands that media and politics often make for strange bedfellows that can harm each other. Certainly, the phenomenon is aggravated by contemporary political leaders, as well as those who covet their office, who for instance agree to be the target of insults on live talk shows that resemble more closely modern circus performances than televised political debates.

This explains the numerous critiques directed at modern political communication, held to be responsible for the banalization of modern political discourse, the escalation of campaign costs, and so on. "Due to political marketing, ideas are no

Campaign Communication and Political Marketing, First Edition. Philippe J. Maarek.
© 2011 Philippe J. Maarek. Published 2011 by Blackwell Publishing Ltd.

longer enough to get you elected", is something one hears all too often, in all the possible meanings of this phrase.

Paradoxically, to offset this criticism, political marketing increased its hold over politicians, and a change in modes of political communication became inevitable. The rapid development of mass media and the growth of so-called "new media" in contemporary society have relegated to the garbage can "classic" means of communication – those, in any case, which have not been backed by more up-to-date marketing strategies. Modern political communication can no longer continue, as in the past, to rely only on the literary quality of political discourse and the rhetorical competence of its orators when the growth of new electronic transnational media has provoked a now unavoidable "globalization" of mediatized political information to the public.

We can date the first genuine manifestation of modern political marketing as an organized overall strategy back to 1952, with the United States presidential campaign of Dwight D. Eisenhower. It also marked the appearance of the first of innumerable political anecdotes which would contribute gradually to the devaluation of politicians, when the latter allow themselves to be guided by communication advisors: the former Supreme Commander of NATO was instructed never to lower his head in front of TV cameras or photographers, so as to reveal as little as possible of his bald head.

Of course, political communication is not an invention of the twentieth century. As far back as Antiquity, for example, kings and princes knew how to exploit their reputation as warriors as a preliminary scare tactic aimed at potential adversaries, and as a device to raise taxes. And in the way he ritualized all his public (and even private) functions at the court of Versailles, literally "staging" every aspect, Louis XIV of France can be said to have been the first modern promoter of the notion of the politician's image – an idea already found in Machiavelli's *The Prince*, in which the Italian political theorist openly supported the idea that appearance was more important than substance for a politician.

But the notion of political communication, and, *a fortiori*, political marketing, are clearly products of the second half of the twentieth century. Of course, politicians were often making unconscious use of political communication methods, when, for example, they would have political notices posted around their districts. But, in fact, political communication was previously limited to basic advertising, that is using communication means in a unidirectional and unilateral way, without following any real communications strategy.

The introduction of political marketing came with the elaboration of a policy of political communication, so to speak: a global strategy of design, rationalization and conveyance of modern political communication. To devise and implement such a strategy of political marketing is necessarily a complex process, the outcome of a more global effort involving all the factors of the politician's political communication so as to avoid any conflicts among the various modes of action employed.

Politicians, especially non-American politicians, have often harbored a kind of shame – or mistrust – as regards the use of political marketing. It is often reduced to a basic pretense of "political campaigning," where the candidate professes to learn and practice modern means of communication only in order to enhance his or her action. In fact, this book will show that political campaigning extends well beyond what is usually claimed, which justifies our use of the term "political marketing."

This book will deal mainly with communication strategies of the individual political figure, encompassing both the campaign for public office and the public relations campaign designed to improve that person's public image. Thus, it does not deal with the public relations efforts of governments or public institutions, which are of a very different nature, both in terms of their form and content:

- As regards content, the aim is to get a politician elected, or to improve his or her reputation, and not to support a public service action, anchored in the global nature and the lifespan of a national government.
- As regards form, the sense of urgency surrounding the marketing of a politician is also quite different. If the results of a public relations campaign are negative, a politician may remain in the shadows, not win a seat, or lose it. Campaigning for election is a "winner takes all" process. There is no prize for second place. A poor marketing campaign for a government policy will not have such immediate or drastic consequences: the state will remain as such, and a cabinet reshuffle may even be avoided; one of the state's many activities will only have missed its target. This naturally explains why this book does not deal with all that relates to the communications efforts of a politician while in office apart from his or her specific efforts to maintain his or her personal image in order to be reelected in the future.

This volume is divided in four parts. The first part consists of a single chapter providing a brief overview of the rise of modern political marketing in the United States, its country of birth and early development, and, so to speak, its greatest level of achievement. The second part, divided into two chapters, deals with the foundations of political marketing: its general functional framework and the survey and study methods that help build it. The third part analyzes the main tools of political marketing in four chapters: classic instruments, audiovisual methods of communication, methods known as direct marketing tools, and the more recent new media, namely the Internet. The two chapters of the fourth and final part outline the particular aspects of the actual running of election campaigns as such, be they problems of infrastructure or the specific difficulties of local elections, as distinguished from national ones.

Part I

The rise of modern political communication

1

Birth and rise of political marketing in the United States

There can be no doubt that the genesis of modern political marketing is entirely rooted in the history of political communication in the United States. Owing, mainly, to the early development of mass media and later the Internet, the United States was the first country to experiment with modern political communication techniques, and then apply them systematically. These methods have since been imitated throughout the entire world, western democracies being the first to adopt them, as they are quick to share new improvements in media systems.[1]

Though the intent of this book is by no means to trace the history of political marketing across the globe, we will nevertheless devote this preliminary chapter to a brief overview of its development in the United States, where it all began.

US domination of modern political marketing was quickly established. Within less than a decade, between the presidential elections of 1952 and 1960, it became an incontrovertible practice, the recent years confirming its significant expansion. But this rapid growth owes nothing to chance. We will first demonstrate that it was fostered by several characteristics inherent to the political information system in the United States before examining the main growth stages of modern American political marketing from infancy (1952/1960), through the formative years (1964/76), to today's relative "maturity."

1.1 The grounds for development of modern political marketing in the United States

Three main factors explain the early development of political marketing in the US: its electoral system, its tradition of "political public relations," and the rapid expansion of modern media.

Campaign Communication and Political Marketing, First Edition. Philippe J. Maarek.
© 2011 Philippe J. Maarek. Published 2011 by Blackwell Publishing Ltd.

1.1.1   The particular nature of the electoral system

One of the main causes of the fast growth of political marketing in the United States certainly has to do with the system of primaries in the early stages of presidential election campaigns.

The two major political parties that have shared the favors of American voters since the nineteenth century choose their candidates during their party conventions, the delegates of which are not selected solely by regular party supporters (few in number, except in election years). There are two ways of appointing delegates, depending on the rules that apply in a given state:

- During caucuses, meetings of the local political party members or sympathizers. In the past, these gatherings received little media attention, since they were a relatively small-scale event.
- During the primaries, in existence in some states since 1903, which are virtually early elections. Traditionally, the first primary takes place in mid-February in the small New England state of New Hampshire, thus giving its inhabitants a vastly disproportionate influence in the country's political agenda. Some of these primaries, including the one in New Hampshire, are "open," meaning that any registered voter may vote for the candidate of his choice, despite the voter's stated party preference, while in the other "closed" primaries, ballots must be cast only within the voters' registered political preference.[2]

By its very nature, the primaries system encourages the consumption of immense amounts of political information:

- First, on a quantitative level, given that the primaries system duplicates each electoral campaign, the primaries campaign sometimes lasts longer than the actual campaign for the seat. For instance, the presidential primaries run from January to June every four years, whereas the actual campaign starts only mid-July, after the appointment of the candidates by their party convention, and runs until the first Tuesday in November.
- Second, on a qualitative level, since to be designated as party candidate, politicians must not only obtain the endorsement of a few followers, but must undertake a full-scale campaign among their party's sympathizers to persuade them to tick their name on the primary ballot, rather than another member of their own party, with whom they are bound to share many of the same opinions. This kind of campaign therefore paradoxically requires a much greater public relations and political communication effort from a qualitative standpoint than the actual campaign to come: it is considerably more difficult to convince voters to choose one candidate over another who expresses similar political ideas than it is to convince them not to vote for a politician from an opposition party, in which case arguments can easily be based on ideological differences.

The influence of the mix of "open" and "closed" primaries carries some weight, particularly when no party candidate clearly emerges from the start, and may also endanger the candidate more or less tacitly endorsed by party officials. For instance, in 1992, initially an obscure outsider alongside his seasoned Democratic opponents, Bill Clinton slowly rose above them through the primaries trail to become the Democratic candidate.[3] Similarly, among the Republicans, John McCain's first attempt to run for president in 2000 was initially aided by some "open" primaries, in which he outbalanced a more traditionally positioned George W. Bush: more than one Democrat sympathizer was then able to cast his vote for him![4]

This basic fact alone explains the over-consumption of political information in the United States, and also the speed with which new political marketing methods are adopted. This over-consumption has continued to rise from year to year due to the increasing number of primary elections throughout the country. During the 1970s, several states decided to ingratiate themselves with the media coverage that goes with holding a primary election, rather than to hold a simple caucus. In 1976 only 29 states held primaries and/or caucuses, whereas 40 were held in 1992 and now 63 in 2008 including 38 primaries! Today, the primaries system had been implemented in most states, with very few exceptions.[5] The most influential of the caucuses takes place in Iowa, mainly because it occurs traditionally at the beginning at the electoral year, before the New Hampshire primary, and also because not only regular activists, but also sympathizers, may take part in it.[6]

Lastly, it must be noted that the focus on primaries and caucuses has annoyed many states which are now trying to dispute the chronological precedence of the Iowa Caucus and the New Hampshire Primary. To continue to be first, for instance, the New Hampshire primaries had to be moved forward to January 27 in 2004 and even to January 8 in 2008! The rush to organize primaries – or caucuses – as early as possible certainly changes the balance of the contest: with such an accelerated process, the gradual emergence of "outsiders" over several months has become less and less easy to achieve.

1.1.2   The tradition of elections for all public offices

As soon as the United States came into existence, when it broke away from British colonial rule, it became routine to hold elections for most major public offices: from the local sheriff, mayor or judge, to the president. Although a relatively new country, the United States was forced relatively early on to practice what might be called political communication: the obligation to use a minimum of public relations methods applied to politics in order to be chosen for any elected office. A strong executive branch, with the president elected by universal suffrage (although a two-step process), enhanced this tendency, because it created both a bond and an obligation to campaign.

Therefore, it is not surprising that, in the nineteenth century, as soon as railroad tracks were laid across the country, potential presidents got on board trains to meet their voters. Who does not recall Abraham Lincoln's famous speeches delivered from the rear platform of the campaign train, scenes reconstructed in John Ford's famous movie *Young Mister Lincoln*?

By the same token, the use of radio for political communication increased rapidly in the twentieth century. The first regular radio stations were founded in 1920, and as early as 1924, John W. Davis and Calvin Coolidge bought airtime in order to broadcast their speeches. The first political spots as we know them today appeared as early as 1928, sponsored by the Republican Party, while Democrat Governor and Senator Huey Long made extensive use of radio speeches as early as 1924.[7] President Roosevelt's well-known radio "Fireside Chats" were a natural part of this tradition of political PR: since he was directly elected by the citizens, he felt he owed them regular accounts of his acts, reaching an audience of more than 60 million listeners in the 1940s. But he was also concerned with measuring their efficiency and Roosevelt himself was the first president to commission public opinion polls on a regular basis to assess the evolution of his popularity.

This tradition of widespread political communication formed a very fertile ground for the development of modern political marketing in the United States. The over-consumption of political information in there is in fact partly a result of the increase in the number of primaries for local elections: already in 1917, primaries had been held for either local or national elections in all the states of the union but four. Nowadays, in many states, primaries are organized for the election of state governors and mayors of major cities, New York City being a case in point. These factors further increase opportunities for political marketing to develop: in 2010 the American Political Consultants Association had no fewer than 1,331 members, not counting those that were unaffiliated.[8]

1.1.3   The early development of modern media in the United States

The third element that fostered the expansion of modern political marketing was the rapid growth of modern media in the United States with regard to all the other democratic countries. In 1952, there was already a television set in nearly 40% of American homes. This figure rose to 60% in the northeastern states. In France, by comparison, the figure of half a million sets was not reached until 1957 (about 4%).

A related factor is the large degree of freedom in commercial advertising in all American media, a freedom that political marketing has always exploited to its advantage. This explains why the growth of American political marketing has always paralleled the evolution of the broadcast media, and particularly its use of commercial spots. Most other countries in the world, including the major democracies, heavily regulate political advertising, or even forbid it, which in turn has delayed the political use of audiovisual methods.

The same phenomenon occurred in the 1990s with the fast growth of Internet use in the United States, way before its expansion around the world. The Internet burst into the US presidential campaign in 1996 and its share of political communication has never ceased to grow.

1.2   The main stages in the evolution of political marketing in the United States

We will review these stages with special emphasis on the successive presidential elections. Of course, political marketing is not limited to them, as we have already mentioned, and more than one innovation first took place in local elections in one state or another. But the fact is that only when new methods of political communication are used during presidential elections, with their incomparable media visibility, do they really become a permanent addition to the tools of the trade.

We will also take a keener look at the use of audiovisual media, namely television, by the political parties, because these media are the most representative tools of modern American political marketing. Naturally, the evolution of political marketing in the United States is not limited to audiovisual media. For instance, direct marketing by mail was also used for the first time in the United States as early as 1952, when a mailing campaign was organized in order to help choose which issues Eisenhower's campaign should focus on. When appropriate, we shall therefore also mention other innovations in political marketing in the United States, with a particular emphasis on the Internet in recent years.

1.2.1   Infancy: 1952–1960

1.2.1.1   1952: Instant success for Eisenhower and Nixon
The 1952 presidential election marks the start of modern political marketing in the United States. For the first time, the two main parties earmarked a special budget for political communication. To support General Eisenhower's candidacy, the Republicans went so far as to enlist the services of the public relations firm BBDO (Batten, Barton, Durstin, and Osborne). They also hired one of the pioneers of audiovisual commercial marketing, Thomas Rosser Reeves Jr., at the time an employee of the Ted Bates Agency.

Access to television broadcasting at the time meant that politicians had to "buy back" television shows: United States media regulations allow politicians to preempt television time on any network, at any moment, the sole obligation being adequate financial compensation for the producers of the show which had been scheduled to be broadcast.

Both parties put together several long television broadcasts during which their candidates either addressed voters at length, or debated with other politicians who more or less cleverly played up the candidate's image. But Reeves' influence on the Republican campaign was essential: at his request, around 30 commercials were designed, identical in style to ones for consumer goods, a fact that at the time spurred more than one jab at Eisenhower as a pure product of merchandising. These short, twenty-second tailor-made spots, entitled *Eisenhower answers America*, showed one or two ordinary citizens asking the General a question, of course carefully prepared beforehand by the future president's advisor, showing him at his best, often answered by humorously sidestepping the question. These spots were aired among the usual group of commercials, before or in the midst of the most popular television programs, which thus allowed a much broader target to be reached than the far fewer number of viewers interested in political newscasts and programs.[9] In this way, according to Reeves, the candidates could benefit, at no extra expense, from the efforts made by the television networks to increase their audience. Also for the first time, Reeves directly influenced the substance of political discourse, imposing on "Ike" a simplification of his message and a change in its very substance.

As to simplification, while working for Ted Bates, Reeves had been one of the first to promote the "Unique Selling Proposition" (USP) for consumer products. Transferring this method to the presidential campaign, he requested that Eisenhower never develop more than one category of arguments in any given speech, press conference or television appearance.

And as to changes in substance, for the first time, several public opinion polls were commissioned to decide on the issues that would be developed in the spots. One poll, to which we will return later, even tried to correlate differences in voter behavior with geographical factors (this was another first, since it was done through direct mail).

Eisenhower was also required to change his very physical appearance, with the idea that he should try to conceal his age. He was also asked to use only notes for his speeches, and not the fully written texts that had been drawn up for him that he would simply read in front of the cameras.

While the Republican Party's use of modern marketing was right on target from the start, the Democratic candidate, Adlai Stevenson, was hindered by a series of errors in judgment and spells of bad luck, which meant that his television campaign broadcasts were confined to night-owls. His advisors thought that quantity was preferable over quality and calculated that, rather than investing in a limited number of (more expensive) television shows on prime time, it was better to count on regularity and quantity: they booked half-hour shows twice a week, broadcast between half past ten and eleven in the evening. Bad luck came into play when Stevenson's excellent acceptance speech during the Democratic Convention, broadcast live by the major networks, was only watched by the same late-night audience. Prior to his speech, the whole first part of the program was devoted to the state-by-state vote of all the Democratic delegates, all of whom took their time, in order to remain longer on their constituency's television screens!

The presidential elections of 1952 will also go down in the history of modern political communication as the first time when … animals were used. Vice-presidential candidate Richard Nixon was publicly accused of having received a large quantity and variety of gifts while holding elected office. He appeared on television and gave the now famous address in which, "looking the viewers in the eye," he admitted having once, but only once, accepted a gift: a puppy that his 6-year-old daughter had immediately loved and christened "Checkers," and that, "regardless of what they say about it, we are going to keep it." The so-called "Checkers Speech" reached nearly 50% of the television sets then in American homes, thereby paving the way to the vice-presidency for Nixon.

1.2.1.2   1956: triumph of the political commercial

On the basis of the experience gained in the previous campaign, the communication consultants of the two main parties decided to abandon the practice of half-hour television broadcasts for the presidential campaign of 1956. Instead, they made massive use of short advertising spots, strategically broadcast as close as possible to the most popular television shows as previously advocated by Reeves.

That year, 1956, was also the year of the first so-called negative commercials. Just as in ordinary commercial advertising practices, the Democrats' marketing consultants (Norman, Craig, and Kummel) suggested presenting the opponent (Eisenhower, who was running for a second term) in a negative light. Their technique was elementary: to use spots from Eisenhower's 1952 television campaign. Whenever the General made specific promises, they simply added a voice-over that whispered "How's that, General?" before demonstrating that he had not kept his promise during his term. This negative campaign is still known today under this very name: "How's that, General?"

1.2.1.3   1960, or the birth of the decisive debate

The campaign that led John Fitzgerald Kennedy to the presidency is a model one. From the start, Kennedy had the insight to enlist the help of two brilliant public relations consultants, Pierre Salinger, who managed relations with the printed press, and Leonard Reinsch, who took care of television. It seems that Kennedy himself was the first major political figure willing to undergo intensive media training to learn how to act in front of the television cameras and this was a considerable asset during the famous televised debates with Richard Nixon.[10]

Because of these debates, 1960 is generally considered as the birth of modern political communication. At the time, a very narrow difference in voter intentions separated the candidates. Nixon agreed to the idea of holding a series of four televised debates with Kennedy, thinking that he would easily come out victorious, since he was much more experienced than his opponent (although his consultants had advised him that Kennedy, less well-known, probably stood to gain more).[11]

In fact, Nixon performed poorly in the first debate. He did not stand up to the comparison with his younger adversary: the latter's ease was obvious to the viewers. In truth, it was not Richard Nixon's luckiest day: he was suffering from a knee inflammation, had a fever, and was physically worn down, which was quite perceptible on the screen, in contrast to the young and sun-tanned Kennedy. Nixon's make-up was also deficient, making the vice-president look as if he had neglected to shave and the sharper lenses of the new cameras on the set were not to his advantage on that point. To add to his uneasiness, the studio was apparently too warm for a man who was already running a temperature, and Nixon was caught perspiring and wiping his forehead, quite a demeaning image for the audience.[12]

Part of his uneasiness also derived from an error in judgment: believing that the audience would increase from one debate to the next, he had agreed to dedicate the first one to topics he was least fond of, keeping his favorite, foreign policy, for the last broadcast. But he was quite mistaken. It was estimated that about 70 to 75 million people watched the first debate, a figure that was never to be matched: the audience grew smaller and smaller, most of the citizens being satisfied with their first impression for the duration of the campaign.

Since Nixon missed the presidency by fewer than 100,000 votes, a ridiculously narrow margin on the scale of the United States, the first debate has generally been considered the reason for his defeat. Even if the real influence of this debate was never really assessed, it is likely to have contributed in part the minimal difference in scores between the two leaders.

That explains why the televised debate between the main candidates on the eve of election day has taken on a mythical value in the eyes of political PR specialists as well as in those of political leaders throughout the world. Since the Nixon-Kennedy debate, this televised debate has been considered the most important stage of the electoral campaign in most of the world's democracies.

One must finally note that one innovation of the 1960 Kennedy campaign in was the production of the first political commercials intended for ethnic minorities of his country, one of these being the Hispanics.

The 1960 presidential campaign thus marks the end of the infancy of modern political marketing in the United States. In 1948, Harry Truman was still proud of having been in direct contact with 15 to 20 million voters in his presidential campaign, having attended some 356 public meetings, and having traveled 31,000 miles and shaken 500,000 hands within three months. His campaign is the last one that did not rely on modern political marketing. In the eight years, between 1952 and 1960, political PR had discovered television and had invented its two main tools : the political commercial and the decisive debate.

1.2.2   Adolescence: 1964–1976

In these years American political marketing experienced its period of adolescence, a time in which it explored the full range of techniques at its disposal, but also their limitations.

1.2.2.1   1964: the first stumbling block: the "Daisy Spot"

In the the presidential election that year, Lyndon B. Johnson, who had stepped into the presidency after Kennedy's assassination, stood against Senator Barry Goldwater, a very conservative Republican. At a time when the United States was becoming entrenched in Vietnam and the Cold War was at its height, Goldwater made it clear that he was in favor of the systematic use of tactical nuclear weapons whenever the military thought it wise.

Advertising specialist Tony Schwartz, hired to help Johnson's public relations team, designed a very elaborate television spot which became famous overnight, known as the *Daisy Spot*. It showed a little girl peacefully plucking the petals from a daisy, counting from one to nine. Just as she reaches the number ten, we see a close-up of her eye, and hear a booming voice through a loudspeaker. The voice now counts down: "Ten, nine, eight, seven ..." At the end of the countdown, we hear, and see, the reflection of an atomic explosion in the little girl's eye, who naturally seems terrified, and we hear a voice-over saying: "These are the stakes – to make a world in which all God's children can live ... or to go into the dark. We must love each other or we must die." This is followed by: "Vote for President Johnson on November 3rd. The stakes are too high for you to stay home."

The spot was only broadcast once, on September 7, just before the famous CBS prime time show *Monday Night at the Movies*, and immediately gave rise to so many phone calls that the White House switchboard was jammed. The Republicans, starting with Goldwater himself, complained that Johnson had exceeded the limits of the "normal" negative spot. The *Daisy Spot* was never broadcast again. The Democrats claimed that it would not be shown anymore, realizing, in fact, that they overstepped the boundaries of fair play. But they had also achieved their goal: the image of Barry Goldwater with his finger on the button was once and for all instilled in the American public, starting with the some 50 million viewers who had seen the *Daisy Spot* (press commentaries of course also conveyed the idea to many more). Goldwater was never to recover.

Unlike the 1960 campaign, the 1964 presidential election did not resume the practice of the decisive televised debate between the two candidates. Johnson thought, probably rightfully so, that he stood more to lose than to gain in such a debate, because he was somehow in the same position as Nixon in 1960: elected only as vice-president, and serving as interim president but not elected as such, he was in fact competing for the presidency on the front line for the first time.

1.2.2.2   1968, or the invention of the close-up

No decisive televised debates took place in the 1968 or 1972 campaigns either: one might surmise that candidate (then incumbent president) Richard Nixon did not want to play this dangerous game again.

The 1968 election gave televised political communication an opportunity to explore the entire scope of its possibilities, thanks to Richard Nixon's close relationship with a young 27-year-old television producer, Roger Ailes, the future chairman of *Fox News*. Ailes was able to convince Nixon to take a natural pose in front of the camera and to agree to be filmed in close-up, in short, to accept the hints which still today enhance the popularity of today's television stars. All television directors know that close-ups suit the television screen much better than the wide- angled shots used for cinema.

Incidentally, it was later revealed that many of the Nixon ads had been deliberately designed not to show the candidate they were campaigning for: the appeal of the commercials was deemed stronger using his voice alone.[13]

1.2.2.3   *1972: alliance of text and image*

One of Senator George McGovern's spots in his campaign against Nixon in 1972 was especially striking: a long speech giving apparently objective figures on inflation over the four preceding years with an emphasis on the state of the American economy was read by a voice-over as it appeared on screen. The rise in the cost of many basic household products that all American housewives buy in their neighborhood supermarkets were stigmatized, with the forceful conclusion: "Can you afford four more years of Mr. Nixon?"

This adaptation for television of a technique, invented in the 1960s by French filmmaker Jean-Luc Godard for filming text, demonstrated forcefully that a spot can be effective, even if it conveys fairly complex statistics.[14]

1.2.2.4   *1976: televised political communication comes of age*

Modern American political communication completed its initiation stage in that year for two main reasons:

- the practice of decisive televised debates was revived and has endured since then;
- the remaining restrictions on political advertising were removed.

Two televised spots broadcast during the 1976 campaign illustrate the latter point, marking the end of adolescence for televised political communication.

First, a spot for Ronald Reagan, then candidate for the Republican Party nomination, innovated by portraying the candidate with the same style of images as those that the viewers grant the greatest credibility: the news. Reagan's public relations team staged one of his public appearances using the same technique employed to film the nightly news report: the camera was placed directly on the set and technical defects were voluntarily inserted. In short, it was a very good imitation of what can be seen on television every day when the news is broadcast. The spot was naturally programmed immediately before or after the evening news to maintain the confusion.

Second, a spot made for Malcolm Wallop, Republican candidate for the Senate in Wyoming, a state where the rodeo is popular, marks this coming of age by the use of theoretically less credible images: television commercials. The would-be-senator was shot leading a stampede on a white horse, imitating in the style of the famous "Marlboro Man" commercials.[15]

Televised political marketing had thus come full circle: by imitating the most credible images shot for television, and even those viewers knew to be contrived, political advertising had reached adulthood.

But in 1976 American televised political communication came of age in another way. For the first time since the famous Kennedy-Nixon debate in 1960, decisive debates between the two main candidates were held in formats and frequencies which are mostly still used today. Gerald Ford and Jimmy Carter met three times before the cameras. Handicapped by his position of "interim president," since he had replaced elected vice-president Spiro Agnew, forced to resign because of a financial scandal, Gerald Ford felt that he had to agree to participate in some decisive debates, which did not turn out to his advantage. Republicans and Democrats also even staged a debate for the first time between the two candidates for the office of vice-president, Bob Dole and Walter Mondale: recent events had shown clearly that vice-presidents could step into the foreground much faster and much more frequently than generally thought.

1.2.3   Adulthood: political communication and campaigning in the United States since the 1980s

Six main characteristics that have marked the recent years may be observed in the current stage of the evolution of political communication in the United States, a stage we will consider as being the "adulthood" of modern campaigning:

- a still dominant application of the "Unique Selling Proposition" principle leading to the greatest possible simplification of campaign themes;
- a still prevailing part played by television, but at greater costs and with some new "trends";
- the overall increase in the cost of campaigns, leading to greater fundraising needs;
- legal loopholes are allowing a rather more and more aggressive campaign tone;
- the integration of new media particularly the Internet, in campaigns, as soon as they were even hesitatingly regarded as fit to use;
- the recently increased personalization of campaigns, enhanced by the introduction of "*storytelling*" in modern campaigns.

1.2.3.1   A recurrent simplification of campaign themes

Modern political marketing owes of course much of its achievement to Ronald Reagan's two successful campaigns for the White House. Political communication specialists consider both campaigns as the victory of the Unique Selling Proposition.[16] The candidate was portrayed as having a very clear and simple conservative profile with a very sparse political platform: reduce taxes and federal government intervention, except for defense, where the budget was increased. Many political communication experts also made sarcastic remarks regarding the fact that, for the first time in history, a national political figure hired Hollywood gagmen to write jokes for the future president.[17] Computerized help for campaign themes was also tested for Ronald Reagan campaigns in order to determine which policy could be chosen during this simplification process.

The same decision to reduce campaign themes and to simplify the campaigns in order to facilitate their understanding by the "average" citizen marked most of the following campaigns. Both of Bill Clinton's victorious bids for the presidency, in 1992 and 1996, similarly applied USP principles and were orchestrated using a single word, "*economy*."[18] As for George Bush, his pattern of systematically implying in 2000 that he did not belong to the "Washington politicians" clique may be likened to a clever USP – all the more so as he managed to keep it credible in spite of being the son of a recent president, and hence far from being as distant from the "Washington politicians" as he claimed.

Finally, the 2008 campaign can be considered as another triumph of the USP. Barack Obama's winning streak in that year was also placed under the sign of a USP quite cut down to size: the superb slogan "Yes we can" is probably one of the best campaign themes ever devised from a USP standpoint. On the other hand, his opponent, John McCain merely managed to confuse voters, by choosing Sarah Palin as his running mate, whose political opinions were very different from his own, in order to soften-up the opposition of the most conservative segment of the Republican electorate.

1.2.3.2   Television domination and its new "trends"

Television is now so common in North American political communication that it has become its principal medium: since 1980, nearly half the federal campaign funds allocated to presidential candidates have been spent on television airtime. Its supremacy is still uncontested, and it remains the prime medium sought by politicians, through three main kinds of broadcasts: debates, commercials, and talk shows.

1.2.3.2.1 Debates   Since 1976, the practice of the decisive debate has been maintained systematically, though the frequency of debates and their format has varied slightly depending on the agreements made between candidates. Debates among vice-presidential candidates have also grown popular, as proven by the exceptionally high audience figures for the debate between Joe Biden and Sarah Palin, which attracted more than 70 million viewers.[19] As can be seen in Table 1.1, the 1976 format now seems to be becoming a permanent fixture, with three debates between the presidential candidates, and one between the vice-presidential candidates in 2000, 2004, and 2008. It should be noted that in many elections for state governors or municipal elections, televised debates on local television stations are also now frequent.

A new addition to the debates was Bill Clinton's initiative to organize the second 1992 debate in the form of a town hall meeting, with "representatives" of the people asking the two candidates questions directly. Quite at ease on the set, Clinton easily gave an excellent performance opposite George Bush, Sr., and literally managed to steal the floor from Bob Dole in the following 1996 town hall meeting debate, squeezing himself on the images behind Dole to blur his appearances on camera without the latter even noticing that he was played on like a second category actor on stage with a veteran.

While no debate seems to have had as much alleged influence as the famous first televised debate between Kennedy and Nixon in 1960, debates continue to be a cornerstone of campaigns. They throw politicians' potential weaknesses dangerously into the spotlight, which can sometimes be damaging. It happened in 1980, when

Table 1.1 Presidential debates in the United States

Election	Number of presidential debates	Number of vice-presidential debates
1960	Four debates between Richard Nixon and John F. Kennedy	None
1976	Three debates between Gerald Ford and Jimmy Carter	One debate between Bob Dole and Walter Mondale
1980	One debate between Ronald Reagan and Jimmy Carter, One debate between Ronald Reagan and John B. Anderson (*)	None
1984	Two debates between Ronald Reagan and Walter Mondale	One debate between George H.W. Bush and Geraldine Ferraro
1988	Two debates between George H.W. Bush and Michael Dukakis	One debate between Dan Quayle and Lloyd Bentsen
1992	Three debates between George H.W. Bush, Bill Clinton and Ross Perot	One debate between Dan Quayle, Al Gore and James Stockdale
1996	Two debates between Bill Clinton and Bob Dole	One debate between Al Gore and Jack Kemp
2000	Three debates between Al Gore and George W. Bush	One debate between Joe Lieberman and Dick Cheney
2004	Three debates between George W. Bush and John Kerry	One debate between Dick Cheney and John Edwards
2008	Three debates between John McCain and Barack Obama	One debate between Sarah Palin and Joe Biden

(*) Three debates between Jimmy Carter, Ronald Reagan, and John B. Anderson were scheduled and another one between vice-presidential candidates Walter Mondale, George H.W. Bush, and Patrick Joseph Lucey. But only the two debates mentioned could take place because Reagan and Carter did not reach an agreement on Anderson's and Lucey's attendance.

Source: Commission on Presidential Debates – http://www.debates.org/pages/history.html (last accessed December 2, 2010)

incumbent President Jimmy Carter said absent-mindedly that he would consult his 13-year-old daughter, Amy, before deciding on what the most critical political issues were, an astonishing method for a world leader. It happened again when Al Gore looked too aggressive and rather like an unsympathetic "technician" of politics in his first debate with George Bush, Jr. in 2000.

1.2.3.2.2 Political commercials Political commercials remain one of the major tools of political communication. Nowadays, parties and politicians do not hesitate to broadcast new spots practically every day during the final stages of their campaigns, now with special versions for Internet viewers, particularly during the 2008 presidential election.

Last-minute spots are now even hastily produced in the final days of the contests to help ailing campaigns. For instance, a few days before its anticipated loss in the

2006 mid-term elections, the Republican Party thus tried a desperate last-ditch effort by devising and airing a spot mimicking the famous *Daisy Spot*, still present in many memories. Osama Bin Laden and his fellow terrorists were seen threatening the United States. In the background was the sound of a ticking time bomb that finally exploded in a similar way to the 1965 *Daisy Spot* atomic bomb.[20]

1.2.3.2.3 Talk shows   It should be noted that politicians are increasingly attempting to "humanize" their campaigns by accepting invitations to appear in talk shows and similar television programs not primarily dedicated to politics. They are, therefore, following in Bill Clinton's footsteps. The former president famously played the saxophone on the popular *Arsenio Hall Show* during his 1992 campaign. Barack Obama scored a few points against John McCain, so to speak, when he was able to demonstrate his dancing skills on the *Ellen DeGeneres Show*, a performance incidentally later repeated by his wife. The most far-fetched campaign, in that regard, was Arnold Schwarzenegger's first bid for the state governorship of California in 2003, when he refused to take part in most political programs or to honor requests for political interviews, even starting a new sort of trend among politicians by announcing his candidacy on the *Tonight Show* with Jay Leno.

In short, aside from the now inescapable debates leading up to the presidential elections, advertising spots (at great cost) and participation in talk shows (and the like) have been a strong component of politicians' televised political communication in recent years: they have changed the way they use television, but it still remains the dominant medium.

1.2.3.3   Rising campaign costs and the increased need for fundraising
The enormous number of political spots during campaigns does raise some ethical issues, since wealth now virtually appears to be a sufficient criterion to qualify as a politician. After the lavish campaign spending done by Nelson Rockefeller, an heir to the famous oil magnate but who also had true political stature in terms of leadership, 1982 marked a turning point. A complete unknown, Lewis Lehrman, who also happened to be a millionaire, secured the Republican nomination in the primaries for the governorship of New York state by virtue of his campaign spending, and he came very close to winning the election. He paved the way for other followers, since the Supreme Court decided in its *Buckley v. Valeo* ruling that in order to protect freedom of speech as guaranteed by the First Amendment to the US Constitution, unlimited spending was legal as long as the candidate could afford it. The court ruled that only candidates requesting a partial refund from the state for some of their campaign expenditures were obliged to limit their spending to a certain amount.[21] This decision cleared the way for the likes of Ross Perot in the 1992 presidential election. Many keen observers were not surprised: sooner or later, some billionaire for whom cash was no object was bound to make a bid for the presidency. The same kind of spending occurs for all kinds of US elections: media mogul Michael Bloomberg was elected mayor of New York City in 2001 while spending US$73 million of his personal wealth and

more than 66 million to be re-elected in 2005, figures comparable to the amounts spent by Ross Perot on a nationwide presidential campaign.[22]

The cost of campaigning for presidential elections has thus kept growing despite the limitation on private funding when candidates do not reject federal help. Bill Clinton and George Bush spent a combined total of US$155.2 million during the 1992 presidential election. This figure climbed to US$696 million for John Kerry and George W. Bush in 2004. The amount was even much higher for the 2008 campaign, with US$742 million raised by Barack Obama alone, and an all-time high of about US$700 million was spent by all the candidates and the interest groups that took part in the campaign just for television ads.[23]

Furthermore, the money spent on election campaigns in the United States is not likely to diminish. A brand-new Supreme Court ruling on January 21, 2010, the *Citizens United v. Federal Election Commission*, has reversed the former jurisprudence banning corporations from using their own money to help a candidate during campaigns, arguing that the First Amendment to the US Constitution guarantees free speech (only direct help to the candidates remains forbidden). Almost unlimited corporate spending is now possible, as long as they campaign for the candidates but not directly giving money to them,. This somewhat controversial decision came in opposition to the attempts by Congress and the Federal Election Commission to limit campaign expenditure.[24] Attempts by some members of the Senate and the House of Representatives to mellow the effects of the Supreme Court decision by imposing publicity on most of the donations have failed: a "Disclose Act" adopted on June 24 2010 by the House of Representatives has been rejected twice in the following months by a Republican filibustering in the Senate.

This has made fundraising a considerable hindrance for campaigning politicians, sometimes setting unexpected divisions between candidates. The 2008 presidential campaign thus saw Barack Obama easily top donations, and he even disappointed some of his supporters when he decided to reject federal funding for the actual 2008 presidential campaign (not the primaries), since he wanted to be able to spend all the funding he had managed to collect without limitation, a first among major candidates in the 30 years that the electoral federal funding system has been in existence.[25] He was then able to spend most of the huge amount of funding he had raised, which already reached US$600 million in mid-October 2008[26] – not counting the funds directly raised by the Democratic Party. In the meantime, fundraising by his Republican opponent John McCain kept lagging behind, to the extent that he spent US$100 million less than Barack Obama for the fall presidential run.[27] As for Hillary Clinton, his unlucky opponent in the Democratic primaries, she finished her run with a debt of US$20 million, including a personal debt of US$11.4 million, and had to seek help from Barack Obama's campaign as well as to do more fundraising just to be able to recover financially.[28]

1.2.3.4   *Legal loopholes and increasing aggressiveness of campaigns*

Two legal dispositions theoretically meant to protect freedom of political speech in line with the First Amendment of the US Constitution – Section 315 of the Communication Act, 1934 and article 527 of the Bipartisan Campaign Reform Act,

2002 – have given campaigns considerable leeway, leading to the use and abuse of this freedom and heightening campaign aggressiveness in recent years.

1.2.3.4.1 The consequences of Section 315 of the *Communication Act, 1934*

Section 315 of the Communication Act, 1934[29] has been mainly used to free negative political spots from any control: it grants them complete freedom without any possible censorship or liability for the spots themselves or for the TV channel broadcasting them. When the fierceness of the "*Daisy Spot*" provoked a nationwide scandal in the 1960s, some had thought that it would remain a rather isolated event. They were proved wrong, and the American media's tendency to probe into the smallest details of the private life of politicians has made it even worse.

"Low blows" have grown more common than ever, particularly since President Carter's ruthless campaign, despite his incumbency, against his opponent for the Democratic Party nomination. Just before the Iowa caucus and New Hampshire primaries, a spot programmed in those states concluded with a voice-over saying "President Carter – he tells you the truth," a clear allusion to the well-known car accident that involved Edward Kennedy in Chappaquiddick, in which his passenger was killed (Senator Kennedy was, at the time, the most serious contender for nomination among the Democrats).[30]

The George H.W. Bush campaigns of 1988 and 1992 were equally ruthless, relying on vehement negative spots. Some 1988 spots hinting that as former Massachusetts governor, Michael Dukakis had been environmentally irresponsible seriously damaged his image, though it has since been established that the shoreline strewn with alleged radioactive garbage shown in the spots had nothing to do with Dukakis's actions.[31] Even more damaging was the so-called "Willie Horton" spot which attacked Dukakis for a furlough given to a convict who then committed another crime – while Dukakis had been simply applying a furlough program established by his Republican predecessor and who furthermore was far from the only governor granting furloughs to convicts who then committed another crime. In 1992, the same aggressiveness characterized President Bush's campaign while he was still in office: many of his spots and some of his speeches clearly suggested, this time to no avail, that his opponent, Bill Clinton, had been disloyal to his country as a young man, since he had managed to avoid serving in Vietnam and that he had probably cheated on his wife, and also that he might have been a drug addict in his youth.[32]

The harsh tone of the 2000 presidential election, this time mainly from the George W. Bush campaign side, was made even more memorable by an apparent experiment of inserting subliminal images in one of his negative commercials criticizing Al Gore, his Democratic adversary. Visually playing on words, a shot showing "Democrats" in boldface type was followed by another one showing "Bureaucrats," but an intermediary image nearly invisible to conscious perception only flashed "rats" in bold capital letters.[33]

Though the 2002 legislation tried to limit negativity in campaign spots by having candidates stand by their ads with a short statement, usually at the end, it has not prevented them from continuing with strong attack ads, even during the primaries:

some of Hillary Clinton ads were so harsh that it might be one of the reasons she did not become Barack Obama's running mate during the 2008 convention, contrary to what is usually expected from such close second running primary candidates.[34]

The only limit for negative spots seems to be the abuse of images of politicians themselves when they are used without their consent. For instance, during the 2008 presidential election, one of the spots aired by John McCain's Campaign had to be quickly withdrawn when Hillary Clinton threatened to go to court. This spot, *Passed Over*, indeed pinpointed the fact that Barack Obama had not asked her to become his running mate, by showing some of her public attacks on him during the primaries campaign.[35] Similarly, John McCain's campaign was not very fortuitous when its *Celebrity* spot backfired on him. He was attempting to mock Obama's celebrity and good ratings as being stronger abroad than at home, and similar to those of entertainment and chat show stars, but one of the latter, Paris Hilton, was so angry that her image was used in a political context without her consent that she retaliated, so to speak, with a spot critical of McCain, while Hilton's parents, the hotel chain owners, were at a loss, since McCain had negatively used their daughter's image whereas they had supported him.

1.2.3.4.2 The consequences of Article 527 of the Bipartisan Campaign Reform Act, 2002   The new campaign regulations introduced by the Bipartisan Campaign Reform Act, 2002 were intended to avoid unhealthy fundraising and spending. On the contrary, it has increased the harshness of political campaigns in an unexpected way. While this reform, endorsing some previous judiciary precedents, limits the amount individuals can donate to candidates and political parties, it authorizes any grouping of citizens to use any form of political communication they see fit during the campaigns in order to put their views on the political and public agenda. The law only requests that these groups be independent from parties and candidates, and notably do not overtly call citizens to cast their vote for the candidate they favor. The idea was of course that the American citizen could then put pressure on the competing politicians during the campaigns by forcing them to acknowledge the political ideas they were trying to promote.

But the "527 Groups," thus nicknamed after the so-numbered article of the United States Tax Code authorizing them, soon found another *raison d'être* than simply lobbying to advocate new specific policy stands. During the 2004 presidential campaigns, many quickly understood that even if the law indeed forbade them from speaking favorably about candidates, it did not prevent them from speaking unfavorably against them without running the risk of making the candidate they supported look too aggressive, since they were not formally linked to him.

The "527 Groups" supporting George W. Bush in 2004 immediately understood this unexpected side effect and leaped at the occasion: they engaged in a very vicious series of negative spots against his Democratic opponent, John Kerry. His honesty, and the very fact that he had been injured during a heroic action during the Vietnam War were loudly contested, and he never fully recovered from these attacks, his later rebuttals not fully recovering the lost ground. In fact, the Bush-Kerry run is seen by

Table 1.2 Geographical penetration of the Internet, 2000–2008

World Internet usage and population statistics

World Regions	*Population (2008 Est.)*	*Internet Users Dec. 31, 2000*	*Internet Users Latest Data*	*Penetration (% Population)*	*Users Growth 2000–2008*	*Users (% of Table)*
Africa	975,330,899	4,514,400	**54,171,500**	5.6 %	1,100.0 %	3.4 %
Asia	3,780,819,792	114,304,000	**657,170,816**	17.4 %	474.9 %	41.2 %
Europe	803,903,540	105,096,093	**393,373,398**	48.9 %	274.3 %	24.6 %
Middle East	196,767,614	3,284,800	**45,861,346**	23.3 %	1,296.2 %	2.9 %
North America	337,572,949	108,096,800	**251,290,489**	74.4 %	132.5 %	15.7 %
Latin America/ Caribbean	581,249,892	18,068,919	**173,619,140**	29.9 %	860.9 %	10.9 %
Oceania / Australia	34,384,384	7,620,480	**20,783,419**	60.4 %	172.7 %	1.3 %
World total	6,710,029,070	360,985,492	**1,596,270,108**	23.8 %	342.2 %	100.0 %

Notes: (i) Internet Usage and World Population Statistics are for March 31, 2009. (ii) Click on each world region name for detailed regional usage information. (iii) Demographic (Population) numbers are based on data from the US Census Bureau. (iv) Internet usage information comes from data published by Nielsen Online, by the International Telecommunications Union, by GfK, local Regulators and other reliable sources. (v) For definitions, disclaimer, and navigation help, please refer to the Site Surfing Guide. (vi) Information in this site may be cited, giving the due credit to www.internetworldstats.com.

Source: March 2009, http://www.internetworldstats.com (last accessed December 2, 2010)

many observers as the most negative since the 1960s.[36] Altogether, no less than US$100 million is estimated to have been spent by the "527 groups" clearly supporting George W. Bush during the campaign.[37] At the time, the most important group, *America Coming Together*, raised US$79.8 million![38]

Lastly, one might fear that the 2010 *"Citizens United v. Federal Election Commission"* Supreme Court ruling will lead to similar effects, since corporations taking part in political campaigns – without any direct link to the candidates, as for the 527 Groups – will also have much more leeway than the candidates themselves in attack and negative spots and propaganda.

1.2.3.5   Early integration of the Internet and new media in campaigns

Since the 1950s, North American consultants specialized in campaigns and political communication have always tried to employ all kinds of media to aid them in their task. The same has happened for the Internet. And here again, they have somehow unwillingly set the rules for the whole world, since the Internet began in the United States and grew there first and much faster than anywhere, soon providing a new audience for political communication (see Table 1.2).

It is not surprising then to discover that as early as 1996, and then again in 2000, all the US presidential candidates have put out a web site, even if the actual impact on voters was unclear and quite uncertain.[39]

In fact, it is only with the 2004 presidential election that the Internet started to be acknowledged as influential force in the campaigning process. In 2003, some months before the first primaries, Howard Dean, a little-known Democratic politician, outgoing governor of the rather small state of Vermont, was able to benefit from a clever Internet petitioning campaign and a bold use of networking web sites such as *Meetup.com,* which was quite successful. To that effect, for the first time, he systematically exploited growing possibilities offered by the Internet to achieve true interactivity. He was the first major politician to develop what is known today as a *blog,* an interactive web site, which was judiciously used in conjunction with his flagship Internet web site. The Internet also unexpectedly helped him raise a considerable funding for his campaign. Of course, Howard Dean was not able to capitalize immediately in 2004 on the good results of his preparatory Internet campaign, but it transformed him and turned him into a major American politician: it very quickly propelled him to the helm of the Democratic Party as Chair of the Democratic National Committee, a position he held until Obama came to power. At the same time, the huge amount of money he managed to raise through the Internet decisively established the medium as one of the new channels of political fundraising.[40]

Also helped by the leeway given to political communication's use of the Internet by a 2006 ruling of the Federal Elections Commission,[41] Barack Obama's 2008 campaign went one step further, exploiting the extension of its possibilities. He created a "profile," an account, on most of the brand-new Internet social networks, from *Facebook* and *Twitter* to *YouTube* and *MySpace,* thus building up a considerable following.[42] His team was also very efficient in building up a positive rumor effect on the network, following the Howard Dean model of multiplying blogs. He was helped to that effect by no less than Chris Hughes, the co-founder of *Facebook* and Joe Rospars, a member of Howard Dean's 2003/2004 campaign staff, the latter acting as new media director. Although the electoral effect of this vast investment on the Internet cannot be directly measured, the high number of web surfers who connected to his various Internet actions obviously had non-negligible effects: around 1.5 million accounts were opened on his campaign web site, he got nearly 3.2 million "supporters" on *Facebook*, and nearly one million "friends" on *MySpace*.[43] Similarly, a rather strong hint as to the effectiveness of Barack Obama's Internet campaign is provided by the fact that he was able to collect an unexpectedly high level of funds through this medium for his campaign, as we have already mentioned.

Here, in fact, the globalization of political marketing methods definitely played a part in this decision to bank on the new possibilities opened by the Internet. It is well known that some Democratic and Republican representatives had been following closely the 2007 French presidential campaign, in which both of the main competitors, Socialist candidate Ségolène Royal and future President Nicolas Sarkozy, made extensive us of the Internet in a manner similar to the one initiated by Howard Dean. Ségolène Royal's team notably imitated Dean's brilliant idea of imposing a candidacy by Internet blogging and petitioning, thus wining by surprise the Socialist primaries, with the help of a series of blogs intertwined with a main one, *Désirs d'Avenir*. On Sarkozy's side, the first French political spam was sent out to more than 1.5 million unwilling recipients, and later, his Web-TV, NSTV.com, received quite a respectable audience during the actual campaign.

1.2.3.6   *The recent increase of personalization of campaigns: "storytelling" in modern campaigns*

American politicians have had a longstanding tradition of associating their household to their campaigns: Mamie Eisenhower and Jackie Kennedy had set a clear trend there, and even the Nixon family dog, Checkers, was part of the 1952 campaign, as already mentioned.

But a new turning point of the personalization of political communication was reached with Barack Obama's 2008 successful presidential campaign. In his case, very thorough image-building helped him considerably by somehow establishing a parallel between his own personal life and not less than the history of the United States. While his racial and partly foreign origin might have been seen as negative factor, he successfully used them to appear as a symbol of the building of America. In telling the story of his personal life, from his Kenyan father to his white grandmother who raised him in Hawaii, he brought personalization to a new level, "storytelling": fictionalizing the campaign by personalizing a kind of modern hero of History. This image-building started right from the very beginning of his political life with the first book he wrote, *Dreams from My Father: A Story of Race and Inheritance*, which was published in 1995 when he became the first African-American to preside over the *Harvard Law Review* and began his political career. A new edition of the book was published in 2004, right after his famous keynote address at the Democratic Convention which gave him momentum for the next presidential race.

In 2006, a second book, taking its title from the 2004 Convention speech, *The Audacity of Hope: Thoughts on Reclaiming the American Dream*, put the final touches to this image-building campaign a few months before Barack Obama announced that he would be a candidate in 2008. The book was one of the year's bestsellers and remained in the front shelves all year long.

Here again, the parallel between Barack Obama's 2008 campaign and Nicolas Sarkozy's victory a year before is quite interesting, clearly showing that political marketing has now generalized this new trend of personalizing campaigns to the point of having the politician's image being built-up as a fictional role model. In a similar way, Sarkozy regularly repeated during his campaign how proud he was to be able to be a candidate to the presidency of France when he was only a second generation migrant of Hungarian descent, and later also managed to put his marital distress in a positive light by explaining in his first campaign speech that it had helped him gain a better understanding of life and newly acquired wisdom befitting a man who was to lead the country.[44]

***

Devised and implemented first in the United States, modern political marketing techniques have been widely imported by most of the world's democracies. Three factors determine how quickly the techniques have taken root:

- The development of "mass" and "new" media, from television to the Internet, in the different parts of the world: countries in which means of mass communication expanded rapidly, such as the United Kingdom and France, have logically been the first to import modern means of political marketing.
- The extent to which political communication is subject to government regulation, especially during election campaigns: for instance, in some countries, such as France, where there is no question as to the strength of its democracy, stringent regulations forbid any form of political commercials sponsored by political parties or leaders on television and radio channels (both publicly and privately owned). This has for years been partly compensated by the excessive use of political posters on huge billboards in the country's city streets and on roadsides:[45]
- the country's level of development: curiously, this last limitation is not always significant: many not-so-rich democracies, such as most of those in Latin America, use many of the modern political communication techniques, and campaigns in many European countries look quite pale in comparison.

Incidentally, the lowest common denominator of nearly all democratic countries might well be the practice of the decisive televised debate between the main candidates for major office, usually the presidency, in countries which are republics, or parliamentary elections in countries where the head of government is the prime minister, as head of the parliamentary majority, like in the United Kingdom. In both hemispheres, it is now by far the most important step of any political campaign for election, and the example set by Kennedy and Nixon in 1960 remains fresh in the minds of politicians and political marketing specialists around the world 50 years later.

Notes

1 More detail on the globalization of media systems and its consequences can be found in the extensive comparative research done in 18 countries by Daniel C. Hallin and Paolo Mancini 2004.

2 The system is in fact even more complex: for instance, some states allow voters to write in the name of a politician who is not officially a candidate for nomination. This is known as a "write-in" ballot.

3 Bill Clinton's race to win the 1992 primaries has even been the direct inspiration for a popular novel, *Primary Colors: A Novel of Politics* (Joe Klein – initially as "anonymous," Random House, 1996), which in 1998 Hollywood made into a movie with John Travolta as leading actor (*Primary Colors*, by director Mike Nichols).

4 For instance, in Michigan, on February 22, McCain got about 80% of the Democratic votes and Bush 67% of the Republican voters, a typical case of "cross-over" allowed by an open primary (see http://usgovinfo.about.com/library/news/aa022100a.htm (last accessed December 2, 2010).

5 Some American political scientists also explain this increase by the weakening of party organization in the period between elections: neither party has ever maintained a very strong structure on a permanent basis, and the number of permanent activists is continuing to fall.

6 For more details on the US election system, see Dave Leip's well-documented Atlas of US Presidential Elections, http://www.uselectionatlas.org/ (last accessed December 2, 2010).

7 See K.H. Jamieson 1996.

8 From the AAPC web site, http://www.theaapc.org/ (last accessed December 2, 2010).

9 These spots were produced in the same way as regular commercials: alleged "citizens" of the United States were in fact little-known hired actors and tourists deemed representative of "average" Americans; shot after shot was taken with them to try and assess who was most able to be shown questioning Eisenhower who had already filmed all his answers to them in a few hours, without even knowing to whom he would be answering.

10 Kennedy is also the first politician who publicly admitted that he did not write his speeches himself, but was aided by a speechwriter (Ted Sorensen).

11 The first formal political debate on radio for US presidential elections apparently took place on May 17, 1948, between Thomas Dewey and Harold Stassen during the Republican primaries. Though this broadcast got a wide audience, it did not seem to have influenced the final result of the primaries and did not leave such a lasting memory as the 1960 Kennedy-Nixon debate (see Minow and Lamay 2008).

12 For more detail, see for instance Diamond and Bates 1984; Schroeder 2000; Minow and Lamay 2008.

13 See Joe McGinnis, *Selling of the President 1968*, Penguin reprint, 1988.

14 Twenty years later, Bill Clinton's 1992 campaign extended the process by adding "footnotes" to some spots in order to try and reinforce their content exactly as an academic would do in a book.

15 A scene from Sidney Lumet's *Power* is a direct take-off on this spot, ridiculing the candidate who is shown falling off his horse because he does not know how to ride.

16 For further detail on the USP, see Chapter 2.

17 Ronald Reagan was also probably the first president of the United States who kept one of those gagmen on the White House staff payroll.

18 Bill Clinton's two main communication advisors during the 1992 campaign, George Stephanopoulos and James Carville, notoriously kept sending him messages before his main meetings with a bluntly phrased cue, "It's the economy, stupid" (see the Chris Hegedus and Arthur Pennebaker 1993 documentary on the campaign, *The War Room*).

19 From "Audience USA", http://www.audiencesusa.com/80-archive-10-2008.html (last accessed December 2, 2010).

20 The title of the spot *The Stakes*, was even taken from the beginning of the *Daisy Spot* voiceover.

21 See Lynda Lee Kaid, "Political advertising," in Nimmo and Sanders 1981.

22 *New York Daily News*, December 9, 2003 and November 9, 2005.

23 See Lynda Lee Kaid in Denton 2009 and M. Currinder in Nelson 2010.

24 The decision was taken with a very narrow 5-4 majority, with a huge 90 pages of dissenting opinion by Justice John Paul Stevens, joined by his three other dissenting colleagues. President Barack Obama even declared publicly three days after the 5-4 court decision was announced that "[this] ruling strikes at our democracy itself" (see for instance, *The New York Times*, January 24, 2010, *USA Today*, January 25, 2010, etc.).

25 The "*Federal Election Campaign Act*" (FECA) of 1971, started in fact to be considerably amended in 1974 and in the following years, encompassing the consequences of the Watergate scandal in order to try and redeem US politics. Most of the current legislation can be found on the Federal Election Commission web site at http://www.fec.gov/law/law.shtml (last accessed December 2, 2010).

26 *The New York Times*, October 19, 2008.

27 See Lynda Lee Kaid in Denton 2009.

28 See http://www.bloomberg.com/apps/news?pid=20601103&sid=aPKtsGLZmHZM (last accessed December 2, 2010); also M. Currinder in Nelson 2010.

29 With the arrival of the first TV broadcasts, it replaced Section 315 of the previous Radio Act 1927, which was similar.

30 A second spot along the same idea was also aired.

31 See for instance K.H. Jamieson, (1996) and Paul F. Boller, Jr. 2004.

32 George Bush went so far as to insult Bill Clinton, calling him a "clown," for instance, toward the end of the campaign, when he was trying to make a comeback on his opponent, who was still leading in the polls. During the same 1992 campaign, some sort of investigation was even commissioned by some of Bush's partisans, seeking to prove that Clinton had tried to abandon his American citizenship to escape the draft.

33 Questioned by journalists, Alex Castellanos, the Republican consultant behind the spot, denied any specific intention while admitting that the insertion of the word "Rats" was "a visual drum beat ... [trying) to get [people] interested and involved." (*ABC News*, September 12, 2000).

34 See for instance her Wisconsin primaries ad, accusing Barack Obama of deliberately refusing to hold public debates with her, or the beginning of March attack on alleged inactivity of a Senate Commission on Afghanistan Barack Obama had been chairing, etc.

35 "You never hear the specifics," "We still don't have a lot of answers about Senator Obama"(about the Roscoe scandal) etc., were two of Hillary Clinton's soundbites in the *Passed over* spot. The same method, incidentally, was used in Ronald Reagan's winning campaign against Jimmy Carter in 1980, when he aired negative spots taken from Ted Kennedy's attacks on Carter during the Democratic primaries.

36 See for instance Geer 2006.

37 See Lynda Lee Kaid in Denton 2009; altogether, the top five 527 Groups allegedly spent nearly US$170 million during the 2004 campaign, according to N.T. Kasniunas and M.J. Rozell (in Semiatin 2008). The spending was much lower for the 2008 presidential campaign, part of the reason probably being that artificially spontaneous anonymous ads were now shown on *YouTube*, when formerly, only costly ads showed on paid airtime on "traditional" television were possible.

38 Source: http://www.opensecrets.org/527s/527cmtes.php?level=C&cycle=2004 (last accessed December 2, 2010).

39 For more detail, see Chapter 7.

40 He allegedly raised more than US$3 million in a single week (in Benoit 2007).

41 See Chapter 7; the FEC ruling may also be found in Appendix 2.

42 One of the main initial 2008 primaries candidates, Democratic Senator John Edwards, was also rather active on Internet social networks, for instance also creating a *Twitter* profile.

43 See Denton 2009.

44 "I have changed" ("J'ai changé") was the peak of the January 14, 2007 meeting speech, in order to convince his audience – and the French voters – that he was no longer the rather agitated Interior Minister always keen to appear before TV cameras, but a more sedate and experienced person. For more on "storytelling," see Salmon 2007.

45 A law passed in France in early 1990 further restricts the possible uses of political posters as well as any campaign advertising medium within three months preceding election day.

Part II

The foundations of modern political marketing

As we stated at the start of the present work, political marketing can be defined as a genuine policy of political communication, a global strategy involving the design, rationalization and conveyance of political communication. We shall trace its main stages in Chapter 2 and examine in Chapter 3 the soil in which it takes root: the means of analysis and information.

2

Political marketing: a global approach

2.1 The foundations of political marketing

Contrary to common belief, political marketing consists of more than a set of hints and formulas discovered empirically and re-utilized: it obeys a number of precise basic principles that apply in almost all the cases, both specific and general.

Two fundamental ideas must be kept in mind; they will be the subjects of both parts of the present section:

- even if political marketing often replicates the methods of commercial marketing, it possesses methods specific to its field, owing to its sphere of action;
- whatever the type of communication, several guidelines must be strictly observed.

2.1.1 The originality of political marketing

2.1.1.1 From commercial marketing to political marketing
In recent decades, promotional and sales techniques of commercial products have undergone a complete transformation due to the development of new methods, pigeonholed under the generic term "marketing." A conventional definition of this term would be "the set of means by which a business venture may create, maintain and develop its market, or, if one prefers, its clientele."

Without claiming to summarize modern sales marketing in a single phrase, one can nonetheless provide an accurate idea of its evolution. Whereas sales representatives formerly saw themselves as middlemen intervening in the final stage to get a product

Campaign Communication and Political Marketing, First Edition. Philippe J. Maarek.
© 2011 Philippe J. Maarek. Published 2011 by Blackwell Publishing Ltd.

from the manufacturer to the consumer, sales and marketing are now an integral part of the production process. Marketing begins at the design stage of a product, and can even lead to modifying its design according to its perception of customers' needs, or to desires it has created, both being inextricably linked today. It follows that the field of marketing has come to cover much ground, from a product's genesis to the end of its life cycle, when after-sales services take over. Marketing also claims to be rational, even "scientific": charts and equations assessing the plausible life span of new products are nowadays commonplace.

But adapting marketing to the sector of political communication stumbles on an unavoidable difficulty: applying commercial marketing methods directly to developing what is termed "political marketing" by definition adulterates them. Replicating relatively tried-and-true methods of commercial marketing is a hazardous enterprise in view of the fact that the object in question is of a fundamentally different nature.

In the case of consumer products – be it a vacuum cleaner, a home to be built, or an automobile – the aim is to plant in the consumer's mind a desire to purchase the said product as something that will be of use to him, and to determine in advance, if possible, certain product features as they may relate to a consumer's needs (needs either objectively identified by a preliminary survey, or previously created by some promotional means). This is the classic case sociologists have well described (Figure 2.1): marketing increases the symbolic value of a product (or a service), which will add to its potential practical value, to encourage the consumer to purchase it by reinforcing the satisfaction it will provide:

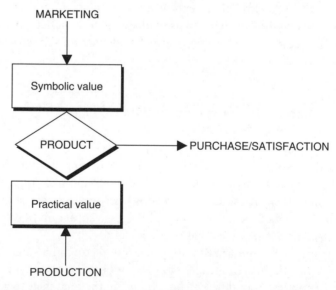

Figure 2.1　Commercial marketing, symbolic value and practical value.

Conversely, in matters of political marketing, the problem is to define a politician's objectives and platforms and to influence the way citizens are to respond, particularly during the approach of an election. Thus, the terms of the above equation are rendered false by the simple fact of a politician's practical value to the voter being nearly nil. In most cases, for instance, the citizen can expect no direct concrete benefit from the results of an election in the short term; there can be no tangible satisfaction. The only exceptions are local elections, particularly in small constituencies, where the bond between politician and voter is still very strong, on a person-to-person basis, and the stakes involved for local life much clearer; this means that voters in this situation have a clear idea of what would change in some aspects of their day-to-day life because of the outcome of the election; for example, garbage collection taxes being used to pave their street. But in most cases, those involved in political marketing must take into account that it is not simply a matter of transposing commercial marketing, which has a clear and precise end: the purchase and use of consumer products (or services).

This also means that it would very difficult to adopt, as is, the entire array of instruments and methods used in commercial marketing, since political marketing cannot make use of a large number of its usual criteria of choice and prospects: there are no charts showing sales curves or the size of the potential market, and so on. Public opinion polls, for example, do not provide any information as reliable as sales statistics for commercial marketing, as we shall see in Chapter 3 and political events are quite unpredictable, whereas consumer behavior is generally easier to anticipate.

Moreover, in most cases, the failure of a commercial marketing campaign simply means a decrease in sales or a lesser increase than expected, but very rarely the disappearance of the product and even less of the company that manufactures it or sells it. On the contrary, the failure of a political marketing campaign will mean that the politician in question has not managed to be elected, and this will have extremely harsh consequences. At the very least, the politician will endure a long wait until the next election,[1] and, even worse, this might end his or her political career if he or she is not able to gain again enough credibility for another campaign, which is very often the case in the United States where the high number of potential candidates for the same job makes it very difficult to "return" after an electoral misfortune.

2.1.1.2 Political marketing, advertising, propaganda, information and communication

Before we begin our explanation of the political marketing process, we must remove one final problem: terminology. Political marketing is often mistaken for political advertising, and "information" is frequently confused with "communication."

But these notions are of fundamentally different natures:

- for commercial products:
    - "marketing" is, succinctly, a general, systematic method of redefining, backing and promoting a product in view of increasing sales;
    - "information" is a one-way process of "communication," one of its tools being called "publicity," or "advertising," when it is paid for by the advertiser.

- in matters of political communication, one can similarly establish the same kind of differences:
  - ○ "political marketing" is the general method of "political communication," one of its means being,
  - ○ "political advertising," which is a paid type of unidirectional "political infor- mation." Originally, and up to the Second World War, this form of unilateral communication was usually designated as "propaganda."

The parallel between modern communication for commercial products and political communication can be visualized thus in Figure 2.2:

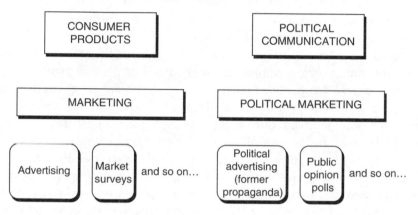

Figure 2.2   Commercial and political marketing: two parallel strategies.

Today, with marketing and media both evolving as rapidly as they do, to limit oneself to the term "political advertising" is to employ an ill-adapted, not to say out- dated, category. Political communication no longer means merely designing and printing a message on posters without consideration of whom they are addressed to. It encompasses the entire marketing process, from preliminary market study to testing and targeting.

In one sense, we could say that "advertising," as practiced by its pioneers, has today disappeared, even from the commercial sector. In any case, the very term "advertis- ing" has, in the eyes of the general public, a negative connation: that of distorted, if not biased, information – a fact blatantly played on by the television series *Mad Men*. In fact, advertising dates back to the beginnings of communication, just as propa- ganda, its equivalent in the political communication sector. Propaganda was nothing more than the adaptation of old-time conventional "advertising," generally employed by government institutions: partial, one-way communication trying to impose opinions. Whether it is "advertising," or "political propaganda," the mechanism is identical, and not unrelated to proselytism, in the original sense of the term.[2]

Modern political communication makes less and less frequent use of political advertising and its means, posters, commercials, and so on, without a major effort of preparation, which amounts to a genuine political marketing operation. We will thus tend to employ the terms political communication and political marketing interchangeably, since both are now inextricably associated, or nearly so. On the other hand, we will only use the terms publicity and advertising, in their restrictive sense, meaning unidirectional information.

2.1.2   General rules of conduct in political marketing

Transposing the principles of commercial marketing to politics creates an obligation to observe a basic code of conduct, composed of a limited number of ground rules. There are four abiding principles that are always applicable to the political marketing process and, paradoxically, they form two symmetrical pairs of rules often difficult to reconcile: Though these are called "rules," they are in fact principles to check rather than mandatory laws: one might decide not to respect them, or some of them, providing that the decision is made consciously, in the frame of a well-thought-out decision-making process and not inadvertently.

2.1.2.1   *Coherence*
The principle of coherence requires that no campaign decision can be made before it has been correlated with all others. This rule must be followed at every possible stage of the political communication process, from the eleventh-hour addition of a new line of communication in response to the allegations of a political opponent to the apparently banal decision to employ a new medium, and so on. The rule of coherence must also apply with regard to any previous campaigns conducted by the politician in question, or his party, especially when the said campaigns are of recent memory.

A surprising breach of coherence sometimes comes from incumbent politicians who think, usually wrongly, that they should start "afresh," and decide not to mention their past actions during the new campaign, a move often illegible in the eyes of the voters. Al Gore thus became hard to decipher when in 2000 he decided to dissociate himself from Bill Clinton's past two presidencies and did not boast about the improvement of the country's economy by saying that America had a lot to do to improve its "bad" situation. Similarly, two years later, French prime minister Lionel Jospin did not campaign on his societal achievements during the 2002 French presidential race, and that may well have been one of the reasons he lost his bid for the presidency.[3] More recently, in 2008, when John McCain chose Sarah Palin as a vice-presidential candidate, this was a clear example of too strong a breach of coherence, since the political outlook of the governor of Alaska was somewhat remote from his; this last-minute decision was not prepared well enough in advance to offset this lack of coherence.

2.1.2.2   *Systematic re-examination of earlier campaigns*
An effective campaign demands that the entire communication process be redefined, thus ruling out the unmodified repetition of an earlier campaign strategy, even if it was successful. While abiding by the rule of coherence, the politician must

resist the temptation to repeat a political communication campaign identically, which is not always easy. Almost inevitably, a change in any one factor (a new opponent, a new medium with a larger audience base, a disturbing new development of any kind, etc.) will quickly invalidate the candidate who merely falls back on an earlier campaign strategy. Thus, in his 1992 campaign against Bill Clinton, President George H.W. Bush probably made one of the fatal decisions that cost him a second term by disregarding this rule and reusing the kind of negative campaign he had employed against Dukakis in 1988.[4]

2.1.2.3   Minimal differentiation

Whatever the campaign and the choices made, the angle decided on must grant the politician an advantage on a specific point. Why should voters be inclined to vote for him if no specific factor differentiates him from his opponents?

This minimal differentiation must be emphasized throughout the political campaign process, even if at times it tends toward sophistic reasoning rather than a genuine advantage. This means that features that could be viewed both as qualities and defects may be (similarly) utilized as differentiating factors. For instance: a politician's youth or long experience; his excellent grasp of economic issues, or the excellence of his advisors given his conspicuous lack of knowledge of such issues; his past experience in holding office, or his lack of it, making him the right man for a "new" kind of leadership, and so on. For example, in 2000, Al Gore boldly put to use in his favor his rather negative reputation of being a fairly remote politician by publicly endorsing it during the Democratic Convention and stating that this was caused by his workaholic capacities which would then aptly help him to serve his country if elected – a clearly differentiating factor from his Republican opponent.

2.1.2.4   Maximum security

Sometimes difficult to reconcile with the preceding rule, the obligation of maximum security warns against adopting a communications strategy that could put the candidate at a disadvantage. Marketing consultants thus refrain from anticipating a future event if it is not absolutely certain to materialize: it is for instance unthinkable to speculate on an economic index unless inside information obtained prior to its publication certifies the direction it will take, and so on. On Monday, September 15, 2008, sometimes nicknamed the second "Black Monday" by the financial world, John McCain thus lost most of his credibility in economics when he boldly stated against all odds that "The fundamentals of the US economy are strong" at a town hall meeting in Florida, only minutes before Lehman Brothers collapsed.

Nor is it considered wise to speculate too boldly on the direction the campaign of a rival candidate will take: the latter need only alter his objectives in mid-campaign with respect to what has been anticipated for such speculation to produce negative effects. This explains why politicians already in office who have easy access to inside information, are often in a better position than their rivals.[5]

2.2 Main stages of the political marketing process

Being an overall process, political marketing can be broken down into two main stages, each divided into two steps:

- deciding on a strategy, and establishing its main line;
- deciding on a tactic and its application.

The following diagram (Figure 2.3) represents the overall process, which we will now examine in detail.

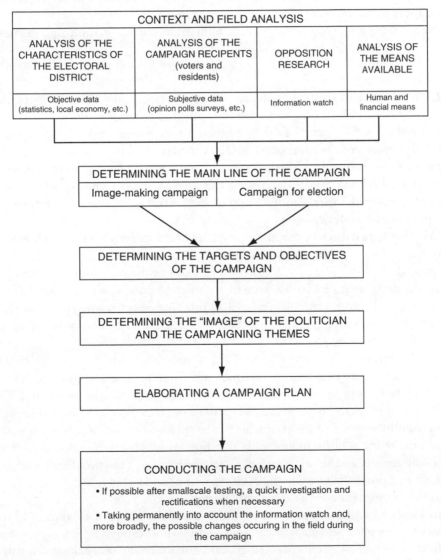

Figure 2.3 The main steps of the political marketing process.

2.2.1   Planning a campaign strategy

Like commercial marketing, political marketing is not neutral, since it does not function as a simple promotional method but affects all the components of political communication. This intrusion of political marketing into the very core of politics, under the pretext of improving communications, is quite new. It gives political marketing another dimension that is strategic, rather than merely tactical.

The planning of a strategy follows the following steps:

- first, the basis is established in light of the campaign line and field analyses (from the potential communication recipients to the opposition, that is the political opponents in the event of an election campaign);
- second, the actual objectives are determined: targets, image, campaign themes.

2.2.1.1   *The basis of the strategy*

2.2.1.1.1 Field and context analysis   The first stage in the political marketing process is field analysis (or geodemographics): studies made of the aspirations of the population, the candidate's public image, the platforms and possible opening campaign moves of the adversaries, and so on. Mastering the analysis is the foundation of the political marketing process: most political marketing specialists draw a medical analogy in describing this step as the "diagnosis." This step is crucial, because the whole equilibrium of the marketing process depends on the accuracy of the analysis.

Whether for a national or local campaign, the field analysis is a thorough investigation of the electoral district (the whole country's current specifics in the case of a national election). The politicians' local contacts or the party's local activists are asked to draw up a district assessment in order to put forward the local socio-economic and cultural specificities, and so on. This objective analysis of the field may be helped by all the available statistical data on the electoral district (census, hospital activities, and so on.).

As in commercial marketing, specialized consultants conduct systematic benchmark surveys of the campaign field, which involve an in-depth study of voters and inhabitants of the geographical area in which the campaign is to be carried out. This gathering of subjective data on the electoral district constitutes an invaluable aid to understand the mood of the recipients of the communication campaign. It makes use of the many public opinion study instruments which have developed over the past half-century and should give a complete panorama of the peculiarities of each district in a profile delineating the socio-economic and cultural features of what is commonly called the local geographical cluster.

In view of its vital importance, we shall devote the whole of Chapter 3 to this analysis, since poor field analysis can invalidate a whole campaign.

In the event of an election campaign, and not a mere image-making campaign, special attention must also be given to what is known as opposition research: the analysis of political opponents who may compete against the candidate, or who have already announced that they are candidates for election. It will be important to get as precise information as possible on the way they conduct their campaign. The main tool to that effect is the "Information Watch," mainly achieved by constant monitoring of the media, including of course the now essential Internet.

Finally, an initial assessment of the means available for the campaign should be made, taking into account the initial funds the candidate (or the party) may use, but also the human factor, meaning the local network of party activists and sympathizers. Obviously, this initial assessment must be updated throughout the duration of the campaign, since funds and sympathizers may come to the campaign as it unfolds – or pull out if things are not going well...

2.2.1.1.2 Determining the main political marketing campaign line Political marketing is applicable in two main areas: image-making campaigns and election campaigns. The first choice to be made resides here and dictates the ensuing logic of the process.

Determining a campaign line is not as easy as it appears. A candidate might start an election campaign with the knowledge that he stands no real chance of winning: in such cases, his campaign is in fact an image-making campaign and must be planned as such. But in the event that a candidate occupies an intermediary position as an outsider with slim, but not impossible, odds of winning, conducting a victory campaign, with the aim of winning the election, could help him achieve his goals, but also carries the risk, in the likely event of his losing, of diminishing his chances for a long career in national politics (his defeat then appearing exaggerated). So the option between the two postulates implies serious consequences.

A good example of an election campaign that was, in fact, an image-making campaign preparing the way for a later victory, was Ronald Reagan's campaign in the 1976 United States presidential primaries. Endorsing Gerald Ford's victory at the Republican Convention strongly and graciously enough to acquire an image of fair play, Ronald Reagan cleverly managed to maintain all his chances for the future. In the same manner, the campaign of the future French President François Mitterrand in 1965 against General de Gaulle, at a time when he knew he had very little chance of winning, was skillfully designed to maneuver him into position as the opposition leader for the years to come (and which paved the way for his eventual victory in 1981).[6]

Finally, it must also be noted that in some cases, campaigns are not conducted in order to build a politician's image but to focus attention on the political issues he stands for. This has been for many years the case for ecologist parties and their leaders all around the world, from Daniel Cohn-Bendit in Europe to Ralph Nader in the United States, who have continued to campaign for the sake of environmental protection rather than on their own personal ambitions. The same can be said about Ross Perot's two presidential campaigns in the 1990s, when he was arguing for transformed economics without claiming to have a chance of winning or of becoming a "true" politician. In that case, of course, the choice is clear, and "image-making" rather than winning the election, is the goal.

2.2.1.2   Determining the strategy

2.2.1.2.1 Target research   One of the major difficulties facing political marketing is the researching of targets, meaning the location of those segments of the general population which might be subject to the influence of political communication. Even if marketing can increase a politician's reputation considerably, it does not automatically win him an election: knowing of a politician's existence is not tantamount to believing that he is the best man, nor, of course, if anyone is going to vote for him.

In fact, a large portion of the electorate is very difficult to influence, because it is unlikely to change its mind. According to the country, or the kind of elections, no more than 30 to 40% of the voting population would be amenable to changing their opinion about their future vote (but this percentage is often much lower).

This explains why political marketing depends a great deal on an understanding of the recipients of communication: besides above-mentioned field analysis, much depends, too, on an estimation of the number of people political communication can affect, and a precise idea of their attributes and motivations. This means too that field analysis can be used simultaneously to determine a campaign's goals and issues (which implies good coordination, since certain targets are better adapted to certain objectives, or more receptive towards certain campaign issues, etc.).

THE NECESSITY OF SEEKING PRIME TARGETS   Political communication cannot simultaneously affect a very wide audience reliably: by its very nature, mass media do not allow much effective communication because of the diversity of the audience. On the contrary, when the message is addressed to specifically predetermined groups of recipients, known as segments of the population, it can be much more effective, since it is diversified according to the characteristics of the target segment.

But, in almost all cases, it is virtually impossible for a candidate to effect a communication with an ideal segmentation of recipients: to do so would mean his having to visit every home, since the family unit is probably the smallest useful segmentation of the population for the purposes of communication. Only a selection of new media, usually grouped under the generic heading direct marketing, and now the Internet, can begin to allow this approach to be implemented.

Whatever the kind of segmentation chosen, every target, every segment will nonetheless be subject to the most precise delimitation possible (using criteria established by preliminary benchmark surveys) and a suitably adapted marketing policy.

THE DIFFERENT KINDS OF TARGETS   The segmentation of communication recipients generally involves two options:

- either to organize a structural segmentation, by defining a certain number of prime communication targets: the so-called "opinion relays," with the hope that they will influence other recipients, who are their usual customers in questions of communication;

- or to establish a qualitative segmentation, by modifying certain aspects of communication according to the characteristics of fairly precise but relatively large segments of the population.

The search for opinion relays   It is an abiding paradox that one of the best methods for reaching communication recipients can be indirect. It is a long established fact that the direct effects of communication, especially when mass media-conveyed, are feeble, "neither very strong, neither very decisive," as the famous media theoretician Joseph Klapper termed it.[7]

In a good number of cases, the effects of the perceived message are quite indirect. The recipients make up their minds only after having listened to the people to whom they concede, consciously or not, an influence in such matters: the opinion leaders or "relays." The communication process thus breaks down into two successive steps, which make up the celebrated "two-step flow of communication" first expounded by a group of North American analysts on the influence of mass media, as can be seen in Figure 2.4:

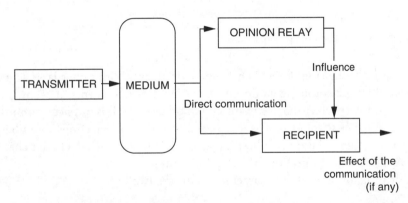

Figure 2.4   The role of opinion relays in the communication process.

Naturally, this phenomenon is most useful to political marketing. It is a fact that sometimes the only way of guaranteeing effective impact among the targets is to discover how to influence their opinion relays, exactly in the same way as a detergent salesman tries to convince housewives that the women who peddle their products on television are not professional actresses, but genuine housewives who are an example to be followed.[8]

Obviously, among the possible opinion relays, journalists form a category that is particularly valued and sought out by politicians, since their job is indeed to act as opinion relays towards their readership or audience, which makes press conferences and interviews a prime tool for reaching them.

Segmenting the population   There is another possible procedure for researching targets: instead of seeking out prime relays for the message, one can attempt to adapt it to various previously determined segments of the public. In this case, the candidate's communication will multiply messages which vary according to the previously determined segments of the public (as shown in Figure 2.5):

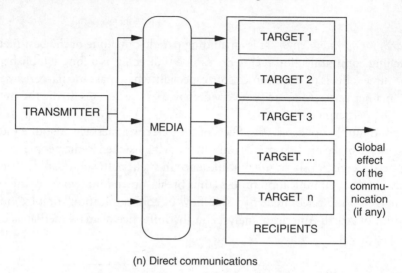

(n) Direct communications

Figure 2.5 Segmenting the population.

Naturally, the division of recipients can be done only with rather large segments of the population: some media do not allow for narrower forms of segmentation (general-audience television, for example); in other cases, it is physically impossible for the politician to hold non-stop communications (at meetings or rallies, for instance). So segmentation is at best imperfect, but it does afford a better chance at improving the communication's penetration power.

The criteria for division into target segments are twofold:

- either the standard sociological indicators;
- or, more inherent to political marketing, an affinity with the politician.

i *Segmentation by sociological indicators*   Most standard methods of targeting communication are based on the sociological characteristics of the recipient:

- sex;
- age;
- socio-occupational category;
- life style, or consumer habits;
- (level and type of personal expenses…), and so on.

A number of opinion polls in recent years have empirically confirmed the constancy of certain types of behavior peculiar to each socio-cultural category. In the field of political communication throughout the democratic world, for example, women appear to be more steadfast in their main choices than men. Similarly, both young people under 30 and the elderly seem less certain of their choices than people of intermediate age groups.

Pollsters today are even formulating new, more complex kinds of socio-cultural categories in order to correlate individual lifestyles with their socio-political context. Thus, people have been classified as "defensive individualists," "neo-rural," "indifferent conservatives," "social egoists," "enlightened consumers," "serene hedonists," "bobos" (or "bourgeois bohemians"), "early adopters," "daddy boomers," "dinks" (i.e. "double income, no kids"), "weekenders," and so on, according to the survey, the pollster and the country. Any recent book on commercial marketing will parade this kind of fashionable new categorization, which is also used for conventional marketing techniques, and varies almost from day to day, in order to follow as closely as possible the changes in social habits and patterns of consuming.

ii *Segmentation by political affinity* Another way of segmenting communication recipients stems from research conducted into their political affinities, when this is possible, of course. Opinion polls then try to establish previous political affiliations, political issues at the time of the poll, interest in political events, and so on.

When such data is at hand, political marketing can decide:

- either to neglect the segments sympathetic to the candidate, since they seem already won over to the cause, and to concentrate on a victory campaign among undecided voters: these persuadable voters, known as "floating" or "swing" voters, often constitute the main target of a communication campaign;
- or to address only those segments sympathetic to the candidate, in order to ensure their continuing fidelity, and also to try to have them serve as opinion relays for less accessible targets; in this case, the more vulnerable voters are the specific objective.

Two separate kinds of communications may then be tailored to the two main target categories, based on their affinities for the candidate in question:

- the "maintenance communication," aimed:
  - mainly at vulnerable voters who would probably vote for the candidate but are unsure; also at floating voters;
  - secondarily, at his steadfast supporters, in order to reassure them;
- the "conquest communication," directed:
  - mainly at floating voters
  - but also at less committed voters leaning toward a rival politician.

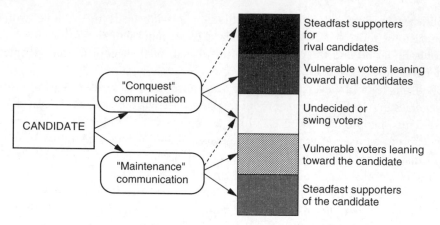

Figure 2.6   Targeting the communication recipient by political affinity.

Both processes can of course be activated simultaneously if it is deemed necessary, a task done carefully to maintain the coherence of the campaign.

Political marketing very often selects its prime targets among abstentionists, or the undecided, the persuadable or swing voters. Due to the very narrow margins that often separate the main parties or leaders at the polls, it is more productive to try to convince those marginal citizens who, in fact, will often cast the decisive votes. It explains why this method is so hard to manage, since politicians use a political communication campaign precisely to reach those who are least interested in politics!

In all circumstances, the candidate's communication should not be limited to one or more specific target categories, even if surveys indicate that they appear to be the most interesting in view of an immediate gain. Completely ignoring the rest of the voting population can be hazardous, since it gives them the feeling that they have been abandoned, and may produce a negative effect that could cancel out the potential gain of a few new voters.

This is the old problem for conservatives conducting their campaign on a liberal platform or liberals conducting theirs on conservative platform to win new voters: by pretending to favor ideas alien to their beliefs, they sometimes end up exhausting the patience of their own habitual sympathizers. For instance, during the 2008 US presidential elections, we have already mentioned that by choosing as his running mate Sarah Palin, a politician much more conservative than him, John McCain probably lost some of his usual support based on his usual "liberal-Republican" stands.[9]

But obviously, this kind of targeting outside one's own ranks, usually towards less politically committed positions, in order to capture the swing voters, may help politicians win by finding the "missing" voters where they are. Bill Clinton's bold campaigns focused on economics, a field traditionally left to the Republicans, are good examples of politicians using "conquest" across targeting with successful results, pulling the rug out from under their opponents.[10] One of his advisors, Dick

Morris, was known to regularly encourage Clinton, while president, to surprise people by standing as much as possible for issues usually defended by the Republican Party in addition to traditional Democratic issues, nicknaming this cross-targeting "triangulation." The word stuck and is now commonly used. More recently, French President Nicolas Sarkozy became an expert in triangulation, campaigning in 2007 with unexpected positive statements on historical Socialist Party leaders such as Jean Jaurès and Leon Blum being a significant part of France's past, and then, when elected, appointing many of their former Socialist opponents to government jobs.

On the contrary, it is very rare to stick to maintenance communication. This is usually confined to cases in which very popular incumbent politicians make a bid for re-election: being endowed with a high level of support and voter intentions, these politicians feel they should derive more harm than good from looking for more votes. They then deliberately conduct a demure maintenance campaign in order to avoid taking any risk. An extreme case of this can be seen in German Chancellor Angela Merkel's 2009 parliamentary campaign, during which she communicated as little as possible, to the dismay of her party, because she felt that her strong personal popularity lead over her opponents made it useless and even dangerous for her personal success to undertake any stronger kind of campaigning.[11]

2.2.1.2.2 Determining the image and themes of the campaign

Once the campaign angle is known (an image-making or an election campaign with its sights on victory), once the recipients' temperature has been taken to reveal their concerns, once opposition research has determined what field the opponents have chosen to concentrate on, once the targets of the campaign have been made clear, the politician's objectives must be decided, including his or her image and the issues to be taken up – this is why politicians already benefiting from a strong and positive public image usually start to campaign rather late.

At this stage of the political marketing process, two different operations take place:

- Even before the precise objectives of the campaign are known, the politician's so-called image must be created, redefined, or reaffirmed; unless the candidate is inexperienced, political marketing must take into account the fact that he or she is surrounded by a preexisting image. Many political campaigns have been doomed to failure for overlooking this fundamental factor: they had created campaign objectives and themes that were hardly reconcilable with the candidate's previous political image.
- The objectives can then be determined, namely the "campaign themes."

CREATING THE POLITICIAN'S IMAGE More and more these days, as campaign personalization grows in importance, the politician's image is a key factor in the electoral process. In some cases, the politician's image has even been credited as one of the major factors of victory: for instance for the 2004 US presidential election, in the aftermath of the September 11 terrorist attack, Bush's character traits caused him to be perceived as stronger and more able to lead than Kerry's, compensating for other weaknesses of the incumbent president's previous term.[12]

But image-building is quite difficult for three reasons: it is a subjective, slow and complex process.

A subjective process: a politician's image has to be constructed as much on the projecting end as on the receiving end: its components, of course, are predetermined with more or less precision by political marketing specialists, but the image only takes its real form after it has been decoded by the communication recipient. This means that if the making of a politician's image is "objective," in the sense that political marketing attempts to work with concrete elements in order to enforce the politician's subsequent communication, the final effect is subjective, since the image is reconstructed in the mind of the individual recipient.

A slow process: image-making does not come easy to politicians. They have to enjoy a certain reputation to start with for the communication recipients to have a clear idea of the elements of that projected image, which they will then try to correlate with the current ideas and the personality of the politician. Any attempt to change an image too quickly is constrained by this slow pace.[13]

A complex process: the politician's image is going to be the result of the sum of the many subjective images reconstructed by all the various recipients of his communication, which is impossible to really assess ahead of time.

Thus, the initial objective framework of the communication must take into account the essentially subjective nature of how it will be received; which forms the basis of the image that will henceforth accompany the politician. This also obliges him or her to build a suitable image – a truism that is not systematically complied with.

Framework for image-making   Given such a complex process, it is not surprising to see that to construct a politician's image, political marketing often makes unhesitating use of a well-known commercial marketing formula: the "unique selling proposition" (USP). The USP comprises two levels: the search for a differentiating factor, and simplification.

i) Highlighting the "difference"   The word "unique" in the USP formula has a double-edged meaning. First, it implies greatest effectiveness when the image clearly demonstrates that the product in question possesses at least one factor differentiating it from all others of the same kind. This factor can then be pitched to consumers as the product's specific advantage. This is the "instrumental difference," in the jargon of some marketing specialists.

Applying this concept to political image-making means that the marketing process must emphasize a unique characteristic that is truly the politician's, be it youth, age and experience, grasp of foreign or economic affairs, and so on. Naturally, the playing up of this characteristic must be carefully prepared. First, his advisors must ensure that the factor is really original to the politician. But they must also judge if the recipients (the voters) are indeed going to interpret this factor positively: unless it is considered a sign of maturity and experience, there is no need to draw attention to the fact that the politician in question is the only bald one!

During the 1992 American presidential election campaign, independent candidate Ross Perot made particularly clever use of this kind of image-making: he and his partisans systematically played on the fact that he was the only candidate who was a political "virgin," thus making him, they alleged, much more sensitive to the "genuine problems" of the average American, unlike his two "professional" opponents, who had lost touch with reality. This same notion is frequently used today in Europe to strengthen the appeal of far-right or ultra-nationalist politicians, who have been absent from government since the Second World War: it is easy for them to hold the democratic parties in power responsible for the current economic and unemployment crisis.[14]

More recently, the appearance of high-ranking female politicians in several countries has made this new factor of differentiation appear very strong, though not always carrying enough support for the candidate to win. Michelle Bachelet indeed won the Chilean presidency in 2006 with a surge of popularity apparently increased by her gender – unlike Laura Chinchilla who apparently rather won the elections in Costa Rica thanks to the support of the still very popular incumbent president, Oscar Arias. In France, in 2007, Ségolène Royal clearly played on her gender as a differentiation factor by implying that the fact that she was a woman, and that no woman had ever been elected president, was indeed in itself a factor of change – a change that the French voters at the time supposedly longed for. But her bid for the presidency, even though it dominated the front pages of magazines and newspapers around the world, failed to convince enough voters. The last-minute choice of Sarah Palin as John McCain's running mate in 2008 was also an obvious attempt to differentiate their "ticket" from the traditional-looking ticket with a seasoned male politician, in contrast to the choice of Joe Biden by Barack Obama.

ii) A desire for "simplification"   "Unique" has another meaning in the USP formula: the simplification of the image. Modern mass media do not convey complex messages well: the simpler the message, the easier and more effective its transmission. This explains why it is usually considered unwise to convey more than one message within a single act of communication (the same selling proposition). Similarly, the image of the politician would be more effective if it were as simple as possible. On that account, Barack Obama's 2008 campaign, which had at some point narrowed his image down to his concise slogan "Yes we can", is probably one of the best examples of effective simplification of a politician's image.

The difficulty of maintaining an image made   The above subheading may strike one as paradoxical. But political marketing has quite a major obstacle to overcome once the image of the politician has been designed. Inherent in the image is a commitment to the communication recipient: a promise of earnestness, of modernity, and so on. This promise is all the more difficult to keep in that it is basically a subjective construction: any rather minor incident can instantly destroy an image that has taken a long time to cultivate. The image of having a complete, in-depth grasp of every issue, for instance, can be killed on the spot when a journalist's overly-precise question throws the politician off-guard, who then refuses, or is unable, to supply an immediate answer.

A politician's image is much more difficult to supervise than, say, his electoral promises: unless some basic mistake is committed, the recipient will only be able to "judge" the validity of those promises when the communication campaign is concluded, after election day, whereas his judgment on the validity of the image is made immediately and possibly irrevocably.

Two kinds of rather uncontrollable factors characterize the difficulties of political image-maintenance:

i) Compatibility problems between the politician and his image   Of course, political communication advisors would never be so foolish as to design an image totally out of keeping with the personality of the politician who hired them. Thus to proclaim that there might be a compatibility problem could seem excessive. But the problem does exist, for two reasons.

First, the compatibility in question is not between the image of the politician and his true personality, in fact, but between his image and his personality *as perceived by the recipient,* a completely subjective phenomenon over which political communication can exercise little control (all the more so because recipients' subjectivities naturally differ). Thus the image can finally prove incompatible with the communication recipient's perception of that image.

Second, while being obliged to respect the politician's personality to the extent possible, hired consultants are nonetheless compelled to try to eliminate, so to speak, some of his less "telegenic" traits, particularly when they do not conform to what popular opinion expects of a political figure seeking public office. Sometimes, the gap between these two factors is so wide that the politician finds himself unable to behave in a way that corresponds to his own image: such an eventuality has come to be termed the "Ottinger Syndrome," well-known among North American political communication specialists. Richard Ottinger was a member of the House of Representatives aspiring to become a New York state senator in 1976; since he was younger than his opponents, his advisors tailored him an image of a bold, young executive in shirt sleeves, an image which he lost in the space of a single evening, during a three-way debate with his rivals, in which he appeared colorless, lacking in confidence, and nearly unable convey his opinions with conviction.

Political marketing specialists cannot always avoid the Ottinger Syndrome: the image they construct is usually the result of a more or less successful compromise between the true personality of their client and the characteristics the voter subjectively expects of a political personality. It explains why the risk of sudden revelation of incongruity is genuine, and why the Ottinger Syndrome still strikes from time to time, whatever the precautions taken. It occurred in 1984, for example, in the presidential campaign of former astronaut John Glenn: his qualities of political leadership came out less forcefully that his reputation as space hero had led one to think, which strongly disconcerted the American public. More recently, General Wesley Clark, while former supreme chief of the NATO forces in Europe, suffered the same fate when he appeared unable to speak up against his political opponents in television debates and was then never able to be a serious contender in the 2004 US presidential primaries.

ii) Impossibility of absolute control over how the image evolves We must finally stress the point that even if the politician's image is in harmony with his personality in the eyes of his recipients, genuine control of its evolution and its perception in the long term is impossible. A seemingly insignificant incident, a slight detail, can suddenly take on enormous proportions and thus destroy the cogency of the image.

A good example is former French president Valéry Giscard d'Estaing. Aware that he might be resented as being too "grand bourgeois" by many citizens, this politician went to great lengths to cultivate an image which included certain characteristics that made him appear more attractive to the middle class: for example, during an appearance on a popular television show, he played the accordion, an instrument associated more closely with French popular culture. But this somewhat forced sense of neighborliness vanished instantly the day when, fielding questions during a live television program, he was unable to say how much a Paris metro ticket cost. Another notorious mishap of the same kind occurred in 1976, when Swedish Prime Minister Olof Palme, during a debate with Thorbjörn Fäldin, could not quote the average rent of a flat. Lastly, everyone still remembers how Howard Dean suddenly tainted his image of a rising Democratic candidate during the 2004 US presidential run when he uttered a wild scream that flabbergasted everyone during his final speech at the Iowa Caucus contest.[15]

This only goes to show that formulating an image to give a politician is no minor affair. The subjective perception of the image by the public at large makes it a difficult factor to elaborate and even more problematic to control in its evolution.

DETERMINING THE CAMPAIGN THEMES The choice of the campaign themes, namely the issues the candidate is to develop, is the part of the political marketing process that most endangers his autonomy. Politicians today retain very little freedom of maneuver because they have to struggle against four categories of forces:

- the media only question politicians on their own "agenda" and leave little if no room to discuss other issues; politicians are hence tempted to develop only campaign themes that fit the media's agenda and therefore seeming more apt to be relayed by them;
- surveys also push politicians towards campaign themes corresponding to what they deem to be voter preoccupations, in order to avoid risking a conflict of interests with the electorate's beliefs. It then becomes difficult to maintain any original and more personal campaign themes;
- politicians' advisors, fellow party leaders, cabinet, and hired political marketing and communication consultants, despite their good intentions, also put pressure on politicians to choose campaign themes, either because they think that the politician they support should satisfy the two previous categories of forces, or just because they hold on to their own thinking on political issues, which might not be identical to the candidates' wishes (previous candidates, or earlier party policy, lesser resistance to some lobbies for other reasons than what is useful to the candidates' campaign, etc.);[16]
- lastly, the arguments of a politician's adversaries curiously have a strong influence on the politician's choice of campaign themes, since it is difficult for the candidate to keep developing issues that never answer the opposition, unless the candidate is willing to look marginalized.

This explains why the choice of campaign themes is the element of the political marketing process that puts at greatest risk the politician's autonomy. The political ideas he or she stands for can often turn out to be in contradictory to the four main forces pressuring her, whether systemic, personal, antagonist, or opportunist: though they appear to help her, if she wants to stick to her "own" campaign themes, she will need a lot of energy to get out of these traps – systemic forces being stronger than personal ones, as shown in Figure 2.7.

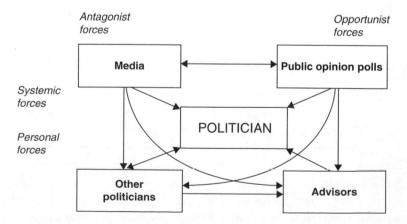

Figure 2.7   The forces hindering the choice of campaign themes.

Conversely, it is very tempting to adopt as the main themes of the communication campaign those issues that dominate public opinion, as indicated by polls. Some politicians today never even risk any other kind of campaign issue. One of the reasons for Al Gore's loss in the 2000 US presidential campaign was for instance allegedly the pressure of his advisors not to insist on environmental issues, since at that time they were not regarded as vote-winning issues – a decision that took away from him a considerable share of his authenticity, as clearly demonstrated in the following years when his popularity rose with the stand he took on the environment.[17]

On that account, French Socialist presidential candidate in 2007, Ségolène Royal, went even a step further, deciding to leave the decisions regarding some of her main campaign themes to groups of citizens gathered around France in a so-called "participation" process.[18]

These general considerations aside, the choice of campaign themes and issues to be put forward remains beyond the scope of the present book, and is obviously to be decided, case by case, by the politicians and their advisors: sticking to overtly political or social problems, playing up local or national issues (in the case of local elections), or adopting an ideological or a pragmatic platform, and so on.

It should be noted, however, that some political advisors do not observe this warning, and claim to offer politicians help in matters of campaign theme selection. Each has a different formula, creating criteria that correlate the popularity of certain issues with the credibility they would have if espoused by their employer-candidates. Such a method can only constitute an empirical process which presumes to be rational: it is not possible to know in advance if a politician will indeed be credible with a new campaign theme, since he has no precedent to go on, and the polls on which the study is based deal only with a potential situation. This undoubtedly sets the limit political marketing consultants are not to exceed, as decision-making aids cannot replace actual political decisions.[19]

Technically speaking, however, political marketing not only provides useful information through opinion surveys, it also offers two useful guidelines for choosing campaign themes, while complying with the two basic rules outlined above:

- simplification, by limiting the number of campaign themes;
- overall harmonization of the campaign, through the choice of a general theme.

Limiting the number of campaign themes   In any case, and whatever his final decision about the issues he will publicly endorse, the politician will have to observe the same golden rule that also underlines the construction of his image. To the extent possible, he will have to limit the number of different campaign themes to avoid giving his communication recipients the impression of being too dispersed: modern mass media are sometimes even less conducive than the older forms to the transmission of complex messages, a fact which strongly argues in favor of taking the Unique Selling Proposition (USP) as a guideline.

The best recent example of successful application of the USP in a general election campaign was probably that adopted in the United Kingdom by Prime Minister Margaret Thatcher in 1983 just after the Falklands War: she was portrayed by and large as the person who had defended the last vestiges of the British Empire, so to speak. The emphasis on economic issues by Bill Clinton in the 1992 election is another good example of the triumph of the USP for limiting the range of campaign themes.[20] Clinton's mastery of political marketing went even a step further when he cleverly distinguished himself by very early on by devising a very thorough government program and had the idea of sending copies of it free of charge to all public libraries. In a way, this shipment became a campaign theme in itself: the idea that he had a program that any American citizen could find in his own town, also implied a credible relationship of proximity.

Of course, one can sometimes find examples contrary to this line of conduct. In 1981, for example, during the campaign that led François Mitterrand to the French presidency, he set out an imposing list of "110 propositions," most of which were often too complex to be fathomed via the communication process. In any case, there were too many for the voters to remember! Yet the very fact that there were more than 100 "problems" facing French society in 1981 was clearly a way of emphasizing a single political campaign issue which, in a way, was derived from the "110 propositions": the candidate was clearly perceived in the public eye as one whose policy, if elected, would differ considerably from the one that had formerly dominated. In fact, the very figure "110" proved to be François Mitterrand's USP in 1981.[21]

But even if there are exceptions to the rule of limitation, the rule of thumb remains that, the fewer the objectives, the more effective the campaign. Ronald Reagan's election campaigns will remain models of this kind, notably that of 1980, built around a small number of clear-cut campaign issues, beginning with tax reductions.

It must be said that reducing the number of issues or oversimplifying the contents of the modern political campaign to facilitate their dissemination in the media, is probably one of the main causes for the reduction of content in a political communication, which is related to the so-called "end of ideology" nowadays stigmatized by some political analysts.

The choice of a tone for the campaign　　The positioning of the communication campaign often results from this decisive choice. Are the main themes of politician's campaign to have a polemic turn, or rather will they presume to be "neutral" or pseudo-objective?

Here again, the choice of the campaign's tone reveals how political marketing choices interlock with the political choices themselves. Running an effective communication campaign means having a strong internal coherence between the essence of the politician's discourse and its form. It is quite difficult to opt for relatively aggressive campaign themes if at the same time one seeks a friendly image in order to win over the persuadable voters who might otherwise be scared off by an overly aggressive approach. Likewise, a dynamic, innovative image is unlikely to serve the candidate if his campaign themes are too commonplace, and so on.

So the choice of campaign tone is closely linked to that of the politician's image: the subjective dimension of the interpretation of these two elements binds them together. It thus becomes indispensable to establish a perfect homology between the politician's image and the campaign themes he develops, so as not to weaken the quality of his communication.

As with the problem of maintaining the image, too, the tone of the campaign should respect the same register in the long term, so as not to disconcert the communication recipients.

Finally, the tone should obviously match the previous strategic choices: a conquest campaign with not have the same tone as a plain image-building campaign.

2.2.2   Devising tactics and implementing them: "the campaign plan"

As in any campaign, once a strategy has been decided on, tactics must be devised to implement it, with two main steps regarding political communication:

- charting the campaign timetable;
- defining a suitable "media plan."

Setting up a sufficiently precise campaign plan is essential, because it will allow proper coordination with the candidate who will spend most of his time far from his base, touring the electoral district, or the country during a national election. The campaign plan will then be able to achieve some coherence between the headquarters where the main communication team is working and the candidate. It will also be a good reminder of the core objectives of the campaign, despite the permanent duress coming from the accumulation of disparate news regurgitated daily by the media, and from the candidate's opponents' own campaigns. Of course, the campaign plan might be revised if unexpected events occur.

2.2.2.1   Charting the campaign timetable
Ideally, the campaign should be carried out in several phases:

- time allowing for a trial campaign should first be made;
- after the trial, a campaign timetable should be devised.

This timetable should allow certain components of the campaign plan to be modified if necessary, either in light of the results of opinion surveys, or, in response to the communication programs of rival politicians:

2.2.2.1.1 The trial campaign   Whenever possible, a pilot campaign should be conducted on a geographically reduced scale, preferably in a sector with known political characteristics: towns with a political past markedly linked to the candidate, towns

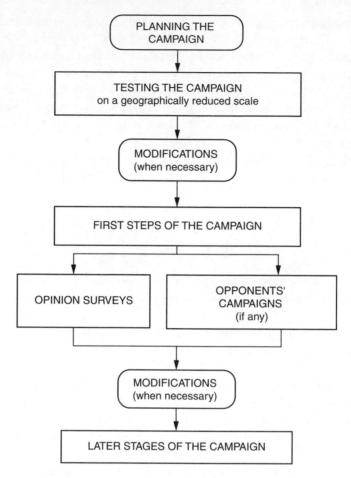

Figure 2.8　The different stages of a political communication campaign.

in which the vote is often indicative of the final electoral outcome, or highly representative of the priority targets of an image-making campaign, and so on.

On this reduced scale, it becomes easier to design fairly precise opinion surveys to come up with a clear idea of a campaign's potential effectiveness, just as commercial marketing runs trial sales of new products in reduced-scale markets, or as Hollywood producers organize sneak previews of new movies with a real paying public.

In certain instances, one can limit oneself to testing a sample section of the campaign to check its positioning, or to know which choice to make when several neighboring options are open. The use of direct mail has been of great service in this kind of experimentation, especially concerning the choice of campaign themes: a few thousand letters with enclosed reply coupons can provide valuable information.

In most cases, a minimal trial is run, with a representative group of recipients receiving the principal communication elements (posters, programs, brochures, leaflets, etc.). The decision is then made to modify or maintain those elements according to five criteria:

- the "recognition (memorization) score," establishes how many people remember the communication element after having been exposed to it;
- the "attribution score" establishes if the recipient can attribute the communication element to the politician (or the party) that sent it;
- the "confusion score" corresponds to the reverse of the preceding one;
- the "approval score," established in the light of recipient's positive response to the communication element;
- the "disapproval score" is the reverse of the preceding one.

We should point out that although these five scoring criteria may seem to overlap, they are in fact distinct: for instance, a high approval score can be judged inadequate if the remaining people questioned register a high confusion score; a slightly lower approval score can be preferable if the disapproval score is significantly lower, and so on.[22]

2.2.2.1.2 Charting the campaign timetable   This seemingly banal step of the process is actually of greater importance than it might seem at first: putting together a timetable for the campaign implies two other choices, which can prove to be crucial:

- the choice of when to start the campaign;
- the choice of when to escalate the campaign.

THE CHOICE OF CAMPAIGN STARTING DATE   This choice can have considerable consequences, and political marketing cannot come up with an appropriate response in advance. Recent history provides as many examples of late campaign starts that resulted in victory as those that ended in defeat.[23]

Nevertheless, most political marketing specialists often advise against starting a campaign at too early a date. But an early campaign start can be beneficial at times, especially in the case of lesser-known candidate (though this can never be taken as a hard and fast rule). The early start of Barack Obama's campaign for the 2008 presidential election is a good example of that kind. Knowing that he would probably face opponents better known than him in the primaries, starting with Hillary Clinton, whose candidacy had long been a probability, Barack Obama's team decided to organize the upcoming campaign as early as in mid-2007, particularly by establishing local relays all around the country, a grassroots campaign at its best. So when his fellow Democratic opponents came as usual to campaign in each state one or two months before their primary, they had the surprise to see that many regular local Democratic activists had already been enrolled by Obama's campaign months ahead, and of course would not commit for another candidate.

The most commonly observed rule as to the timing of the campaign start is indeed to take into account the candidate's situation in regard to the seat he is contesting. If he is unknown in the area, or if he is a first-time candidate, he should probably be advised to start earlier in order to conduct a longer campaign; if he is standing for re-election, he may begin his campaign at a later date, knowing full well he should not leave too much ground to his adversaries.

In the United States, the peculiarities of the electoral system usually oblige politicians to start early, with very rare exceptions. The primaries system encourages candidates for nomination by the two leading parties to make a major effort from the very first primary elections, even if, technically, the stakes are low, as only a small number of delegates are to be appointed for the final convention. For example, getting ahead in the New Hampshire primaries in the 1976 presidential elections, Jimmy Carter, made the wise decision to campaign actively to be the first to choose convention delegates for the Iowa Caucus. No serious candidate up to then had devoted any real attention to it. A small series of televised advertising spots, costing a mere US$8,000, in this small state of under three million inhabitants, made him one of the more serious contenders for the Democratic nomination in the eyes of the media and the public at the very start of that election year. Bill Clinton's long fight on the 1992 primaries trail is another example of an early start for a little-known candidate, former governor of a "small" state, Arkansas, who was thought to have little chance since he was not initially supported by the Democratic "establishment."

THE CHOICE OF WHEN TO ESCALATE THE CAMPAIGN   Again, this is a crucial step, just like following a doctor's prescription: taking too small a dose has no effect; too large a dose is harmful. This means that the choice of stepping up the campaign can only be empirical; political marketing consultants have to rely on their know-how, which includes a good deal of intuition!

Four main types of timetables are possible:

- A *gradually escalating campaign* aims for a relatively regular presence in the field and intensifies as election day approaches. This is the most common kind of campaigning; it relies on a corresponding increase in voter interest from day to day, in accordance with the theory that the greater the media interest in the election, the greater the number of people who pay attention to it (which peaks, of course, in the final days before the election).
- A *"blitz" campaign* aims at media saturation through short-term concentration, with all forms of media and communication instruments brought into play simultaneously, as in the second part of Ross Perot's campaign for the presidency in 1992, or French President François Mitterrand's late blitz campaign for re-election in 1988.
- A *step-by-step campaign* is probably the most difficult to get off the ground, but it can prove to be among the most effective kinds of campaign; the candidate's image takes shape as the campaign progresses, with the help of "pseudo-events" carefully programmed in advance which help focus public and media attention;[24]
- A *"stop and go campaign,"* often opted for when the politician lacks adequate funds, starts up again every time a particular event can potentially boost its impact (publication of public opinion survey results, TV broadcasts with the candidate as a guest, and so on). Such tactics liken the politician to a surfer, who uses the energy of the waves to propel himself forward.

Political marketing consultants do not tend to limit their escalation choices to only one of the kinds defined above, preferring to combine several for greater effectiveness. In any case, the campaign calendar must be kept relatively flexible, in order to be able to respond to any of the unforeseen events which can crop up in the political arena, for example consequences of new opponents on the scene, or a rival campaign, new national or international incidents, and so on.

But one must be fully aware that certain choices about campaign escalation can hamper subsequent maneuvers during the communication campaign. For instance, late escalation impedes the mobilization of activists and volunteers,[25] and their ability to serve as relays for the central campaign organization.

ASSESSMENT OF THE END OF THE CAMPAIGNING PERIOD   When preparing the campaign schedule, one must also assess when it should end since there is significant inertia that is part of the complex political communication process. It brings about a long latency period, which might forbid any evolution in the final days of the election period, the so-called "time's up" moment, as North American political analysts have dubbed it.

A good example of "time's up" is George H.W. Bush's last-ditch effort to change his campaign methods during the final fortnight of his 1992 campaign, which did not help him win (although it did stir some movement at the polls).[26] Similarly, when John Kerry had clearly lost ground to George W. Bush at the end of the 2004 US presidential campaign, even producing nearly a new advertising spot a day did not help, since obviously the end of the "useful" period of campaigning had come early.

In some countries where it is forbidden by law to publish the results of surveys of voter intent during the last few days before the election, politicians and parties are then compelled to sponsor specific "private" surveys in order to assess if it is still worth making last-minute campaigning efforts.[27]

2.2.2.2   The media plan

Deciding on the actual channels to convey the candidate's communication is the second tactical aspect of the political marketing process. But before we examine how this decision is made, we must recall some of the general principles of the communication process in general.[28]

2.2.2.2.1 Media and effective communication

THE DRAWBACKS OF COMMUNICATION SELECTIVITY   Political marketing cannot function without a preliminary knowledge of the basics of the media it is to employ. Whatever the message the politician wishes to convey, his communication must be made through a medium, whether a narrowcast, interactive one (face-to-face verbal communication) or a unidirectional broadcast mass medium with practically no interaction (television, posters, etc.).

The political message will thus necessarily follow the standard process of all forms of communication (see Figure 2.9):

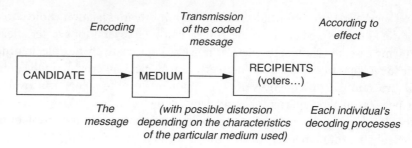

Figure 2.9   Coding and decoding: from candidate to recipient.

As indicated in the caption to Figure 2.9, it is now an established fact that, as Marshall McLuhan's famous intuitions maintained, each medium leaves its mark on a communication, sometimes reinforcing the message's effectiveness, sometimes weakening, even contradicting it, depending on the medium's psycho-sociological and psycho-physiological peculiarities.

Even with the exception of examples where the message does not reach the intended recipients (for some reason they do not see the posters or watch the TV program, etc.), political marketing specialists are well aware that their communication, once perceived, runs a high risk of a loss of effectiveness, with more or less favorable variations depending on the singularities of each medium.

The chief factor of dispersion is undoubtedly the very selectivity of the communication process. Media specialists, as well as neurophysiologists, concur that, in all regards, the recipient of a communication exposes himself to it, perceives it, and decodes it only after a series of choices, conscious or not, of three different kinds:

The selectivity of media exposure   First, many surveys since the Second World War have confirmed that voters, when political communication is involved, are clearly inclined to seek exposure only to issues they identify with: conservative sympathizers will probably change channels when a liberal politician begins to speak, and, of course, would not attend his meetings, and so on.

This first choice, usually made consciously, is one reason for the loss of effectiveness in communication campaigns, the very intent of which is to change the preferences of recipients with previously clear-cut political opinions. This phenomenon also inhibits political communication as a whole: voters who are not interested in politics tend not to expose themselves to this kind of message.[29]

The selectivity of communication perception   This second contingency is much more difficult to assess, as the operation is an unconscious one: even when exposed to a communication, recipients with very different opinions are strongly inclined not to take notice of it, like a driver cruising down a road flanked by numerous billboards:

although he is exposed to the communication, he often chooses to not "look at" them, not perceive them.

The selectivity of decoding and memorizing communication   The third selectivity factor occurs during the decoding of a communication: each recipient deciphers and interprets it in the light of his own previous experience and ideas, in short, according to his previous referents, retaining essentially those elements that reflect his own ideas, interests or tastes. Memorization and consequently the effectiveness of the communication are directly at stake here. As early as the 1950s, Paul Lazarsfeld's political science research team had clearly delineated this process in a series of highly detailed surveys.[30]

WAYS OF IMPROVING THE COMMUNICATION PROCESS   Two main tools are likely to limit this dispersion:

- feedback;
- redundancy.

Feedback provides the transmitter with the opportunity of clarifying, if necessary, the communication in light of the recipient's requests, as Figure 2.10 shows:

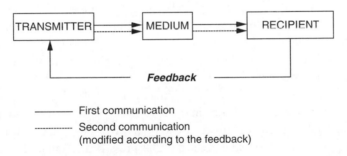

Figure 2.10   Feedback and the communication process.

Thanks to feedback, it is then possible to improve the effectiveness of the communication process significantly, by reducing misunderstanding; of course, this bidirectionality in the communication process is conceivable only when the politician employs marketing instruments that allow direct contact with those he is trying to reach.

"Redundancy" is a method of reformulating the initial communication by modifying only those components that will improve comprehension among the recipients. These modifications are generally based on indications furnished in feedback (which also provides a means to assess the recipients' misunderstanding).[31]

The inevitable distortions in any communication process can thus be highly inimical to political communication and must be taken into account in political marketing. Thorough knowledge of the particular characteristics of each medium is therefore indispensable, since each medium will affect in its way the effectiveness of the political communication: the more "precise" the media employed – "precise" meaning limiting the risks of dispersion, or misunderstanding – the better the potential effect of the political communication.

2.2.2.2.2 The resulting choice of individual media   The media plan, or "communication mix,"[32] as commercial marketing specialists call it, is, empirically, a kind of media "cocktail," mixed in terms of what the real imperative is judged to be:

- to reach a limited number of recipients with maximum effectiveness, since it is understood that it is nearly impossible for the message to be immediately and genuinely effective if the recipients are too numerous;
- to reach as many people as possible, repeatedly, in rapid succession, to enhance the "agenda-setting effect"[33] which is the usual result of increasing the range of communication recipients.

The choice of the actual communication network is made in two steps:

- first, determining the media priority;
- second, choosing the exact channels to use.

DECIDING THE MEDIA PRIORITY   For each campaign, the choice of media priority is made in direct relationship with the differentiation of the "communication quality" they allow, as we have just mentioned. Certain media, due to their characteristics, will then be obvious first choices for specific priority targets or objectives in the communication campaign.

For example, an image-making campaign aimed at strengthening the position of a politician among the upper classes, in order to obtain funding and set up a number of "clubs" or "political circles" for future support, will not need such mass media methods as posters or advertising in the popular press, but can make satisfactory use of the fame televised appearances offer, and personalized contacts facilitated by the modern means of direct mail, and so on.

Decision based on target type   The more precise the knowledge of the communication recipient, the greater the communication's effectiveness potential. To this effect, Table 2.1 on page 63 shows the distribution of media according to the target types.

Choice based on the nature of the message   It is sometimes preferable to select the medium in view of the nature of the communication and its complexity. A communication with a precise message, a non-complex unit of information, will then best be served by posters, radio or television. On the other hand, a more

Table 2.1 The distribution of media according to target types

Objective	Media	Target
Reaching the opinion relays of the different socio-occupational categories, possibly collecting donations from sympathizers	Meetings, conferences, direct mail, direct marketing methods in general, the Internet	Precise "external": recipients differentiated by occupation or social category, etc.
Mobilization of activists and volunteers	Election rallies, television spots, video tapes, Intranet (*)	Precise "internal": favorable recipients
Conquest communication, marking a difference from political opponents	Posters, printed press and public relations, radio, television, (political advertising if paid access to those media)	Not precise "mixed": general audience

(*) If the activists who support the politician are well organized and equipped, then "Intranet" means in fact communication to these precisely identified supporters through e-mail lists, etc. (which would be called "Intranet" in any organization, company, etc.).

complex communication, linked to campaign issues or a candidate's platform, will come through better in the printed press (daily newspapers, weekly news magazines, specialized periodicals), or through a complete program sent directly by mail or distributed by activists and volunteers, and so on.

Here, the Internet provides an incomparable quality of communication for complex messages, but will only reach potential voters already favorable to the politician, (though now *spam* and new forms of Internet advertising may help to reach other categories of voters). This does not make Internet use easy for conquest communication, except in the world of the so-called *Web 2.0*: here, as we will see later, various kinds of "social networks" may more efficiently reach people not initially interested in political communication.

But if the intention is to help build the politician's image, those media that directly bring out his personal qualities, such the audiovisual media, which give a sense of proximity to the audience, will usually be preferable.

The quest for speed The quest for speed leads to another media classification: direct-communication media, particularly electronic, are preferable. If we combine the two criteria of a communication's complexity and its intended speed, we obtain what is shown in Table 2.2 on page 64.

CHOICE OF EXACT COMMUNICATION CHANNELS Once the kinds of media have been decided on, political marketing consultants must select the precise channels they will use for each kind of medium: choice of title(s) in the daily press, television network(s), billboard network(s), etc.

Table 2.2 The two criteria of a communication's complexity and its intended speed

Objective	Media	Kind of communication
Transmitting a simple communication, a non-complex message (slogan, etc.)	Unauthorized posters or billboard advertising, advertising in the printed media, advertising in general, television spots, radio	Fast
Transmitting a more complex message (program, etc.)	Meetings, conferences, rallies. direct mail, leaflets, election press in general, most direct marketing methods, some radio shows, video tapes, or DVDs, the Internet (web sites).	Slow
Establishing the "image" of the politician, or strengthening it	Public appearances of the candidate throughout his constituency, "canvassing"), grassroots campaigning, meetings …	Slow
	Public relations, press conferences	Slow and indirect(*)
	The Internet (blogs, Web 2.0.)	Fast but indirect (*)
	radio, and mostly television	Fast

(*) Indirect means here the necessity for the politician to pass trough "independent" intermediaries without being able to "control" the quality of the way they are relaying their communication

Problems of duplication among channels Choosing the media in view of their supposed suitability for a specific communication is not enough. It is also necessary to ensure that the different channels will not overlap.

In general, an effort is made to limit the risk of duplication among the different channels used. If the intended target is middle and senior business executives, it would be pointless to advertise in more than one of the main business papers (*The Financial Times* in the United Kingdom, *The Wall Street Journal* in the United States, or *Les Echos* in France, for instance) unless one's intention is in fact to create a redundancy effect (deliberately duplicating a communication in order to reinforce it).

Media specialists know for a fact that it is impossible to avoid overlapping different media audiences completely if most of the desired recipients are to be reached. The readership of a daily paper, for instance, changes more or less from day to day: some buy it only on a certain day for a particular weekly supplement (literary, cultural, economic), others because of a special news interest, etc. Usually then, several insertions are made, even if it means heavy duplication.

This makes it necessary to carry out a thorough preliminary study of the audience the political communication campaign would reach through a particular channel, because it will help decide which channel (medium) will have the highest penetration rate in relationship to the target. For the upper socio-occupational category of target, for instance, the "prestige" newspapers, such as *The Times* or *The Guardian* in the United Kingdom, *The New York Times* in the United States, or *Le Monde*, in France, correspond best, because they are read by the leading opinion makers, and so on. To make this choice, political marketing specialists often employ numerous readership surveys commissioned by their counterparts in the commercial marketing sector.

Seeking a synergy among channels In some cases, political marketing tries to obtain an acceleration of the communication process, and to create redundancy artificially, by speeding up the agenda-setting effect. The task of choosing the channels then becomes quite intensive, requiring an in-depth knowledge of the target audience. Knowing the recipient's form of leisure allows for a contact to be made not only through the newspapers they read for their work but through the magazines they read for their pleasure, etc. It is plain to see that the targeted recipients can be thus closely circumscribed.

The complexity of factors that can play a role in the choice of media and the exact channels political communication will employ, partly explains the presence of professional marketing consultants in a politician's entourage: given their direct access to data banks on the general population, and their expertise with communication channels, they can quickly and effectively suggest an immediately workable media plan, whatever the campaign targets, without having to start from scratch.

Marketing advisors now have available computerized media-plan templates and related decision-making aids: within seconds they can provide media channel combinations based on the parameters we have previously stated. Such software can be highly intricate; certain so-called "evaluation and optimization" media plan simulations are even capable of simultaneously evaluating the campaigning plans one is hesitating between and optimizing the final choice in terms of available budget, advertising rates or cost per insertion, and so on.[34] But it must be kept in mind that these systems can only "reason" in terms of previous data, and cannot take into account new factors which might strongly influence a new campaign. Let us again recall that it is always highly risky to merely replicate a previous marketing campaign, as successful as it may have been.

A good illustration of this kind of specific media choice directed by marketing advisors in recent years has been the choice of media made by some politicians to make their candidacy statement. Instead of doing it in a "classical" way, so to speak, and going to one of the main evening television newscasts, some American politicians have announced their candidacy on popular evening television talk shows, targeting viewers not interested in politics who do not watch the news. The example was set in 2003 by Arnold Schwarzenegger, who had announced he would run for election as Governor of California on the *Tonight Show* with Jay Leno. More recently, John McCain announced his candidacy for the presidency on February 28, 2007 at the *Late Night with David Letterman* show. Not only did this broaden their targeted audience, but it also gave a "lighter" tone to the exercise, especially useful in the eyes of his advisors in the case of McCain who was one of the oldest candidates ever to run for president.

Similarly, in France, Jacques Chirac made unexpected but well thought-out choices to announce his candidacy in both his successful presidential campaigns. He made his 1994 candidacy announcement on November 4 of that year in an interview in a regional daily paper *La Voix du Nord*, not distributed at all outside northern France. Similarly, this time in the south of France, on February 2002, in the midst of a routine visit in Avignon to greet the newly elected mayor of the town, a fellow party member, he announced that he would be seeking re-election on February 11, 2002. In both cases, instead of trying to reach a vast audience directly by going to one of the main evening newscasts or by giving an interview to one of the main daily papers, he chose to state forcefully that he was a non-elitist politician who cared about non-Parisian citizens, and obviously judiciously betting on the fact that all the other media would relay his candidacy announcement anyway, thus cleverly connoted.

The final media plan   All the factors we have described finally merge into the media plan which aims to coordinate as well as possible the available means, the intended objectives, and the desired targets, to establish the classification and timetable of the campaign channels. Generally, a regrouping of the channels in three or four categories results in the following:

- compulsory channels;
- complementary channels;
- useful channels;
- negligible channels.

Most of the efforts and financial resources will be poured into the compulsory channels, as well as the complementary channels, which, for example, may be used for their ability to convey certain kinds of messages and to help establish a particularly apt agenda-setting effect.

Some funds might be funneled for communication via "useful" channels, which are often classified as such for reasons other than their direct value to political communication per se. For instance, to help mobilize the candidate's supporters, they can be enlisted to participate in a poster campaign.

On the other hand, negligible channels will not be used for the campaign, and will even be rejected (refusing interview requests from journalists employed by certain channels, for instance – which will require a good deal of diplomacy from the politician's press agent so that the former are not alienated despite the refusal).

Finally, it must be remembered that the choice of communication channel is naturally also made by taking into account local customs or regulations, some democratic nations being quite strict about the use of paid political advertising, or even access to the media. American and British law usually places a ceiling on political campaign spending. Since 1990, French law even forbids any kind of paid political advertising during the three months before the election, and enforces a complete ban on televised political commercials.[35]

In most democratic countries, the media are more or less subject to some independent regulatory body, which defines a charter of political pluralism in the media. For instance, the American Federal Communication Commission (FCC), which allocates radio and television frequencies, has for years established its own precedents on the "Equal Time Rule, stating that a network must allow equal access to all political parties or ideas; France's Conseil Supérieur de l'Audiovisuel (CSA) strictly ensures that the government, parliamentary majority and opposition share equal news time, with some of its staff keeping year-round statistics on how the main television networks respect this "three-thirds" rule, and so on.[36]

* * *

To conclude this chapter, we must note that we have deliberately overlooked one choice factor that usually turns out to be the most important: the problem of cost, which frequently reduces in practice the vast range of theoretically available communication means. Sometimes, conversely, political marketing has to contain the politician or his entourage, who wrongly think that all campaign funds must be completely used up, when the candidate's overexposure could be pointless, if not detrimental.

In any case, the use of media by modern political marketing clearly shows that we are now quite far removed from near-archaic simplicity of communication procedure during the infancy of political communication in the twentieth century: we know for certain today that combining a series of communications through different channels is much more effective than the single predominant use of the leading audiovisual networks. The famous slogan "Dominate the dominating media" coined by one of the first great political marketing consultants, Joe Napolitan, is not always considered the best solution today.

But the previous developments have also demonstrated that political marketing is not a science, with predictable and guaranteed results, any more than communications in general are. In a way, political communication campaigns can only mimic one another empirically, trying to adapt to recent events. This axiom must be kept in mind when activating a political communication process.

Finally, this complexity and these uncertainties explain the double professionalization of political communication in recent years: first, through the systematic intervention of highly specialized political marketing consultants all around the world; but also through the professionalization of politicians themselves, more and more conscious that their job now requires them to master the tools and the processes of today's modern globalized political communication.[37]

Notes

1 French politicians have nicknamed it "desert crossing"("la traversée du désert"), alluding especially to General de Gaulle's long absence from power between 1946 and 1958.

2 The word "propaganda" has a religious origin, since it was first used in connection with the creation by the Roman Catholic Church of the so-called "*Congregation for the propagation of faith*" (*De propaganda fide*) in 1597.

3 See Maarek 2005.

4 Conversely, when Ronald Reagan in 1986 and Bill Clinton in 1996 decided again to focus their re-election campaigns on the economy, their decision merely to repeat what had been worked for them before was based on its positive outcome – as Clinton summed it up in his opening statement of the first of the 1996 debates with Dole, on October 7, 1996: "Four years ago, you took me on faith, now there is a record [on economics]."

5 Of course, lying about a situation during the campaign and hoping it would not be discovered until election day is another risk not to be taken lightly. The Spanish conservatives were thus doomed in March 2004, when their leader, the sitting prime minister, José María Aznar, repeatedly tried to blame the Basque separatists for the terrorist attack on Atocha train station and the Atocha-bound trains which would have helped his party. When it was quickly established, just before the election, that he had lied, and that he had known soon afterwards that it was an Al Qaeda attack, voters abandoned the conservatives in disdain and chose an outsider, the Socialist politician José Luis Zapatero.

6 In 1995, in France, Lionel Jospin tried the same tactics against Jacques Chirac, deliberately letting things go politely during the televised debate with him, in order to maintain his chances for the next elections – with a good result in the the 1997 parliamentary election, but to no advantage for himself, as proven by his defeat in the 2002 presidential election.

7 See Klapper 1960.

8 On opinion relays, see Elihu Katz's famous essay, "The two-step flow of communication," in *Reader in Public Opinion and Communication*, Glencoe Free Press, 1950 (edited by B. Berelson and M. Janowitz) and Katz and Lazarsfeld (1964).

9 The same misfortune happened to former French Prime Minister Lionel Jospin, the Socialist Party candidate for the 2002 presidential elections, who went too far by declaring in his candidacy statement: "*The project I am proposing for the country is not a socialist project*" ... Al Gore's choice of Joe Lieberman, a much more "conservative" Democrat as presidential running mate in 2000 was similarly too far-fetched (Liebermann, indeed, even ended up endorsing McCain's candidacy in 2008).

10 Among many other successful examples of conquest cross-targeting, we might also mention Jacques Chirac's election to the French presidency in 1995 with a "leftist" slogan, "reducing the social breakdown" ("réduire la fracture sociale") and Tony Blair's bold use of certain traditional British values in the 1997 election.

11 This weak maintenance campaign in fact ended by diminishing the chances of many members of her party to be elected to the German Parliament.

12 See Prysby 2008.

13 The 1998 Bundestag campaign, for instance, was fatal for German Chancellor Helmut Kohl who could not manage to change his image swiftly enough of "politician of the past" in spite of a brand new political program, to make the voters forget about his 16 years at the helm of his country.

14   Some of Europe's environmentalist parties tend to employ similar arguments regarding the destruction of the environment.

15   The damage to Dean's image was heightened by the fact that radio and television newscasts kept playing the "Dean scream" over and over again for several days, to a point that some media finally apologized to Dean.

16   Another constraint on politicians may even come from empirical scholarly research positioning the American candidates to the presidency and their chances of winning the race: they have concluded that the economy should always be on the agenda of a campaigning politician. But it remains empirical, and anyway probably does not apply in every country and for any campaign – the successful Bush campaign in 2004, for instance, seems much more related to the fear of terrorism in the wake of the September 11 attacks (see Vavreck 2009).

17   See for instance Medvick 2010.

18   This produced weak results, since the heterogeneous outcome of these consultations made her appear to lack any real program, as opposed to her main opponent Nicolas Sarkozy and his clear-cut reiterations of his well-groomed and planned campaign themes.

19   In a few cases, nevertheless, (Ronald Reagan's campaigns in the 1980s), specific decision-making software has even been openly devised to help decide on the candidate's campaign themes.

20   Chris Hegedus' and Artur Pennebaker's documentary we have already mentioned, *The War Room*, shows how Bill Clinton's two main communication advisors at that time, James Carville and George Stephanopoulos, reminding him on the phone not to forget to mention the economy during each of his public appearances (with a now famous catch phrase: "It's the economy, stupid").

21   In the 1988 presidential election, which he also won, François Mitterrand cultivated another brilliant paradox of a similar nature, by writing a "letter to the French people" ("lettre à tous les Français") as vague as it was long; the real aim (as the campaign theme cleverly suggested) was to suggest that he was establishing a direct link between himself, as "President of the Republic," in all the majesty of the term, and "his" citizens.

22   For example, if there is a choice to be made between two posters, one would make a different decision if only two approval scores were known, say 50 and 40, than if those scores were used in conjunction with disapproval scores of, respectively, 40 and 10: the gain of 10 in approval would probably be deemed less important than the increase of 30 in disapproval.

23   For instance French president Valéry Giscard d'Estaing was convinced that one of the main reasons for his losing office in 1981 was his late campaign start, whereas president François Mitterrand managed to be re-elected in the following elections, in 1988 thanks to a late start!

24   This category can include the "teaser" campaign, which is designed to suggest before showing. This tactic, borrowed from commercial marketing, may even involve momentarily holding back the name of the candidate or a political party.

25   All through this book, we will make a difference between party "activists" on the one side, and "sympathizers" or "volunteers" on the other. "Activists" are the individuals who are regular (local) supporters of a party (usually) or sometimes of a prominent politician; they are generally card-carrying members of the party, to which they pay an annual subscription. "Sympathizers" or "volunteers" are less regular supporters, often drawn to a specific campaign by the charisma of the political leader currently campaigning, and they might

very well stop being "active" after this specific campaign (we will come back later to these differences and their consequences on the running of the campaign).

26 Another example of "time's up" occurred on the eve of the 1988 French presidential elections, with the liberation of French hostages in Lebanon negotiated by the then prime minister and presidential candidate, Jacques Chirac. He nevertheless lost the race to François Mitterrand.

27 These last-minute surveys have to be taken very carefully, since their results may be misleading. For instance, when they reveal a high number of undecided voters, it might nevertheless mean that the "useful" campaigning period for some candidates is over: the alleged "undecided" voters might in fact have decided not to vote for a specific politician, but not yet for whom they will cast their vote *against him*! This happened for instance in France in 2002, when many voters had decided not to vote for the Socialist party candidate in the presidential election, Lionel Jospin, but had not yet decided which other "leftist" politician they would vote for, and sometimes even made their decision at the last minute in the polling station.

28 For further on the broad notions of communication through media and mass media, see any basic media and communication theory book or textbook.

29 See Blumler, Cayrol et al. 1978.

30 See Lazarsfeld et al. 1948, 1955. The psycho-physiological side of the selectivity problem is now being explored – and confirmed – by neuroscience specialists, who relate this selectivity process to the learning process of the brain cells. See *L'Homme neuronal*," Jean-Pierre Changeux, Fayard, Paris, 1983.

31 A simple example: two persons are talking (medium: face-to-face conversation); one of them does not know the meaning of a rare word his interlocutor has used and says so (feedback); his interlocutor repeats the sentence, but employs a more common word with a nearly identical meaning (redundancy).

32 Commercial marketing specialists sometimes make a distinction between the two terms: "communication mix" referring to the theoretical choice of the kind of media to be used, whereas the "media plan" is the choice of the actual channel for the application of the "communication mix." We will not adhere to this distinction, which is more theoretical than practical, since the choice of media and the choice of channel are usually inextricably linked.

33 "The agenda-setting effect" is, briefly put, the fact that certain issues come to the forefront by the very fact that the mass media have constantly taken them up. See the seminal article on that matter: M.E. McCombs and D.E. Shaw (1972).

34 Any modern commercial marketing reference book will list them in detail.

35 In compensation, some free campaign time is granted to candidates or political parties on television and radio within the two last weeks of the race. Free posting is made available to candidates and one-page leaflets carrying their programs are mailed free to all registered voters.

36 The rule has recently been changing, but has been valid for decades. For instance, in 2009, the CSA decided to include some of the French president's speeches, when deemed "political," in the time allotted for the government and for the parliamentary majority. This contrasts with Venezuelan president Hugo Chávez's 2010 decision to be able to cut any radio program as short when he wanted to speak to the public, at any time of day or night, even calling these appearances "De repente con Chávez" ("Suddenly with Chávez")… (*Le Monde*, February 11, 2010).

37   The same professionalization and attempt to control communication flows is increasingly necessary for politicians when they come to power. Since British prime minister Tony Blair appointed his 1997 campaign director Alastair Campbell as director of communication and strategy in his first ministry, more and more governments have followed suit, using the same tools as the head of state or government used when campaigning. For instance, in 2009, not only did Barack Obama continue to use *Twitter* as president, but he also devised an *iPhone* application for the White House. We won't go further into this because government communication is outside the scope of this book.

3

The means of analysis and information

Designing a political communication campaign cannot be done abstractly. One needs information on the "state" of the recipients, as well as on the campaign ground. Finally, in the case of an election campaign, it is essential to have some data on the opponent's communication policy, or, at the very least, to analyze what information one has about it. In 1928, in his famous book *Propaganda*, Edward Bernays already suggested that "A survey of public desires and demands (should) come to the aid of the political strategist ..."[1]

Thorough knowledge of the analytical tools available to political marketing is indispensable. The best-conceived campaign may well boast the most telegenic candidate, the cleverest posters, and the best possible marketing advisors, but it would take a miracle to guarantee its success if it were based on a faulty analysis.

We will not deal at length with information-gathering about opposing campaigns. In the first possible hypothesis, the analysis of rival political communication is made in the light of that campaign's maneuvers. This simply means assigning a few staffers to follow the rival campaigns, and, whenever deemed necessary, to supply a rejoinder by more or less modifying the campaign plan. The arrival of the Internet has made opposition research a little more complicated. Not only are the opponents' "official" websites, but also social networks such as *Facebook*, *MySpace*, *YouTube* or the so-called "blogosphere" are now part of the survey, thus requiring considerably more dedicated staff. In another hypothesis, which is beyond the scope of the present study, the candidate is helped by contacts in the rival communication teams or by useful tips, which make it possible to anticipate actions by the rival campaigns, a method which can tempt one beyond the boundaries of legality, as the infamous "Watergate" scandal showed.[2]

Campaign Communication and Political Marketing, First Edition. Philippe J. Maarek.
© 2011 Philippe J. Maarek. Published 2011 by Blackwell Publishing Ltd.

In this chapter we shall only discuss the functions of the most frequently used analytical tools. We shall not go into the "objective" means of field analysis, like census or micro-geographic peculiarities of the constituency: this aspect must be dealt with rigorously but does not present any methodological problem. We will instead attempt in this chapter to give a few tips regarding surveys and public opinion polling, which are the main tools for what we call the "subjective" part of the field analysis, meaning deciphering the state of mind of the political communication campaign's potential recipients.

The times when information sources were directly available to the politician himself, who could take stock of the state of opinion by going down to the Greek agora or the Main Street bar, are long since gone (unless it is a local election in a small town). The vast increase in the number of political communication recipients has radically transformed its modes of information-gathering.

In fact, these tools are not numerous. There are only two main categories of information or analysis that will give one an understanding of the state of mind of the communication recipients and their geographical location. Neither can be considered ideal:

- The ballot itself, with its certified figures, is obviously of great precision; but it presents the major drawback of being altogether too infrequent and hard to decipher. Besides which, it comes too late to be of use in planning a campaign.
- Public opinion polls, or surveys,[3] a second source of information, are, in a way, just the opposite; their chief advantage is their great flexibility; their main drawback: their lack of reliability, not so much for technical reasons, as we will see, but simply because they are mere simulations, and not a record of real behavior. Moreover, they are often quite costly, and must be carried out within a certain time span.

This chapter will first define the framework in which these two main methods of analysis and information become operative, then explain them in greater detail.

3.1 The general operative framework for informational and analytical tools

3.1.1 The operational chronology of informational and analytical tools

Political marketing employs opinion analysis tools at two (or preferably three) stages during the communication process (see Figure 3.1):

- During the selection of campaign themes and targets; this includes the indispensable "benchmark polls," the results of which often have a major influence on the main campaign decisions.
- After a "trial campaign," limited in time and place, for so-called "follow-up polls," in order to modify some previous campaign decisions.

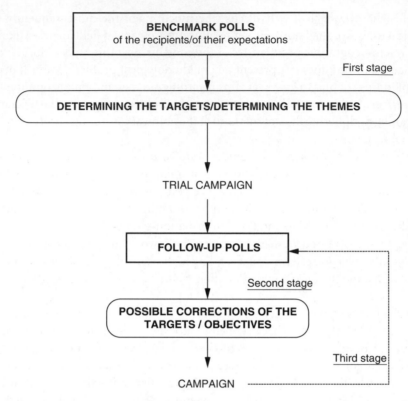

Figure 3.1   The different operative stages of informational and analytical tools.

- During the campaign itself, for so-called "tracking polls," in order to improve the positioning of the campaign, or to modify it, if feasible; in this case, it is usually best to retain the same panel, the same representative cross-section of the population, which is to be consulted periodically in order to trace possible voter evolution during the campaign with greater accuracy.

Naturally, if the candidate is handicapped by a lack of time or funds, informational and analytical tools will be reduced to the first stage of preliminary benchmark information (or, in the worst case scenario, to an analysis of the available statistical data which can be consulted at little or no expense: previously published demographic statistics, professional data available in certain countries or states on voter registration, and so on).

3.1.2   The kind of information expected

Since they constitute its obligatory starting point, political marketing expects to gain a good deal of information from public opinion analytical tools, such as:

- a better knowledge of the potential communication recipients, in particular those from whom the political message stands a good chance of eliciting a positive response; this helps to determine the political communication targets;
- a better notion of what drives public opinion, in order to establish the line of argumentation that a political communication can use to reassure recipients their needs are being looked after; this helps to establish the political communication objectives.

3.1.2.1 Aid in establishing targets

Much of the knowledge about political communication recipients is to be found in the socio-political characteristics of the population. Major expenditure is therefore not always necessary, since much useful data is usually already available, as for instance:

- general census records;[4]
- reports on the results of preceding elections;
- in some instances, tax or real estate registers;
- lists of members of current associations (from sports clubs to art circles), and their leaders, and so on.

Generally speaking, any data on particular characteristics of intended recipients of a communication campaign can be useful for targeting. The fact that a given district has a higher newspaper readership can be a helpful key as to the best media to use, and so on. It can also be very useful to obtain customer data and files from companies or businesses. Some countries, however, forbid extensive distribution of such personal files in order to protect the private lives of their citizens, so this has to be done within the limits laid down by their respective law (renting, buying, etc.).

Polls can then be conducted to determine in greater detail which segments of the intended population are most likely to be receptive to the communication. The polling questions can be dictated by the socio-political characteristics of the recipients; in this manner, new targets can be distinguished as such, or as potential opinion relays.

3.1.2.2 Aid in setting objectives

Knowledge of the motivations and expectations of public opinion gathered through surveys plays an increasingly crucial role in modern political marketing: communication consultants tend to press politicians into setting or redefining their campaign objectives in the light of these polling results.

This means that consultants naturally tend to place great reliance on analytical tools that give them a better understanding of the average citizen's alleged preoccupations and this explains the recourse to surveys that bring to light all sorts of needs relating to physiology, security, membership, self-esteem, accomplishments, and so on.

Objective data on the characteristics of the targeted population alone cannot reveal its expectations or motivations. Quite often, the subjective fears or preoccupations of the population have little rapport with their real objective situation.

There is one well-known example of this dichotomy: few Jews remain in Poland today, but such objective statistical data would not reveal that the subjective, irrational myth of Jewish "power" remains an abiding fear among Poles, as surveys have shown.[5]

Since these surveys seem to reveal the "real" subjective expectations of the communication targets, the temptation would be to make a direct application of them to modify certain themes of the future political communication. Politicians will sometimes have to fight to maintain as the main objectives of their campaign certain ideas not connected with survey results.

3.2   The different types of informational and analytical tools

3.2.1   Past election results

The data provided by previous elections, of course, are the most reliable available to political marketing: in the field of political communication, the election outcome is the best possible transposition of product purchasing process in commercial marketing. While a survey on the probable voting choices does not automatically translate into a real vote as suggested in the polling, the vote itself is concrete and final, exactly like the purchasing process.

Political scientists habitually try to make estimates from the results of previous elections, complemented, when possible, by the results of surveys conducted just after people have voted (known as exit polls). Such extrapolations provide more precise information than the usual surveys. But the process remains imperfect at best, if only because it does not allow access to those who, having abstained in a previous poll, might very well decide to vote in a subsequent election (young people who have reached voting age are also excluded).

Making an extrapolation on the basis of previous election results also creates problems of interpretation, due to two major obstacles:

- The elections providing the basis for extrapolation are usually rather distant from each other in time, except for the relatively rare case of an incumbent politician's sudden death or his resignation, for whatever reason. The election situations thus differ for two reasons. First, new political events occur in the period between two elections, which are naturally not taken into consideration by the electorate during the previous visit to the polls; second, voters are faced with a different choice in the new election, as the candidates are not usually all the same from one election to another.
- Because of this time lag, estimates often must take into account the results of more recent elections of a different kind, which could considerably distort the analysis. Can one really assume that the voter casts his ballot the same way for a national election as he does for a local election?

Thus, though they present the rare advantage of being based on a body of sound and accurate data, the analyses derived from previous electoral data, paradoxically, are not truly reliable.

Nevertheless, they do provide those professionals well aware of this drawback with highly useful information which can have a strong influence on the political marketing campaign, and even more on the campaign's political content itself. In particular, the analysis of previous election results is useful in appraising the potential behavior of voters from one ballot to the other in twin-ballot elections: even if one maintains doubts as to voter constancy from one ballot to the next, one can logically assume that the abstentionists of the first ballot who decide to take part in the second ballot, or the voters who switch from one candidate to another, are likely to behave similarly in subsequent elections. A good analysis of previous vote transfers can thus mean the difference between winning or losing an election: it can make the candidate refrain from introducing into his communication campaign any elements likely to handicap possible transfers in his favor, in the event he is still competing in the second ballot and needs to rely on a considerable number of vote transfers to win.

Although not as accurate as it would seem first, the analysis of the previous election results is nonetheless an essential part of the process of delimiting the political marketing campaign.

3.2.2   Opinion polls

Opinion polls, we know, constitute the main source of data available to political marketing, because of the extraordinary fluidity of the political communication recipients.

A television manufacturer, for instance, can use very precise statistics to estimate his exact sales development potential. The average number of television sets per home and the size of the household can provide a fairly good indication of the potential sale of "second sets," and a survey will give him a closer idea on how large a household must be before the purchase of a second set is considered. Even if the market is not always absolutely rational, manufacturers and their marketing consultants can still devise a fairly dependable production and marketing policy.

In matters of political marketing this is evidently not the case at all: more so than the consumer marketplace, the political milieu suffers from a lack of rationality. For instance, how is it possible to predict what sympathy factor could encourage the voter to prefer one candidate over another, when the latter might theoretically be closer to his ideas or socio-occupational category?

This factor explains why the main information source for political communication professionals, and, beyond them, politicians themselves, is to be found in the analysis and public opinion assessment tools, or surveys, which are only possible way to follow the ebb and flow of attitudes among communication recipients.

3.2.2.1   The different types of surveys
Three main categories of surveys can be differentiated according to the type of data they supply:

- one-time surveys;
- periodic surveys conducted among the same cross-section of people;
- non-directive interviews and focus groups.

3.2.2.1.1 One-time surveys   The one-time survey is the typical opinion poll, which is usually published in newspapers or quoted in television news, and so on.
   Two general options are open:

- The candidate, provided resources are available, can commission a special survey centered on a single objective and composed of one or several correlated questions.
- On the contrary, the candidate commissions the insertion of one or several specific questions in a "general purpose" survey. In most countries, the leading polling institutes organize at least one "general purpose" survey at regular intervals (usually once a week), in which a variety of questions submitted by their various clients are grouped, such as vacuum-cleaner manufacturers who want to gauge their products' reputation, or car rental companies which want to certify if their recent ad campaigns have made an impression on the public, and so on.

This second option will be less costly for the politician than a specially designed survey, but it can introduce two kinds of interpretation problems:

- in some cases, the political question might be misunderstood by the respondent, juxtaposed as it might be with questions on soap or insecticide;
- even more misleadingly, the questions might be inadvertently misplaced in an unexpected context (particularly when a preceding question asked by the polling agent for another client has some political consequence).[6]

3.2.2.1.2 Periodic surveys of the same cross-sections (or "barometers")   This type of survey theoretically offers the advantage of supplying more precise information than the conventional survey since the polling institute rigorously assembles a representative sample of the population, who are asked questions at regular intervals. The same questions are generally asked, thus eliminating as much as possible any factors of distortion. This method makes it possible to chart the evolution of public opinion, at least theoretically, with greater reliability.

Some distortions are, in fact, to be expected, because after a time the panel becomes somewhat more knowledgeable on political events than the average citizen, as a result of being questioned periodically. Polling institutes must take these considerations into account, and adjust them empirically (usually by partially renewing the panel composition at regular intervals).

3.2.2.1.3 Non-directive interviews and focus groups Non-directive interviews and focus groups represent the ultimate survey method: the interviewer conducts an in-depth interview of the people he polls, with certain questions, and even certain subjects, left open, leaving the respondent total freedom in his response. This makes it possible to obtain reliable answers concerning people's preoccupations, since they are not limited to choosing one of several possible replies prepared by the survey institute. When possible, focus groups are constituted for that purpose, in order to also try assessing potential interactions between the communication recipients and their effects.

This method is much more difficult to apply, however, for three main reasons:

- its financial cost is much higher, because the interviewer spends a greater amount of time with each subject, but also because its involves professional, thus better paid, interviewers;[7]
- the diversification of responses is much greater, which can lead to non-significant results, no more than a collection of overly-asserted individual particularities;
- qualitative individual interviews, and even more focus groups, need great technical expertise to be usefully put to use.

One particular variant of the non-directive interview, a cross between the survey with prepared questions and the open interview, can avoid some of these drawbacks: this is the "associative" interview, where words, images, adjectives, and so on, are proposed to the respondent, who is then asked to associate them with certain politicians, campaign themes, and so on.

3.2.2.2   Problems caused by opinion surveys
3.2.2.2.1 Lack of total reliability It is not our purpose here to challenge the reliability of the opinion survey. But, despite utmost precautions, we know they are never absolutely reliable. Some of the notorious survey fiascos remain indelibly in the public mind since their redoubtable breakdown during the Truman-Dewey presidential election of 1948.[8] The polls were for instance notoriously inaccurate in the 1992 British parliamentary election. Even more, in France since the late 1980s, they have in general failed to provide a valid estimate for many presidential candidates on the first ballot. More recently, in the United States, pollsters blatantly failed to predict the result of the 2008 New Hampshire primaries: a few days before the vote, all the surveys gave Barack Obama an 8% lead over Hillary Clinton, whereas she ended up winning by 3%, which is an amazing 11% error.[9]

In political communication, the most credible surveys are usually the exit polls conducted immediately after the actual voting, outside the polling station, where the interviewer queries the voters about the choices they have just made. But even here, some of the responses require correction, as we shall see. All other kinds of surveys are subject to a high degree of error, voluntary or not, for reasons we shall discuss here.

THE SIZE OF THE SAMPLE   It has long been established that survey accuracy does not increase in proportion to the size of the selected population sample, but to the square root of its increase, which is much smaller.

Practically, this means that a sample of 1,500 to 2,500 persons will suffice for countries like France or the United Kingdom if one keeps in mind that a margin of less than 5% between two voting tendencies, or any other result, will never be significant, since any survey findings have to be evaluated within a variability factor of at least plus or minus 1 to 2%.[10]

This alone explains the difficulty of using surveys to evaluate the potential electoral result of relatively unknown candidates or parties, a problem particularly in European countries like France or Germany. There, some marginal parties ("leftists," or "extreme-right," or "green", etc.), usually attract between 1 to 10% of the voters, which means that one-time survey results are quite inoperative for them (barometers being more useful in their case, but which must be interpreted with care). Similarly, when voter intent for two main parties or candidates is very close – which was the case in both George W. Bush's US presidential races – survey results become very difficult to interpret, and, again, particularly the one-time surveys.

REPRESENTATIVENESS OF THE SAMPLE   Survey institutes have long understood that a large sample in no way guarantees representativeness: the empirical selection of 2,000 names from the phone directory, for instance, is futile. Every survey organization has established methods of selection according to a number of objective or empirical criteria, beginning with official census records. These methods are used to help compose samples of which the representativeness is guaranteed by the quota method, the most commonly used. The main differentiating factors of the population (socio-occupational categories, sex, age, income, etc.) are thus proportionally respected when making up the sample. Yet certain geopolitical factors can distort this practice. In each country, for example, inhabitants of certain regions have greater exposure to media than others, by their proximity to a capital city, or international borders, where foreign radio and television can be picked up.

This "customization" of the sample by each survey institute accounts for much of the difficulty of comparing results obtained through several polls conducted by different survey institutes.

WORDING THE QUESTIONS   Three main types of wording exist:

- closed wording, allowing only a narrow range of response ("yes" or "no," for instance);

- "pre-established" wordings, where the premises of the questions are quite directive, implicating the respondent in some manner (as, for instance, in this kind of question: "76% of the population is for the death penalty. Do you think it should be reinstated?");
- open wording, which gives the respondent greater leeway to develop a response.

In all these cases, question wording is undoubtedly the crux for the reliability of an opinion survey. The respondent, by definition, can only answer questions put to him; a survey can be thrown off-balance by the omission or misformulation of a key question with regard to the information being gathered. For instance, the choice of one word over another can have major consequences. French pollsters are quick to recall what has now become a classic example of this problem: in 1969, two surveys conducted in similar circumstances within a few months of each other received different replies because of a slight difference in wording: 81% of the sample answered "Yes" in February to the question "Do you believe in God?" while 66% only answered "Yes" in August to the question "Would you say you believe in God?"[11]

The comprehension of terms in themselves is also a dispersal factor much more important than one might expect, once they are not part of the most "basic" vocabulary (linguists estimate that the basic vocabulary understood by everyone, for the main western European languages such as English, French, German, Italian, or Spanish, is no greater than 1,500 to 2,000 words).

This phenomenon explains why some apparently similar opinion surveys can in fact be of quite different natures, with major consequences for political marketing, in the event of a faulty analysis. For instance, political popularity recorded by surveys can at times have little connection with voting intentions – and the actual ballot itself. Politicians can remain popular, and yet never succeed in obtaining high office, because they are not able to "capitalize" on their popularity. A survey misreading of a popularity factor can thus lead to considerable – and rather negative – consequences for politicians.

On the other hand, whatever the kind of wording chosen, it is difficult to prevent the respondent from giving their own subjective interpretation of the questions, which can produce some nearly inexplicable variations.

Polling specialists therefore know that answers must be correlated to the length of the questions, their sequence in the questionnaire itself, their interrelationship, even if not deliberate, as they will be deciphered as such by the respondent. This point clearly reveals the difficulty of the task and its high degree of empiricism.

UNRELIABILITY OF RESPONSES As if these abovementioned difficulties were not enough, we must deal with one final, and again crucial drawback: the unreliability of responses. Consciously or not, or out of lack of interest, respondents do not always give "truthful" answers, whether for structural reasons, or because of the current political conjuncture.

The structural lack of reliability   *Unconscious "wrong" answers* can be subconsciously deliberate mistakes. For instance, whereas John F. Kennedy received little more than 50% of the American vote in 1960, his subsequent popularity and his assassination so modified public opinion that in a 1964 survey, 64% of the electorate who had voted in 1960 declared they had voted for Kennedy! More often, these unconscious wrong answers arise out of a lack of attention: one remembers the communication but not its real content or aim.

"Wrong" answers can also be made consciously. Survey specialists are aware that when respondents hold opinions that are at the far end of the political spectrum, they have a strong tendency to modify their responses with regard to their real opinion. How many people today would willingly answer "yes" to the question: "Are you a racist?"

Respondent lack of interest – or unavowed incompetence – in the question, is the last and probably most disturbing cause of survey unreliability. Rather than refrain from answering a question, respondents, to show their good will toward the interviewer, will fabricate an answer that, at best, is merely insignificant. This process has long been familiar to commercial marketing specialists. They know, for instance, how problematic it is to ask a male respondent if he prefers liquid detergent to powder when doing his laundry: the number of answers may prove to be greater than the number of the respondents who actually do their own laundry. Examples of this kind are numerous.

The unreliability of responses, in cases of disinterest – or unavowed incompetence – is all the more hazardous because the margin for error is difficult to assess. It can only be limited by other specific questions, which, by their proximity in the questionnaire, gives a better idea of the reliability of the "main" answer (in the above example, one might first ask the male interview subjects if they in fact do their own laundry before asking them them about other detergents).

Unreliability pertaining to a conjuncture   In recent years, several countries have had more problems of survey reliability linked to a specific conjuncture.

The inaccuracy of answers about female candidates has been one leading cause of inaccuracy in recent years. Even if the number of female politicians has increased, that does not prevent some (usually male) voters from ensuring their election, although they prefer not to disclose it to pollsters. Gender remains an issue, and it does cause a certain degree of unreliability in surveys in that case.

The inaccuracy of answers about minority candidates acts in a similar way. "Political correctness" will sometimes prevent voters from honestly stating in a poll that they would vote against a minority candidate despite their usual political preferences. The question arose notably in 2008, when Barack Obama was the first non-White candidate to be a serious contestant for the US presidential election. The results of surveys in some states were questioned, since they seemed too favorable toward him. This was one of the most difficult factors pollsters had to cope with during the 2008 presidential election.

The same question arises frequently in Europe, where some extreme xenophobic parties are now making their presence felt in politics. The actual election results do not always match results of opinion polls. In France as well as in the Netherlands, pollsters have even learned to "correct" the initial poll results to make them come closer to the actual election outcome – an empirical process done according to previous discrepancies between the past election results and what they had predicted at the time. Of course, these "artisanal" corrections are prone to error, which is a secondary cause of poll unreliability in many European countries where this question arises.

Finally the increasing percentage of undecided voters in many countries, is another factor of poll unreliability. Obviously, in that case, the margin of error of the polls being what it is, any close situation can produce erroneous survey results.

Despite their potential dangers, opinion surveys nonetheless represent the best possible analytical tool available to political marketing. Unlike its commercial counterpart, political marketing has no recourse to other sources of information, such as sales charts or inventory control.

Today's survey specialists have nevertheless learned how to limit the risks using the precautions we have just discussed. In-depth qualitative interviews and focus groups are also conducted in parallel to surveys to check on possible inaccuracies in the answers to the poll. But a candidate's political advisors must always keep in mind that even these precautions can be inadequate, because of two obstacles:

- many of these precautions are highly empirical, not scientific, since they are the result of the survey institute's previous experiences (response correction coefficient, method of composing samples, etc.);
- these precautions can be invalidated by the evolution of the political or social context, since, by nature, they have been devised through study of past experience.[12]

3.2.2.2.2 The cost of surveys

The outlay due to surveys during the political marketing process is all the more considerable because it is unavoidable. Unlike other stages of the process, the technical complexity of surveys makes the use of professional polling organizations almost mandatory. If one were to use activists or volunteers to conduct an opinion poll, for instance, it would destroy the credibility of the polling results.

But, obviously, survey organizations do not usually give away their expertise to politicians; their services come at a price. Beyond the cost of computer resources and groundwork for the survey, conducting a survey requires a number of qualified employees: the interviewers.[13] A survey questionnaire that takes some 20 minutes to administer for a sample of 2,000 persons costs between US$60,000 to US$100,000, whereas a single question in a general purpose survey already costs around US$1,500.

Political marketing, then, must provide from the start for a substantial budget for opinion surveys; their high cost can often prevent politicians from using them as much as they would like. Surveys are usually estimated to take a 10% share of political campaign expenditures when, like in the United States, electoral law does not seriously limit spending.[14] In other countries such as France, where since 1990 the total amount of campaign expenditure has been limited by law to a relatively low amount, politicians sometimes cannot afford to commission surveys and have to rely on their own party's "general" surveys or on past results, which is obviously not ideal.[15]

Of course, to alleviate costs, political surveys have started using the Internet, much cheaper and sometimes as fast as phone surveys, for instance. Though some have been close to actual results on several occasions, pollsters and politicians do not feel that they have had long enough exposure to solely to rely on them.[16]

3.2.2.3 *Consequences of the existence and use of opinion surveys*

It may seem surprising to find a political communication textbook dealing with a problem more likely to be discussed in more controversial or theoretical studies. But a properly-conducted political communication campaign must take that into account: the topicality and use of the opinion survey has a clear and objective influence, not only on the future behavior of the individuals (which constitutes, in a way, an "internal" effect, the "opinion survey" contributing greatly to creating public opinion), but also in an external manner, in the field of politics itself, were it only because opinion surveys influence the behavior of politicians, their words and deeds.

Two kinds of consequences of the actuality of the opinion survey can be differentiated. Paradoxically, their direct effects now appear less dangerous for political communication than their indirect effects.

3.2.2.3.1 Direct effects of opinion surveys: "underdog" and "bandwagon" effects   It has been understood for years that knowing the results of an opinion survey during an election campaign can provoke changes in voter behavior. Many potential side-effects of opinion surveys have been exposed,[17] but here we will focus on ones that have been commonly accepted for many years: the "underdog" and the "bandwagon effects.

In some instances, the demobilized electorate of a candidate in distress, learning of the latter's poor showing in a survey's results, will be encouraged to go out and vote for him (or even, in a smaller proportion, change their vote in his favor). This is the "underdog" effect. This phenomenon occurred for the first time in survey history with Truman's miraculous victory over Dewey in 1948 presidential elections.[18]

In other cases, on the contrary, the publication of survey results can sway vulnerable voters in favor of the candidate who is leading at the polls, so as to be among the majority: this is the "bandwagon" effect. The bandwagon effect provided a boost to Ross Perot during the final two weeks of his 1992 campaign: his high standing in surveys encouraged more people to vote for him; no longer feeling part of an isolated minority, they on the contrary had the feeling of being a "useful" part of a strong movement pushing for a change from the two traditional main parties.

The underdog and bandwagon effects are, by nature, diffuse and unquantifiable, since either can get the upper hand over the other without apparent reason; in any case, neither can be identified in time for the purposes of a political communication campaign, as most research into the matter since 1948 has confirmed. But, in many cases, it would appear that the two phenomena tend to balance one another out, and that the direct effect of the public's knowledge of survey findings has a lesser influence than is commonly thought.

Nevertheless, for the politician, the knowledge of favorable survey findings has the advantage of producing a highly useful bandwagon effect on his own activists and volunteers. Good scores can boost the morale of the former, and increase the ranks of the latter, who, as a result, may become more generous with campaign donations: "good surveys make a good campaign funding" is a saying often voiced by political marketing consultants. This phenomenon alone explains why candidates can become so eager for statistics and survey results during their campaigns: if the figures are good, more sympathizers will sponsor their campaign much more easily, in order to be on the winning side after the election.

In some countries, like France, laws and regulations have attempted to stem the last-minute effects of surveys by forbidding their release in newspapers or on television during the final lap of the campaign (which, in France since 1977, is the last week before the vote.) Most politicians and observers complain that this remedy can turn out to be worse than the original problem: instead of quoting, or being influenced by the most recent surveys, one has to fall back on older surveys, which, for one reason or another, may by now be outdated; thus the phenomenon that led to Truman's surprise election in 1948 could occur again. Similarly, the non-release of survey results close to polling day also leads to the media exaggeration of discrepancies between the latest voter intentions and the real vote, which may be considerable. Also, in democratic countries, there is no law against the richer political parties commissioning their own "private" surveys, to the detriment of those with lesser means, not a very democratic practice!

Anyway, this ban became obsolete with the Internet: surveys may now be published in nearby countries where the law against publication of the polls obviously does not apply and citizens can easily get the results (this was for instance the case for some years in France: when the last-minute survey results started to appear in some newspaper websites in Switzerland, the law had to be amended in 2002: the ban is now only limited to the last day before election day and election day itself, obviously).

3.2.2.3.2 Indirect effects of opinion surveys Contrary to what one may think, the main difficulty with opinion surveys stems from their indirect effects, and, especially, the excessive use politicians make of them. Political communication can thus be heavily influenced, if not diverted, for two different reasons:

- because of the irruption of surveys into the "traditional" political communication circuit;
- because of the "demagogic" excesses in their interpretation by politicians or their advisors; this is the consequence of the endorsement of surveys by the candidates themselves, especially when decisions are being made on campaign issues.

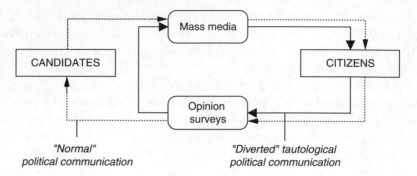

Figure 3.2 Diversion of political communication by opinion surveys.

IRRUPTION OF SURVEYS IN THE POLITICAL COMMUNICATION CIRCUIT As media in their own right, opinion surveys sometimes end up completely redirecting the political communication process to the point where they become the core of the political debate itself: too often, debates and commentaries are no longer focused on the political action itself, but on a kind of metacommunication on the communication tool they form. The media become tautological in a way, since the communication is composed of the elements on which it is based (see Figure 3.2 above).

Figures clearly corroborate this phenomenon: in the United States, we know, for instance, that television networks have been directly involved in the preparation of surveys since the early 1980s, more than 75% of the polls quoted in newscasts of the main networks having in fact been commissioned by them.[19]

With greater frequency, politicians are asked by print or broadcast journalists to comment their rises or falls in popularity in the most recent polls. This manner in which the media dwell on commentaries about survey figures has been termed by the Americans the "Horse race story." The phenomenon becomes particularly acute in the pre-election period, when the media devote more and more time to analyzing the least significant variations in the popularity figures of candidates, rather than devoting time to the real political issues. This "horse race" communication is today one of the main reasons for the weakening of the political debate: in many western nations, each point won or lost in the polls assumes a greater importance in the media than the reason behind the evolution. In reality, as we already explained, it is pointless to attach any real importance to a shift in voting intentions of less than 5% between polls.

Still, candidates and their advisors leap at the chance to exploit the symbolic dimension offered by favorable polls. Since the actual survey results are in figures, they are used in an effort to benefit from the aura of arithmetical credibility. In this abusive assimilation of sorts, politicians and journalists in fact have a joint stake in making the voter believe in the exactitude of the reasoning (since childhood, we are taught that arithmetic is an "exact science").

Because of the excessive use of survey figures, some political analysts now denounce the "dictatorship" of the opinion survey, even the concept of "public opinion" itself, since so-called public opinion is in fact made up only of the sum of individual responses to different recently conducted surveys. Survey institutes' frequent use of the term "public opinion" attempts to impose this presumed truth on the political milieu.[20]

INFLUENCE OF SURVEYS ON CAMPAIGN ISSUES   In the media's defense, it should be noted that politicians themselves are not the last ones to make immoderate use of opinion surveys. Certain results can even become issues in their communications, and deliberately so, when they incorporate them into their campaign platform. It could be said that the overzealous use of polls by candidates is the demagogic form of the late twentieth century. Rather than promoting a clear, predetermined political program, it is much more easy to wave a few general ideas as campaign issues, and to ride on what the surveys reveal to be the voters' major fears, in order to piece together the results like some haphazard but efficient puzzle.

In this respect, a disturbing sign of the excessive importance given to survey results is the manufacture of computer software to help decision-making which today is used by certain political parties, notably in North America. The first example of the kind apparently dates back to Ronald Reagan's 1980 presidential campaign. His advisors used a computerized Political Information System, designed by Richard Wirthlin. It entered on a day-to-day basis the results of a daily phone survey conducted in each state by several hundred persons, the accumulated responses of several segments of the population previously effected, the "advice" of a number influential advisors, and factual data about the means at the disposal of the candidate. This computerized system came up with analyses that aided political decision-making.

Politicians are well aware that they should not expect miracle solutions from the opinion surveys. But as surveys can trace the likely evolution of the electorate in relation to their communication, even with a considerable margin of error, and since they in the very least indicate which objectives or campaign issues are to be avoided so as not to alienate their communication recipients, such opinion analysis tools are of undoubted value. Much more so than the spies who were sent out among the populace by certain rulers, or the intelligence networks created many nations in the early years of the last century, such as the American FBI, or the French *Renseignements Généraux,* for example.

3.2.3   Other types of information and analysis tools

Data on previous elections and opinion survey results, the two main information sources that the politician has at his disposal for his campaign, are not the only ones. Any kind of information, or feedback obtained in response to the political communication, can prove to be highly useful. The warmth of applause that greets key points in a speech delivered at a public meeting, the questions most frequently asked by sympathizers during election rallies, the questions of journalists – all these can prove to be, if interpreted correctly, rich sources of information, which correspond, in a sense, to the traditional channels of information used by politicians before the audiovisual era.

Three information sources, among others, can be cited here for their ease of use, as empirical as they may be:

- *responses to direct mailings* can considerably help gauge the viability of certain campaign elements: it is even possible to test certain elements, by sending out letters worded slightly differently, and analyzing the quantitative and qualitative differences of the replies;
- *spontaneous mail or phone calls,* when properly exploited, can also be very useful; good campaign management should even delegate a special team to oversee responses to spontaneous mail or phone calls; one could also deduce useful information from a precise analysis of the number of connections to specific toll-free numbers, each being allotted to different campaigning issues, etc.;
- *demands of activists and volunteers* in the field, lastly, also provide data which, unfortunately, is frequently overlooked.

In these cases, politicians will nevertheless have to be careful and must take into account that these last kinds of data have to be analyzed with great caution, since the feedback they provide only comes from motivated citizens (even more when they are activists backing the politician), who do not properly represent the global recipients of his communication.

✳✳✳

The analytical tools at the disposal of political communication, then, are far from being absolutely reliable. The most precise data (past election results) is often dated, or rendered useless, because of socio-political developments.

As for more recent material, it is usually subject to analysis and reliability problems inherent in opinion surveys. Nevertheless, politicians cannot do without them, because they give them a kind of objective view of the effects of their campaign on the public and therefore an evaluation tool of its efficiency. Given the great difficulty of gaining an understanding of the full range of subjectivities of the recipients of political communication, surveys thus appear as a way of objectively assessing the situation despite their imperfections.

This lack of reliability of basic information explains why candidates with previous campaign experience have a clear advantage. Unlike many other activities, political communication experience is indispensable, since it allows one to remedy the uncertainties of analysis by empirical compensations based on the earlier campaigns. Also, incumbent politicians can use more precise data for their campaigns, since they had previously run for election in a similar race. Obviously, this means they do not have to bother with a risky interpretation of previous electoral and campaign results, unlike new candidates who must assess if they can postively use their predecessor's campaign data or if these are not too biased by the fact it was not them, but a fellow politician of their party.

This also explains why the talents of political marketing consultants are increasingly sought after by the politicians of democratic nations. The participation of these professionals partially compensates for the inadequacies of opinion analysis tools, which recent communication school graduates could certainly use, but, because of lack of experience, do not always interpret them correctly.

Notes

1   Bernays 2005, p. 113.

2   In this respect, the most amazing event of the 1992 American presidential campaign was the notorious love affair between the campaign managers of the two main leading candidates, Clinton and Bush. It was was regarded with disapproval by their respective teams, who feared involuntary leaks of crucial information between them. The couple had to solemnly swear that they never discussed their employees during their romantic interludes! (see Matalin and Carville 1994).

3   We will use both terms indifferently, the minor difference sometimes observed by some specialists as being too artificial.

4   In many countries, census data is now easily available on the web. This is for instance true in the United States where census data for campaigning politicians may be found on http://www.census.gov/ (last accessed December 2, 2010).

5   See for instance http://orgs.bloomu.edu/gasi/Proceedings%20PDFs/Mihulka.pdf (last accessed January 20, 2011).

6   For example, questions about extreme-right or ultra-conservative parties might elicit different responses as part of a general-purpose survey that also includes questions on immigration or unemployment, etc. This is why the polling organization must be a serious one: in such cases they should defer certain commissioned questions – at the risk of forfeiting income – in order to avoid this kind of interference.

7   The need for professional interviewers is dictated by the attention and patience that are required for the job and also by the trust the surveying institute must have in the persons it employs: an interviewer can be tempted to falsify an interview, or, more insidiously, to "suggest" certain answers to the respondent as a time-saving device.

8   On the failure of the 1948 surveys, see Norman C. Meier and Harold W. Saunders, *The Polls and Public Opinion*, Henry Holt and Co., New York 1949.

9   The fact that Hillary Clinton for the first time had removed her "armor" so to speak, and had a short crying spell on television two days before the vote was deemed to be a partial explanation of the apparent last-minute "swing" of some voters that the surveys had been unable to foresee.

10   Pollsters usually assess the error margin for countries the size of the United Kingdom or France at less than 3%, for a sample of 1,000 persons or more, this margin increasing to 5% for a sample of 400 people.

11   In French, the first question was "Croyez-vous en Dieu?," and the second was "Est-ce que vous croyez en Dieu?"

12   In certain countries, such as France since 1977, any time a newspaper or newscast announces survey results, they are obliged by law to report the conditions under which they were carried out and the precautions taken, and the law has even established a specific state body, the "Commission des sondages," to supervise the process.

13 We have mentioned that the reliability of the survey depends heavily on the reliability of the interviewers. In order to ensure their seriousness, most survey institutes regularly "test" their interviewers' results, usually by confirming with the alleged respondents that the interview did in fact take place and was properly conducted.

14 See Shea and Burton 2006.

15 The cost of a survey in a big electoral district for a parliamentary seat would require the all the funds allocated to the campaign.

16 See for instance Nelson, in Semiatin 2008.

17 For instance, the "Spiral of silence" theory propounded by German researcher and pollster Elizabeth Noelle-Neumann suggests that knowledge of survey results causes people to refrain from stating their opinion publicly for fear of expressing a minority viewpoint. This silence would then create a discrepancy with the outcome of the vote (see Noelle-Neumann 1993, *The Spiral of Silence: Public Opinion – Our Social Skin*, University of Chicago Press).

18 There, the underdog effect was even more obvious, due to the fact that the polling institutes had stopped polling two weeks before the actual vote, thinking the outcome to be evident.

19 In Jerry L. Yeric, "Television's reporting of campaign polls: the new political communicator," paper prepared for the Eighteenth Conference of the International Association of Media and Communications Research, São Paulo 1992.

20 France's oldest polling institute, established as recently as 1938, is even called IFOP, (French Institute of Public Opinion) thus artificially conferring a symbolic "official" status on a private organization through its name.

Part III

Political marketing tools

Political marketing can employ most existing means of communication. They can be grouped into four categories, which we will deal with in the next four chapters:

- the traditional modes are, in a nutshell, those which were in existence before the advent of mass media, some even dating back to the dawn of mankind; political communication still uses many of them, often in new ways;
- audiovisual means are increasingly used today in most countries, following the example set by the North American political communication field;
- the third category is made up of direct marketing methods, which can be briefly described as the attempt to renew contacts without intermediaries, mostly through the revised utilization of older media;
- the Internet and "new media" form the fourth and final category.

4

The traditional tools

Many of the tools used by modern political marketing have been around for a long time: political posters were in use throughout the nineteenth century, and pre-electoral meetings date back to Antiquity, or even further, when the potential successors of deceased tribal leaders tried to gain recognition among the Elders.

The traditional means of political communication can be grouped into two categories, according to their operational manner (and the – decreasing – quality of the communication):

- interactive tools;
- unidirectional tools.

4.1   Interactive tools

Interactive tools have the clear advantage of being the most accurate, and, potentially, the most effective: the politician meets directly with his electors, offering them the opportunity to react immediately to his communication.

Their common drawback is that the politician must devote a great deal of time in putting them to use, since direct interactive communication permits only simultaneous communication with a limited number of interlocutors. For this reason, modern political marketing distinguishes between two forms of traditional communication means:

- actual direct contacts, reserved for a relatively small number of special interlocutors;
- various forms of direct contact substitutes, systematically employed for the general masses of political communication recipients.

Campaign Communication and Political Marketing, First Edition. Philippe J. Maarek.
© 2011 Philippe J. Maarek. Published 2011 by Blackwell Publishing Ltd.

4.1.1   Actual direct contacts with the voters

Direct contact with voters is naturally the oldest form of political communication: "going out to meet the people." However brief it might be, this direct face-to-face method is, in essence, the most powerful way of communicating.

But the politician is limited on genuine direct encounters during a political campaign, because time is lacking. Nevertheless, he continues to practice direct contact in two instances: to maintain special relationships with his main campaign contributors, and in the case of a local campaign, which we will come back to in the final chapter of this book.

4.1.1.1   Special relationships with main contributors
The politician cannot help but maintain close ties with a highly select category of persons, those with whom special relationships are sought:

- the wealthiest financial donors;
- prestigious supporters.

The need to maintain direct contacts with large financial contributors is obvious. But contrary to other individuals he meets during the campaign, directly or not, the candidate does not always publicize these encounters. They supply funds, officially or not, or, at times, material help of some kind. This can range from the free, unlimited use of a fleet of rented cars or a private plane, to the loan of a professional bodyguard. Thus these relationships often remain cloaked in secrecy, but are perpetuated by all politicians without exception, as one can guess, despite what they might publicly claim. Their help is particularly useful at the start of the campaign, when far-reaching fundraising campaigns are still to come.

For the prestigious supporters, the phenomenon is exactly the opposite. Here, politicians wish to make public the support they receive from a wide variety of personalities: famous basketball players, eminent surgeons, respected police officers, and, of course, movie stars or other celebrities from the artistic or cultural world. In many instances, the candidate, in order to obtain their endorsement, must obviously meet with such personalities in person. To save time, a well-organized political marketing campaign will devise ways of grouping these various direct contacts by organizing support brunches, luncheons or dinners, or closed meetings with different types of prestigious supporters in the measure that their sensibilities and sense of diplomacy will allow. For instance, some Hollywood personalities are well-known go-betweens able to set up these kinds of gatherings – usually in favor of the Democratic Party candidates.[1]

4.1.1.2   Canvassing, grassroots campaigning and other forms of direct contact with communication recipients
Canvassing, calling on people at their homes or workplace, is theoretically the ideal political communication tool: the ideal opportunity for face-to-face verbal communication. But this form of actual direct contact with voters can only be exercised by

the politician himself in the case of local campaigns, where geographical proximity and the relatively low number of recipients allows, and even impels candidates to visit the electorate in person.[2]

Yet a summary form of canvassing can be carried out in the event of national political communication campaigns, when the politician enjoys a strong local infrastructure. In such a case, local activists and volunteers can practice canvassing, going around the homes of their neighborhood co-constituents, and delivering brief messages on behalf of the politician. Political communication specialists have empirically established that this method is particularly profitable when the visit leaves a concrete trace (fliers, leaflets, election programs or publications, etc.).

It should be stressed that activists who canvass require a minimum of training: to be effective, canvassing should not involve long discussions with the voters, but simply be restricted to eliciting voting preference, along with some kind of printed matter. Should a real discussion take place, the canvasser loses valuable time, and also risks being unable to supply the right answer to some highly detailed question, which would create a negative effect. The training of canvassers involves learning the basics of the communication process, and of psychological evaluation, so as to avoid overestimating any favorable impressions they might have had during while canvassing.[3]

Properly carried out, canvassing not only allows the campaign staff to relay a message to the recipients, but also, to obtain feedback by giving the politician information similar to the kind he would get from a conventional survey. To this end, canvassers are usually asked to update a "canvass card" immediately after visiting the voter. The main information indicated on the canvass card is the apparent degree of support for the politician:

- highly favorable;
- favorable;
- indifferent, undecided, or impossible to ascertain;
- unfavorable;
- hostile.

In this way, the views of residents in neighborhoods which have been canvassed can be put on file, and the next stage of canvassing can be conducted with the help of the results from the preceding round, according to the kind of campaign:

- "maintenance communication" or the search for financial donations, where a return call is made on people having expressed support for the politician;
- on the contrary, "conquest communication," where pressure will be put on voters who have been indecisive so far.

A strong local activist structure allows for canvassing without the presence of the politician himself. It also allows a more intense spontaneous grassroots campaigning, which marketing consultants often try to intensify into what they call "street marketing."[4] But the contact is clearly of inferior quality when it is an anonymous volunteer who visits voters than when it is the candidate himself.

4.1.2   Substitutes for direct contacts

Canvassing, and even more direct communication with voters, are useless as such on a large scale if the goal is to reach a significant number of voters. In democratic nations, presidential candidates cannot physically visit all the homes of its voters.[5] Beyond the (few) actual direct contacts we just described, political marketing has developed alternate forms of direct communication, which can be divided into two categories, according to the extent of the targeting:

- direct contact substitutes with a narrow target;
- direct contact substitutes with a wide target.

4.1.2.1   *Direct contact substitutes with a narrow target*
This category is closely related to actual direct contacts. The politician meets at the same time with a more or less large group of targeted recipients usually chosen by affinity, or by socio-cultural proximity, and so on, to deliver a precisely tailored political communication.

4.1.2.1.1 Campaign coffees, meetings, banquets and support committees, symposia, petitions   These are highly traditional political communication tools which all share the distinction of allowing for a near direct connection, within a relatively closed circle, between the candidate and a very precise category of communication recipient. Generally, these are people who have already shown affinities with the candidate's ideas or his personality, affinities which the politician attempts to transform into direct support, whether financial or material. Since the politician's time is precious, this way of communicating is usually reserved for known sympathizers, especially those who can provide considerable financial or material assistance. Politicians have used benefit dinners or luncheons since the nineteenth century.

The advantage of this kind of meeting is that it represents a communicating tool that by nature is similar to direct individual contact. Of course, all (paying) guests at a fundraising banquet, or all participants in a symposium, a campaign coffee or tea, or a closed meeting, might not have a chance to speak personally with the politician, but the contact will have been close enough to foster a positive effect. The meeting in itself affords a high symbolic status: even if all the participants did not speak to the politician in person, all theoretically had the chance to do so, and will therefore retain a strong psychological satisfaction, highly propitious for the efficiency of political communication.

Benefit banquets and luncheons function on the same principle, while providing a supplementary form of psychological reinforcement: the sense of communion in "breaking bread together." On a psycho-sociological level, it gives participants a sense of belonging to the same community. The same mechanism is by the way in play when the politician directly encounters selected journalists during a press lunch: the unconscious psychological proximity can lead to more favorable articles.

Those two variants of the closed meeting can sometimes be initiated by people outside the campaign organization:

- they can be initiated by the candidate, of course, as tools of his political communication campaign, and be part of a pre-established plan;
- but they can also be initiated by existing clubs or leagues, who wish their members to meet with political figures.

Even if it might at first seem surprising, this second hypothesis is the most favorable, and this is for two reasons: one of a material nature, the other of a symbolic one. First, this method allows for the reduction of expenses involved in holding the meeting, since the inviting club or league, and not the politician's campaign organization, usually picks up the bill. Second, the politician, in such instances, is able to communicate with recipients who might not have been willing to come if the meeting had been held at his own initiative. This allows his communication to surmount the obstacle constituted by the poor inclination of unmotivated targets to expose themselves to political communication. Members of the campaign organization are often in charge of soliciting invitations from groups of this kind, from executive, professional or investment circles to Rotary International or the Lion's Club. These breakfasts, lunches, and dinners also represent excellent fundraising opportunities, particularly when they are initiated by socialites who invite friends.

It might appear odd to include in the current part of this book the support committees and petition campaigns. But, from the psycho-sociological angle, these communication processes are very similar in nature to the closed meeting. People who sign a petition in favor of the candidate, or who agree to be part of a support committee, have the feeling of enjoying a direct bond with him, since an essential element of their identity, their name, is associated with him. And once the petitions are made public, this bond becomes even stronger; in the eyes of others, it represents that same symbolic sense of belonging as a closed meeting, and thus produces the same kind of positive symbolic satisfaction. The person whose name comes into public view to support a candidate appears to be part of the closed circle of individuals who have directly helped him, as those who took part in closed meetings. For this reason, large donors are often asked if they would agree to have their name and support publicized: not only does it reinforce the campaign itself, but also the quality of their support.

4.1.2.1.2 Public meetings Public meetings – or gatherings with a large audience – represent by nature a more indirect kind of contact with communication recipients, and less precise targeting. They are usually election meetings with a larger attendance. Here, communication is most often unidirectional, but benefits from the considerable feedback of audience reaction to speeches. Of course, the basic participants of mass meetings are no longer interlocutors: they cannot respond directly to, or ask questions of, the candidate. But, here again, they can have a sense of proximity, physical and chronological, since they see the politician with their own eyes, and are physically in the same place as he is at the same time.

There is one caveat though; it is nearly impossible to use public meetings to send messages to citizens who are not already among the politician's followers, the only ones who will come. Meetings will not help conquer new voters, since only people already committed to a politician or at least interested in that person attend them. They constitute an excellent way of heightening awareness and mobilization of the politician's sympathizers, but they will only have an indirect effect on the election result, the people attending the meetings acting here at best as potential opinion relays materializing this indirect effect.

MEETINGS AND TARGETING Even if the targeting of recipients appears relatively imprecise in the case of election meetings, it is nonetheless considerable: those who participate in a meeting have in common the fact that they are sympathizers of the candidate, since they made the voluntary and psycho-sociological effort to attend. Sometimes, this psycho-sociological impact is even reinforced by an obligation to pay an admission fee, however low: the act of payment deepens the participant's favorable conviction, and, consequently, the cohesion of the public at the rally and its psychological closeness to the speakers, making it even more difficult for individuals in the audience to disagree![6]

Targeting for meetings can be improved by inviting certain categories of people exclusively, especially by broad professional fields. The political marketing campaign can then easily prepare several public meetings geared to specific, homogenous audiences. Neighborhood meetings are also in order, particularly for local campaigns, of course.

RALLIES Public meetings in town halls and public meeting rooms have naturally always been the most common communication practice for campaigns set in small geographical areas. But for meetings with a much greater audience, the psychological functioning might at first seem quite far from the direct contact substitute represented by the more intimate, small-scale public meetings.

Yet mass meetings, or rallies, work on the same psychological principle with regard to their participants, and provide the same kind of satisfaction. Physical and temporal simultaneity is the chief motivation for this satisfaction: even if the contact with the politician is theoretical, the very fact of his being present in the same place as the voter, and at the same time, affords the latter a strong sense of gratification, which reinforces the efficiency of political communication accordingly.

Already in the 1930s, the huge Nazi rallies organized by the Minister of Propaganda, Josef Goebbels, notably the annual party congresses in Nuremberg, had systematically exploited this phenomenon for the purposes of political communication. Today's leading pop and rock music stars, building their fortune on a similar mechanism, have perfected the practice of holding rallies with their fans, appearing in gigantic live concerts where the acoustics are vastly inferior to the sound a CD player makes in one's living room, and where the artist is hardly more visible than a small figure in the distance – but the public is nevertheless delighted to be there![7]

One will finally note that the influence of audiovisual media has been felt in the internal functioning scheme of political rallies, which have thus been somewhat distorted in recent years. They tend more and more to resemble TV variety shows, as if this was supposed to give them a greater credibility. Audiovisual spots are now often projected on large screens in order to prepare the public for the arrival of the main speakers, and in some cases, candidates do not even speak directly to the audience, but to "representatives" of the public called on stage, exactly as in popular television talk shows. Since the 2000 campaign at least, when George W. Bush and Al Gore were both filmed stepping out of their cars and entering their respective party's convention hall, so that the audience inside were able to see it on big screens, rallies begin by looking a little like the Oscars ceremony.

Theses rallies take place with a very careful *crescendo* staging. As in rock concerts, lesser known politicians and local hosts speak first and film clips and advertising spots are used to build up the audience's mood, pending the appearance and speeches of the main politician invited. Entertainment may also be part of initial stages of the meetings, particularly in Latin America, where rallies often start with performances by popular singers or dancers on stage. Even the politician's entry to the meeting hall is staged like that of a concert artist, to the sound of some specific enthralling tune. The way the politician steps on the stage is also carefully calculated. A good trick is to have him cross the room from afar, a crowd-pleaser that will increase the enthusiasm of the participants who try to shake his hand, and so on.

Of course, there is a double edge to this, since rallies are as much planned for their direct influence on the participants as for a much broader indirect audience through the television newscasts likely to relay them, at least for a few minutes. The influence of television is also felt on the scheduling of the rallies, always very tight, in order to ensure that the high points, usually the leading politician's speech, are due in time for the main evening television newscasts, even if this means lower attendance since many potential participants would still be at work.

Even the place in the room allocated to the television crews transmitting the rallies is rigidly set beforehand, ever since Ronald Reagan's 1980 campaign, in order to force them to show only packed rows of activists and sympathizers, rather than the sometimes empty back part of the hall. For the 2007 French presidential campaign, Nicolas Sarkozy's team even innovated by "graciously" giving broadcasters the opportunity to take for free their own images, normally intended for the Internet television "network" they had set up for the campaign. Journalists frequently agreed, if only because they could then cut back on crew, and also because the images shot by the campaign staff were much better than their own: Sarkozy's team had a camera fixed on a giant crane giving superb shots of the rallies. Only later did journalists understand that they had somehow been manipulated, since they were now only showing their viewers "official" shots of the campaign!

4.1.2.2   Substitutes for direct contacts with a wide target

4.1.2.2.1 Walking through the crowd   Walking through the crowd is by nature very similar to appearing at rallies. Politicians in every era have empirically understood that it was usually impossible to call upon the greater portion of their potential voters to establish direct communication with them. In addition, they have always experienced the spontaneity of direct contact by these frequent walkabouts by mixing with crowds. Psychologically, the mere fact of direct visual contact, and, a fortiori, the possibility of shaking the candidate's hand, produces a pseudo-communion which can induce an effect similar to participation at a rally. Politicians and military leaders through the centuries have perpetuated the practice, from the Roman legates reviewing their legions to boost morale, to modern political leaders crossing the police security lines to shake hands with their supporters.

Naturally, political communication in such instances becomes something of a caricature. The politician is unable to convey any particular message or communication: the sole message is his presence at the same time and place as the recipients of the "communication," without there being any other kind of communication than a nonverbal one and targeting is now out of the question.

4.1.2.2.2 Media publicizing of special contacts   Even mixing with crowds cannot provide direct contact with all the voters. But a well-designed marketing campaign can attempt to devise a workable pretense, in favoring certain carefully chosen "contacts" and in publicizing them through the mass media for the general public. A series of meetings between the politician and individuals representing specific categories of the population targeted by political marketing is planned. These encounters are fully amplified through the media, in a showcasing effect carefully prepared by political marketing: press photographers are invited, and one sees to it that their pictures are published in the newspapers; sometimes, a television crew from one of the main networks is invited with the promise of exclusive coverage.

In fact, this communication process is indirect: the final recipients identify with those really in the presence of the politician, and the media publicity of this contact creates the identification. In a sense, the media publicity is a two-step process (Figure 4.1):

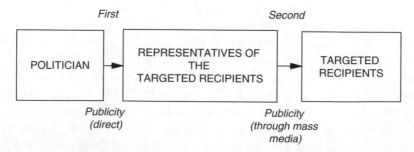

Figure 4.1   Dual media publicity (or second degree political communication).

When politicians invite microphones and cameras for the opening of their encounters with the representatives of such or such category of the population, they are performing, consciously or not, a dual media publicity process of this nature.

4.2 Unidirectional tools

Most of the traditional unidirectional means of political communication are related to the written word in one form or another. Here again, their use is quite ancient: one might even affirm that the earliest written legal codes, starting with Hammurabi's Code, were a way of publicly asserting the pre-eminence of the sovereigns who had decreed them. Unlike the preceding, the standard unidirectional tools of political communication by nature diminish the effectiveness of the communication, as they lower its quality. One cannot be certain as to the very impact of the message, and, *a fortiori*, about what use will be made of it: the poster might not be seen, the newspaper, electoral or not, might not be read, even if it reaches the home of each voter, and so on. No genuine feedback will exist here.

4.2.1   The press and printed matter

There are two categories of press, which can be differentiated according to the quality of their specific communication process:

- the non-partisan press, which affords a better quality communication;
- the partisan press, which, in a sense, is a substitute for the former.

4.2.1.1   *The non-partisan press*
4.2.1.1.1 Continuity of the non-partisan press   The non-partisan press is one of the most productive tools for political communication, even if its role has changed with the evolution of the media. Its relaying of a communication gives it an impact and a credibility which remain unparalleled today.

The non-partisan press must be understood as newspapers and magazines not directly linked to a political party and which the buyer does not believed to be linked to a partisan stance. Readers of *Le Figaro* in France, *El Mundo* in Spain, *The Sun* or *The Daily Mirror* in the United Kingdom, and so on, do not believe they are committing themselves to a party allegiance if they buy such a newspaper, even if they are aware of the paper's political bent. Incidentally, the free dailies now found in the subway passageways of many countries can now be included in this category, even if their readers do not buy them: though their distribution mode is different, the readers mostly acknowledge them in the same way they would newspapers they would have bought.

QUALITY OF COMMUNICATION AS RELAYED BY THE NON-PARTISAN PRESS   The potency of the non-partisan press resides first in its providing candidates with a prime means of access to categories of the population which may be interested in his message, but which might not have felt concerned by it at first, and therefore would not have made effort to receive it. In a way, the reader of the non-partisan press is involuntarily exposed to the political message, since he has purchased his usual newspaper, and thus comes across an article devoted to that message. Thus, independent of its own commentary on the subject, the newspaper is in fact relaying, *nolens volens*, the political communication. This makes it an ideal medium when the campaign strategy is focused on "conquest" communication, and a fairly acceptable one in the case of "maintenance" communication.

The non-partisan press is of all the more interest to the politician as its credibility is greatly superior to that of its partisan equivalent: the reader will put more trust in a favorable article about a politician in "his" paper, than a similar piece published in a partisan newspaper placed in his letter box without any previous request on his part, and which he will most likely consider as an advertising leaflet among others. In the case of the non-partisan press, the recipient feels that what he is reading is neutral, since he knows that the politician in question does not control the newspaper, unlike the partisan press, or even more so, advertising. His defensive instincts against what he is reading are weaker.

EVOLUTION OF THE NON-PARTISAN PRESS WITH REGARD TO OTHER MEDIA A traditional instrument of the political communication process, the non-partisan press was formerly its most valued organ. Access to the columns of *The Times* of London, the *New York Times* or the *Washington Post* in the United States, or *Le Monde* and *Le Figaro* in France, was the natural springboard for the ambitious political figures, as Orson Welles' famous motion picture *Citizen Kane* so accurately portrayed.

One might be tempted to think that the expansion of audiovisual media in today's society has diminished the importance of access to the non-partisan press. This is not the case. True, the non-partisan press, in a way, has lost its autonomy, becoming less and less the provenance for information or commentary. With a few rare exceptions, the main information items developed in today's media begin on television, now the Internet too, and are only relayed afterwards by the printed press. Only exceptionally does the reverse happen, as with the Watergate scandal in the United States, exposed by the *Washington Post*.

But the printed press has become the main arena of discussion of political communications previously transmitted through audiovisual media and now the Internet. It constitutes an important relay of their functions and influence for the latter, an individual component of the agenda-setting process: at once an echo chamber for the communication and opinion relay for readers.

The non-partisan press has thus evolved from being the source in the traditional political communication process, to secondary status as a privileged, if disembodied and impersonal, opinion relay of the audiovisual and electronic media in modern political communication. Its utility to political communication remains, even if its purpose has changed and even if the nature of the coverage is different, this nevertheless serves as an aid to modern political marketing.

It should be also noted that in recent years, politicians have increasingly sought to be featured in mass-market magazines. The increasing personalization of political communication to reach undecided voters and abstentionists by giving them the illusion of a kind of personal proximity with the politicians, has put weekly and even monthly non-politically oriented magazines on the map of political marketing specialists. They are now included in campaign media plans, but this has meant conveying a "looser" image of politicians and their personal life to feed these magazines' needs and readership. For instance, Barack Obama allowed a number of pictures of himself, his wife, and even his two daughters to be taken in private situations and then published, not to mention a cover of *Vanity Fair* dedicated to Michelle Obama after the election, and so on. The same happens in other countries, and for instance photographs of French President Sarkozy openly kissing his new wife Carla Bruni, or public gestures of affection between them, abound in the world printed press, not counting Angela Merkel's one and only gala evening wearing a low-cut dress, and so on. But the consequences are troublesome and the maneuver often backfires: front-ranking politicians are now stalked like movie stars in their private life and are powerless to prevent an invasion of their privacy that they themselves initiated.[8]

Finally, if the printed press has somehow been slow in establishing web sites on the Internet, most newspapers around the world now at least duplicate their output on the Internet, and are even starting to modify coverage of the news for that medium, to make it timely. This shows that political communication still keeps closely in touch with the printed press since newspaper web sites usually maintain a similar level of recognition to their original printed version, despite technical differences. Most of the world's major newspapers have also been quick to catch on to the iPhone's success by shipping their own *iApp*, therefore creating a new chance for politicians to reach their audience with a quality of communication close that of the printed version.

4.2.1.1.2 Difficulties of access to the non-partisan press   The non-partisan press is not easily accessible. Its columns cannot be bought, except in the case of a paid advertising insert, whose credibility is considerably diminished by the fact that the reader immediately understands it to be an advertisement and not a piece of journalism. This brings us back to the low level of quality of the message similar to that of the partisan press.

The best solution open to the politician is to maintain privileged relationships with the journalists in charge of covering his activities. To this end, communication advisors generally prepare a special calendar of interviews with a few carefully chosen journalists from the print media. No politician's agenda would be complete without the periodical press luncheon, during which he can cultivate direct contacts with those journalists. In order to increase the personal flavor of these contacts, one can systematically try to ensure that the politician knows the journalist's name, particulars, and even family situation, as well as the subjects of their more recent articles.

The major leaders of the western world have incidentally made a habit of this method: the American or French presidential planes – even the Pope's aircraft – usually include a handful of selected journalists on board, generally in the rear of the main cabin.[9] Going back to see them a few moments during the flight, slipping them a piece of "confidential information," is part of the game of office.[10]

Another way of gaining access to the columns of the non-partisan press consists in organizing public relations operations substantial or original enough to necessitate journalistic coverage. If an election meeting can muster up a sufficiently attractive array of politicians, stars, and intellectuals, or other distinguished guests and sympathizers, if an open letter to the press, or even a particular stand on an issue or statement, are original enough, journalists of the non-partisan press will usually report it in their columns. In order to keep journalists "informed," trained staffers on the politician's communication team are usually placed directly in charge of non-partisan press relations, under the direction of a public relations officer and a press agent.[11] Of course, the press conference remains the traditional method of circulating a specific message as rapidly as possible among journalists. Predictably, the greater the politician's status, the greater the media representation at his press conferences, and subsequently, the published accounts.

Despite its theoretical independence then, the non-partisan press is relatively influenceable. Good media planning allows the politician's advisors to discreetly choose in advance those speech sections they wish to have the journalist relay, and so to artificially play them up so as give the latter the impression that it is indeed major news – or at least something fit to print.[12] But this practice requires considerable savoir-faire: when overdone, it can alienate journalists, if they feel they are being manipulated.

Finally, we must emphasize that non-partisan press, particularly daily newspapers, have suffered considerable economic decline in recent years, not only because of the financial crisis, but also because of changes in the media system and the proportional reduction in advertising revenues. The fact that many ad buyers changed to television during the 1950s, and more recently to the Internet, has led to a severe reduction of the number of daily newspapers in many countries, not to mention a decline in reading habits, notably among younger generations.[13] Therefore, politicians' access to the non-partisan press is more difficult, and the impact less strong than before, at least as regards the general public (though the media watch by journalists from other media somehow partly offsets the reduction in titles and circulation).

4.2.1.2   The partisan press and printed matter

The partisan press suffers the drawback of having an inferior quality of communication, since it cannot benefit from all the favorable elements we have just cited. Its effectiveness can be divided into two categories, depending on whether the printed matter is paid for or not by the recipient, with, here again, a difference in the quality of political communication based on the recipient's level of involvement inherent in the act of payment.[14]

4.2.1.2.1 Commercial partisan press and books   The commercial partisan press has suffered considerable decline in the course of this century in many western nations due of the drastic economic transformation of the media. Moreover, recently, in many cases, competition from the Internet has forced commercial partisan newspapers to disappear, sometimes entirely, sometimes through absorption by healthier large circulation newspapers, as in France.[15] In some other countries, such as the United Kingdom, the maintenance of partisan newspapers overtly defending one or other political party was only made possible by a lowering of these papers' standards, which remain popular only thanks to the accumulation of artificially inflated scandals.[16]

Politicians have thus lost a very useful organ for reaching the electorate: buying a daily paper on sale at the newsagent's is a routine act much easier to accomplish than seeking out a publication appearing less regularly and more difficult to find – if it is not available only by subscription. It has become more difficult to reach both the general public and the more distant sympathizers and activists simultaneously. The disappearance of many commercial partisan titles has only partially been compensated in some countries by the appearance of new titles sold by subscription. This is the only way of limiting the overhead, since it eliminates the problem of unsold copies at the newsagents. The circulation is calculated according to the demand, but it weakens the possibility of enlarging the readership. The subscription process, in any case, is too similar to a political commitment, which limits the circulation to a small circle of people already close to the politician the paper is supporting.

Naturally, communicating through these commercial partisan newspapers nevertheless offers the advantage of highly accurate targeting: since the recipients are quite clearly identified, the message can be all the more detailed. Recent years have also seen the proliferation of "confidential letters," sent directly to subscribers by many politicians, and made possible by the reduction of publishing costs occasioned by desktop publishing – now increasingly replaced by electronic mailing lists, with lesser impact, obviously.

But a substitute for the partisan press has been used more and more by political marketing in recent decades: the "programmatic book" or the "political essay," if not the "personal biography," usually published by the politician in the early stages of the campaign, if not a few months before. Barack Obama's *The Audacity of Hope*, published in 2006, as a first step into his future campaign, is such an example and was a well designed part of his "storytelling" campaign.[17] It remains to be seen whether Sarah Palin's *Going Rogue*, which unexpectedly hit the 2009 bestseller lists, will be such a cornerstone in her political future, but it was obviously written for the same purpose.

4..2.1.2.2 The freely distributed partisan press and tracts

The free partisan press involves newspapers generally sent without any prior request to the homes of voters in districts the politician is trying to reach. The mailing list is very often based on available listings of registered voters. The use of free partisan press affords a major advantage: since there is no sale, it is possible to reach a large number of voters who normally would not voluntarily buy a paper at a newsagent's or subscribe to it.

But this quantitatively wide circulation suffers from an important qualitative loss, on two accounts:

- free newspapers are often quickly discarded, or merely skimmed over. Even if they are read, readers might attach more importance to the local news or entertainment columns that to the political editorials;
- even if free newspapers are carefully read, their free circulation and the resulting lack of involvement for their recipients reduces their impact. The rather weak symbolic value of these publications entails a reduction of the psycho-sociological impact of the message they carry. [18]

This loss however can be sometimes compensated by targeting properly the recipients of the partisan newspaper. Letters intended for the traders of a district, can be composed or, more generally, according to the socio-cultural characteristics of the targeted geographic (whether they are middle- or lower-class neighborhoods, urban or rural, and so on).

Finally, because of their identical nature as free untargeted printed matter, flyers and tracts function in similar fashion to the free partisan press with regard to recipients. They are useful because they give recipients a written, relatively brief – and therefore easy to memorize – record of the fleeting contact with activists and volunteers who are distributing them. Distributing tracts can also contribute to the cohesion of the campaign organization by uplifting the morale of the activists and volunteers, by giving them work which they tend to consider highly satisfying.

4.2.1.2.3 Campaign literature for internal use   By literature – or printed matter – for internal use, we mean all written political communication media that are not intended for general public distribution, such as leaflets, booklets, programs, and many other kinds of printed documents. All forms of literature intended for undifferentiated outside distribution are excluded from this category (tracts and leaflets handed out on the street, partisan newspapers, distributed free of charge or not, etc.).

Internal printed matter is designed with two main aims:

- *internal circulation within the campaign organization and among activists and sympathizers,* who are thus informed of the substance of the programs, the ideas promoted by their candidate, details and suggestions as to their own participation in the campaign, etc.;
- *semi-external circulation, upon explicit request,* for those wishing more detailed information on the candidate or his campaign (especially voters called on during a canvassing operation who express interest in the candidate and to whom a printed summary of the visit is given or posted).

Today, in matters of literature intended for internal use, communication campaigns tend to be over-productive with regard to the real needs of modern political communication. Many North American political marketing specialists have observed that the printing of numerous tracts and brochures was not entirely justified. Such over-production appears to be more the consequence of the routine reproduction of former campaigning habits than the logical result of the current campaign requirements. In a sense, the printing and distribution of such literature seems at times little more than a routine channeling of the good will of activists and volunteers in the field and who are thus kept busy.[19] In fact, most of this printed literature could also be distributed over the Internet or e-mail lists, but then with a less gratifying effect for the recipients, obviously.

Nevertheless, even if the production of literature is probably excessive, it does help to improve the visibility of the communication campaign. Moreover, printed matter is concrete evidence of the communication campaign, which can be consulted at will, particularly by undecided voters just before polling day. It should thus not be neglected, for it constitutes an advantage absent from many of the media employed by modern political marketing. Finally, campaign literature also allows for much more accurate targeting than most other tools of modern mass media communication. It is possible to print brochures or fliers with program extracts, limited to the politician's proposals that directly concern specific targeted voters. Here, printed matter is irreplaceable.

4.2.2   Posters and billboard advertising

Posters are traditional tools of political communication. As illiteracy decreased, they gradually came to replace the traditional town criers or rural police officers who made public proclamations on the village square. The evolution took place mostly during the nineteenth century, when posters were extensively used in political campaigns in the United States, as well as in British elections, or in France to publicize the "official" parliamentary candidates of Napoleon III. Today, the forcefulness of billboard advertising in the political marketing process is equal to its commercial equivalent.

4.2.2.1   *Characteristics of billboard advertising*
Posters are far from being an ideal means of communication: they do not lend themselves to the transmission of messages of any complexity, and, what is more, they are not always effective. First, in both practice and theory, the message conveyed by posters should be kept relatively simple if it is to be intelligible, especially as the visibility time proper to that media is brief (you see posters at a glance, while walking, or in your car). It is therefore impossible for the poster to be used as the exclusive or main vector of a political communication, particularly a complex one. One must take into account as well that billboard advertising can more easily increase the reputation of a politician, but without insomuch convincing anyone.

Political billboard advertising then is a much more difficult method to employ than it would appear. Political marketing must solve an equation of apparently contradictory terms: make an impression, be simple, and not forget the message to relay. Many techniques have been developed specially in order to correspond as closely as possible to the message to communicate. A billboard "grammar" has been devised to command the recipient's attention. For years, political posters were only used to promote the politician's "self." In playing himself up to excess, the politician indirectly excluded the recipient (the numerous variations on "X, the citizens' candidate," or "X, the best representative").

Today, posters address recipients:

- as individuals, in the second person ("X, who defends your ideas" or "X, who thinks like you");
- or by including them in the communication process through the first person plural, using a "we/us" image (the current posters of politicians in traditional poses with their families, children, or characterized social groups).

Political marketing has also learned to use variations on the theme of the main campaign posters to improve their penetration, in the same way one repeats a leitmotiv or a musical refrain. The major posters will also figure in miniature on campaign letterheads and the tee-shirts volunteers wear while canvassing, and so on. In some instances, political marketing even attempts one final variation of billboard advertising, a bit more delicate to use, "teasing": this consists of putting up a successive string of posters that respond to one other, the first sometimes allusive, in order to pique the curiosity about the subject of the campaign.

4.2.2.2 *Different kinds of poster advertising*

Posters can be divided into two types, depending on whether they are produced through the usual commercial channels, or by activists and volunteers. The difference is not merely financial and material, but also fundamental as well.

4.2.2.2.1 Paid (or "commercial") billboard advertising The traditional use of posters has undergone a radical evolution over the course the twentieth century. In contrast to the home-made posters put up by volunteers, posters are now designed by professionals and circulated mainly through professional billboard advertising networks. This kind of commercial billboard advertising offers a number of advantages. First, the distribution is done through a specialized network of locations. High visibility is guaranteed, since the advertising billboards are located along main public thoroughfares, all duly exploited by professionals. Commercial billboards also allow for the use of larger poster formats than unauthorized posters hastily affixed by activists. The recourse to commercial billboard advertising allows for a better control of the overall process than unlawful posters, whose time of exposure cannot be guaranteed: the volunteers for rival politicians usually make it a point of honor to cover up the opponent's posters as quickly as possible.

The commercial billboard advertising process takes place under the near complete autonomy of the politician: often he only has the right to approve or reject the work carried out by specialists from outside his closed circle or campaign organization. Due to its high cost, commercial billboard advertising design is ordinarily entrusted to specialized commercial agencies: in this way, old hands of this medium theoretically reduce the possibility of errors.

Offsetting these favorable factors is the cost of commercial billboard advertising, naturally much greater than that of unauthorized posters:

- professional advertising agencies charge high prices for campaign design;
- rental of the advertising space is also expensive, although the cost can sometimes be brought down by the circumstantial reductions to which the networks consent (they often sell fewer billboards during the political campaigns because their regular commercial clientele try to avoid putting up billboards during election periods so as not to have their posters covered by illegal poster stickers);[20]
- moreover, since posters are a medium which permits only very fleeting contact, which only becomes effective though repetition, there is the obligation to maintain a quantitatively high exposure (saturation campaigns involving thousands of posters around the country); this too entails considerable expense.

This explains the relatively moderate use of political posters in countries where televised political commercials are authorized, and, conversely, their extensive use in countries such as France, where paid televised political spots are forbidden.[21] In countries of the first category (the United States or the United Kingdom, for instance), political marketing specialists think first about TV advertising spots and devote most of their time – and available funds – to producing these spots and buying airtime. Only the remaining money and attention goes into posters.

4.2.2.2.2 Voluntary or unauthorized posters   In this case, posters are put up in unauthorized places by volunteers and/or activists working for the candidate. Theoretically, the cost of volunteer fly-posting is much cheaper than that of its commercial equivalent, since two kind of expenses are avoided:

- fly-posting is done free of charge (by volunteers, instead of paid workers employed by the advertisement billboard networks);
- as no costs are incurred by putting a poster anywhere there is, of course, the risk of the posters being torn down by the owner of the property, the police, or the activists of a rival candidate.

Generally, the formats of unauthorized posters are much smaller than commercial advertising ones, since A4 and A5 sheets of paper are used.

Beyond considerations of cost, unauthorized fly-posting has two decisive advantages which explain its survival in the face of progress in communication techniques. First, it helps reinforce the cohesion of activists and the local campaign organization by giving them the task of putting their good will to use, a psychological factor which should not be neglected. Also, by usually leaving the design of their posters, and/or the local adaptation of national models, to the initiative of local activists, unauthorized fly-posting sometimes allows a more precise targeting than the commercial billboard advertising devised at party or campaign headquarters.[22] These elements of content and form explain the endurance of unauthorized fly-posting, even in today's multimedia world.

4.2.3   Miscellaneous advertising accessories

It might appear odd to include miscellaneous advertising objects in the category of traditional means of political communication. But they do act as reminders in the modern political marketing process in a way similar to the good luck charms once distributed with many a recommendation by sorcerers of old, or to the religious artifacts emphasized by most religions, or to the coat of arms of a nobleman which his vassal was allowed to place next to his own, and so on.

In a similar way, small trinkets, such as stickers, buttons, balloons, tie-pins, tee-shirts, pencils, key chains, and so on, have been used as campaigning devices in developed countries and have been manufactured in copious amounts.[23] They usually bear the name of the politician or the campaign slogans.

Rather than representing a genuine campaigning device, trinkets in fact are intended to maintain the morale of volunteers and activists, at public meetings in particular. Still, in countries where political opinions are out in the open, when the morale of activists is high, they can serve as a transmitter when these objects are proudly flaunted on their cars or clothes. In such cases, the political campaign enjoys a high visibility. For instance, in the United States and in many Latin American countries (Brazil, Chile), during the major election campaigns, the windshields or the bumpers of sympathizers' cars are festooned with stickers.

In the poorest regions of some countries, distributing gadgets and small gifts is even earnestly awaited during political rallies and meetings. For instance, in Latin America, candidates often throw candies, T-Shirts, pens and other small gifts branded with their names from their cars and at meetings during campaigns, just as bottled water companies and similar enterprises throw samples to the public during sports events.[24]

These objects may also help raise funds for the candidates or parties when they are sold. Many are sold at the entrance to political gatherings and rallies. They strengthen the loyalty of the participants and achieve a kind of redundancy with them. They are often sold to sympathizers via the candidates' Internet web sites.

Practically speaking, we might add these gimmicks and other advertising objects should preferably be made of good quality material, at least something of lasting quality, equal to the duration of the communication campaign, in order to avoid embarrassment, such watches with the candidate's initials stopping after two days.

***

The traditional means of political communication in use up to the mid-twentieth century are thus far from being useless today. On the contrary, modern political marketing has learned to devise a new range of possible uses for some of them, in order to compensate for the drawbacks or impracticalities created by the major increase in scale of the campaigns, when they are not local. The quality of political communication through traditional channels has remained high, a clear compensation for the fact that their audience has sometimes quantitatively declined, such as the printed press. Nevertheless, this change in scale explains why the audiovisual mass media means have been so rapidly adopted by modern political marketing.

Notes

1   For the 2008 US presidential primaries, although Hillary Clinton garnered the support of some of the "old guard" Democrat Hollywood supporters such as Steven Spielberg or Jack Nicholson, one turning point was to discover that Barack Obama had won strong support from popular figures with more up-to-date images, such as George Clooney, Will Smith, Halle Berry and Scarlett Johansson, not forgetting Kate Walsh or Oprah Winfrey for the small screen.
2   See also Chapter 9 of this book for more information canvassing during local communication campaigns.
3   Film director Rob Reiner did a very funny short training clip to that effect for Hillary Clinton's primaries campaign in 2008.
4   Marketing agencies call "*street marketing*," actions where paid or even unpaid persons go into their own communities to relay political communication in any way they can (placing self-made posters all around the neighborhood, discussing with their friends or phoning them, putting up local blogs, giving out pins or autographed pictures of the politician to their friends, bringing them to local meetings, etc.). In short, this is a more professionalized sort of grassroots campaigning. This is in fact a combination of other media analyzed separately all through the present book, with the only peculiarity being that they are combined with a stronger insistence on proximity than usual.
5   One recent exception was the long pre-campaign Jacques Chirac conducted in France between 1993 and election day in 1995, when he traveled all over France for two years, allegedly shaking 2 million hands.
6   France's far-right "Front National" party has charged admission fees for meetings to ensure audience cohesion.
7   A similar psycho-sociological mechanism also comes into play in enforcing the impact of "live" television shows, with regard to pre-recorded programs; broadcasters are perfectly aware of this, and to stress the chronological simultaneity between the show and the viewer, announce this as a "live" broadcast to ensure that the viewer knows it, thus increasing its impact.
8   Sometimes, the appearance of unauthorized images angers politicians, but it somehow nevertheless helps to "humanize" their image, and therefore is part of the personalization process they are seeking. For instance, the notorious paparazzi picture of Barack Obama athletically leaping into the Hawaiian waves in swimming trunks, which was published first by *People Magazine* and then all around the world, certainly helped maintain the image of dynamism his communication team had already built up.
9   If an elected official can afford it, he might even travel with a "second circle" of journalists when he is abroad, in a second plane placed at their disposal. This is frequently the case for long-haul trips by the American president.

10   This method may sometimes backfire, when the politician speaks too carelessly. For instance, during the 2000 US presidential campaign, George W. Bush's advisors notoriously asked him to stop going and chatting with journalists following him at the back of his plane. Similarly, in France, in 2002, French Socialist Leader Lionel Jospin was caught making nasty personal comments about the age of his opponent, the incumbent President Jacques Chirac and had to apologize publicly a few days later (Maarek 2003).

11   The details of this part of the campaign organization will be dealt with in Chapter 8.

12   Even if it is anecdotal, as when Chirac mentioned that he attended a Madonna concert at which she threw her panties from the stage – cleverly indicating to journalists that he had youthful tastes in music and remained young at heart.

13   On that point, see for instance Hallin and Mancini 2004.

14   On the consequences and the self-conviction induced by payment, see Baudrillard 1968, 1970, 1972, Bourdieu 1979, and Maarek 1986.

15   In France, the number of daily newspapers has fallen from 80 titles just before the First World War, to only dozen, so so, today, with commercial partisan dailies remaining only on the extreme right and extreme left fringes (the communist *L'Humanité* and the far-right *Présent*).

16   In particular, the love lives of members of royal families take on an outrageous importance in these papers.

17   Barack Obama, *The Audacity of Hope*, Crown Publishers, 2006. His opponent, John McCain, made a last-minute attempt to fight him on this field with a 2008 September reprint of his *Faith of My Fathers: A Family Memoir* in fact written as a premise of his first attempt at the US presidency, in 2000 (the 2008 paperback reprint was published by Harper).

18   See Bourdieu (1979) and Baudrillard (1968, 1970, and 1972).

19   The same could be said about many trade union magazines, etc.

20   A one-month campaign on most of the billboards of a town of about 1,000,000 inhabitants in the US would cost around US$40,000 to US$50,000 (including printing and paper costs).

21   In France, a law passed in 1990 forbids billboard advertising during the three months before election day, except for a few official advertising billboards freely loaned by the state; this decision put a sudden end to the former extensive use of commercial billboards, as seen in the 1980s.

22   All over the world, during the political campaigns, activists can now download "generic" posters from the candidates' or party's web sites which they can then personalize and localize for their own use, which makes their task even easier.

23   For some amusing illustrated anecdotes of former American presidential and campaign souvenirs, see Gores 1988.

24   See for instance the interesting account of and comments on the 2006 presidential election in Ecuador by C. Torre and C. Conaghan 2009.

5

Audiovisual tools

In the wake of initial attempts during the 1950s, the famous Kennedy-Nixon television debates in 1960 marked the coming of age of television in modern political communication.[1] Since the margin in election votes obtained by the two men had been quite narrow (a mere 100,000), political analysts agree that, as minimal as the genuine effect of the televised debates on the voters would have been, it was probably enough to influence the outcome of the election.

Since then, political communication has never ceased submitting to the growing influence of audiovisual media in general, and television in particular. In most democratic countries therefore, television has become the principal medium by which citizens get information before they go to the polls. Although the actual impact of audiovisual mass media cannot really be gauged, the narrow margin frequently separating political opponents makes their use a must.[2]

Today, in democratic countries, it is almost inconceivable to hold a free election without at least one televised debate between the main candidates, or those still in the running after a first ballot: the pre-electoral television debate has become a mandatory halt on the candidate's political road, both in older democracies such as the United States, and France, as well as in countries with less experience of free elections. In Germany, where there had been no televised debates, and Helmut Kohl had argued in 1998 that "tradition" was against a televised debate, these debates are now the norm. In 2002, Gerhard Schroeder, the incumbent chancellor, agreed to face Edmund Stoiber (knowing that his charisma was stronger and that he would be at an advantage), and did the same in 2005, this time facing a surprisingly good Angela Merkel, who then went on to replace him as chancellor.[3] Finally, a series of debates was launched during the 2010 general election campaign in the United Kingdom. Up to then all incumbent politicians had carefully avoided them, arguing that parliamentary elections

Campaign Communication and Political Marketing, First Edition. Philippe J. Maarek.
© 2011 Philippe J. Maarek. Published 2011 by Blackwell Publishing Ltd.

did not directly elect a leader, as presidential elections did in other countries. The serving Labour prime minister, Gordon Brown, agreed to participate in a series of televised debates with Conservative Party leader, David Cameron, and, the Liberal Democrat leader, Nick Clegg.

In the United States, the "decisive" debates between the two main candidates[4] before polling day have now become mandatory, and 80 million viewers watched the only debate between Ronald Reagan and the sitting president, Jimmy Carter in 1980.[5] The Bush-Kerry debates in 2004 only attracted an average audience of around 50 million viewers, for instance, but this figure still remains high in relation to the number of citizens actually voting. In 2008, the three debates between Barack Obama and John McCain attracted 52.4, 63.2, and 56.5 million viewers and these figures were considered to be above the average of recent years.[6]

In Brazil in December 1989, the two debates between the remaining presidential candidates, Fernando Collor, the "establishment" candidate, and then unknown leftist politician Inácio Lula, tipped the scales in favor of Lula. However, this did not guarantee him enough votes to be elected at the time, but enough to put him permanently on the map of Brazilian politics, before being elected president of the country in 2002.

Conversely, at the beginning of the third millennium, the absence of a "decisive" televised debate, or the refusal by an incumbent politician to participate in one, is now regarded as an essential ingredient of a democratic election. For instance, the opponents of Ion Iliescu's regime in Romania had to live with the fact that the cards had been partially dealt prior to the 1990 presidential elections, since they were denied equal-time access to the television networks. It was also the case for Alejandro Toledo and the other politicians trying to compete against the incumbent president, Alberto Fujimori, in his bid for a third term as president of Peru in 2000.

But the audiovisual media are not particularly easy to use for political marketing. Before looking at the different ways in which they can be exploited, we will deal first with these problems and the need for the candidate to have an appreciation of audiovisual practice. Among audiovisual media, we shall deal mainly with television and video clips in this chapter, media combining vision and sound. Obviously, radio also plays an important part in campaigns, and is a welcome tool for politicians, notably when drivers stuck in their cars in traffic jams have not much else to do than phone, listen to their iPods, or to their radio. But most of what is said in this chapter can easily be applied to radio, with the exception of course of what is related to visuals.

5.1 The complexity of practice of the audiovisual means by political communication

5.1.1 The difficulties of using audiovisual means

We shall concentrate on the two main problems created by the audiovisual media when they are used for political marketing:

- delayed effects of the messages transmitted by audiovisual means, in contrast to the brief duration of the communication campaign;
- the difficulty of exercising control over the audiovisual message itself, because of the major role played by non-verbal communication, which can considerably modify the message, despite all efforts to counteract it, a phenomenon increased by the singular direction of the media.

5.1.1.1 Delayed effects of audiovisual media

Communication specialists understand that the audiovisual media are not always effective vehicles for political messages: being unidirectional mass communication tools, they do not allow for the improvement of a communication, lacking as they do any feedback or true redundancy. This drawback explains the uncertainty about about the direct effects of the audiovisual media: if the message is transmitted concretely, it is not always immediately followed by the anticipated effects on recipients.

E. McCombs and D.E. Shaw have advanced a theoretical explanation for the slowness of this process, explaining the existence of an agenda-setting effect for the mass media. In short, it is constituted by the redundancy empirically produced by the repetition of the same communication via different media. If the message initially transmitted by a television program, for instance, produces an agenda-setting effect, it will be picked up by other network newscasts, then by the newspapers, rebounding sometimes repeatedly in this way, the whole process contributing to heavy penetration.[7] The agenda effect does not change people's opinions directly, but improves their knowledge of various communications, when these latter media gain from it.

To take the example of television newscasts, American political analysts David Paletz and Robert Entman have observed that 70% of the evening news items were identical for two of the three national American television networks.[8] This is where the agenda-setting effect comes into play: from the start, the zapping viewer will be confronted unavoidably by the same images and commentaries. Even the order of appearance of the different news items on the same day is often the same from newscast to newscast.

This slowness explains the difficulty politicians have in modifying their image: there is a long period of time between the actual change of image and the moment it becomes credible. This could also in part provide another explanation for Nixon's defeat by Kennedy in 1960, since his image at the time was clearly that of a sitting vice-president who had been in office for eight years, and not that of a future president. Because of this slowness of audiovisual media effects, it becomes easier and more effective to exploit a politician's known attributes, even if at first sight they may appear as defects, and of course it does then mean exposing them in a more favorable light.

This phenomenon also explains the difficulty of exerting influence directly on the mass media communication process: being empirical, the agenda-setting effect cannot be controlled. Therefore, the media often change the priorities of the political debate without giving candidates the power to stop that change (but we will see later that they still maintain a certain latitude of maneuver in the process). On the contrary, clearly, when a politician happens to benefit from an agenda-setting effect, the media will then listen to him – though not always favorably, of course. His opponents will suddenly be "forgotten," as if they had suddenly become invisible to their eyes, the surveys playing a considerable part in this.

5.1.1.2 Problems generated by the non-verbal element of audiovisual communication

The delayed effect of audiovisual media is not the only obstacle to the effectiveness of political messages. The second main problem comes from the presence of certain components of audiovisual communication that are difficult to control. The effectiveness of a politician's television appearance probably depends as much on his "non-verbal" communication as on his actual speech.[9]

5.1.1.2.1 The importance of non-verbal communication in audiovisual communication Three different aspects of the politician's non-verbal communication can help, or alternatively, harm him:

- physical appearance;
- vocal attributes;
- gestures.

PHYSICAL APPEARANCE We have already cited the now classic example of the embryonic beard of Richard Nixon which made him appear unshaven, and thus not very appealing, opposite John Kennedy during the famous debate of 1960. Even if it was the commentators who, after the event, played up that point, the narrow margin in the number of votes polled by the two candidates will never allow us to judge accurately just how much this apparent carelessness in the Republican candidate's appearance actually influenced the outcome at the polls. Since then, no politician has dared set foot in a television studio without having previously made the effort to look his best with at least a visit to the hairdresser's.[10]

The politician's physical appearance is all the more difficult to control there is not much that can be modified, for good reason. But researchers interested in the problem have noted that the morphopsychology of politicians has major consequences for the quality of their television appearances. Their physical appearance, especially their facial features, lends a subconscious positive or negative connotation to their communication with viewers, and this has nothing to do with the tenor of their speech![11] Some experiments have even demonstrated that the mere sight of a politician's features immediately induces a positive or negative effect in the minds of many viewers. In the United States, this phenomenon considerably helped Ronald Reagan, while immediate negative effects of the same order apparently were prompted by the mere facial appearance of some of his opponents.[12] More recent research led by a team of scholars from the University of Michigan has even indicated that just by watching muted "decisive debates" for state governors' elections on television, a group of 264 students, who did not even know the candidates, was able to predict with an unusually accurate rate of 58% which of them had later won the election![13]

The audiovisual media are formidably effective in inducing this kind of non-verbal communication effect: the close-up shot constituting the main camera angle in televised broadcasts, this easily leads to an audiovisual "iconomorphology" of the political figure.[14]

VOCAL ATTRIBUTES   Many vocal characteristics can modify the meaning of a message, or its interpretation: pitch, timbre, rhythm, inflection, and so on, can be a disadvantage for a politician with a "bad" voice, as as well as an advantage to a politician who knows how to use it, though it cannot be claimed that he has absolute control over it. Indeed, despite good intentions, the politician cannot transform his voice completely as certain human vocal attributes are not alterable. Technological progress has enabled voice analysts to demonstrate the existence of "voice prints" unique for each individual, just like fingerprints. This discovery has already been put into use in computerized security systems, where new voice recognition chips have replaced passwords.

Vocal attributes, then, constitute an individual element of the physical personality of a politician, an element of his non-verbal communication over which the politician cannot exercise complete control (this is even the principal factor in political communication by radio). This has positive or negative consequences for the effectiveness of his speech, just as his "iconomorphology" does.

GESTURES   In a similar fashion, a politician's gestures can reinforce or contradict a speech he is delivering on television. Any movement can make a difference, from a look and the direction of the gaze to a hand movement, or any other body gesture.[15] Of course, we will look at how the politician can control certain gestures with minimal effort. But this requires him to focus the matter.

For instance, strangely enough for such an experienced politician, in most of Hillary Clinton's ads during the 2008 US presidential campaign, she tended to avoid eye contact – that is did not look into the camera lens – a fact which some researchers believe defeated her attempt to seem close to the voters, by making her appear "hard to like."[16] Her infrequent smiling (to look more qualified for the presidency?) increased this distance. Corroborating this is the fact that after her short "crying" episode, she won the New Hampshire primaries against all odds, when the polls had put her way behind Barack Obama.

We term "audiovisual charisma" the set of positive consequences of non-verbal audiovisual communication for the quality of a politician's communication, as described above.[17]

Political marketing strategy thus involves an attempt to encompass a politician's audiovisual charisma as a necessary part of the campaign preparation. One must keep in mind that audiovisual charisma can sometimes be quite different from the usual charisma that comes into play in direct face-to-face communication: they do not always go hand in hand, just as the most attractive people in the world are not always the most photogenic.

5.1.1.2.2 Difficulty of influencing non-verbal communication   It is all the more difficult to teach a politician to amend his non-verbal communication as it is something that happens unconsciously. One of the worst moments in George H.W. Bush's 1992 campaign came during the second of his three debates with Ross Perot and Bill Clinton, when, confronted with a sample of "ordinary" American citizens, the television camera caught him furtively glancing at his watch. Similarly, in the second 1996 US presidential election debate, Bob Dole often gave viewers a bad impression because he always went behind the desk when he was answering questions from the floor while Bill Clinton boldly stepped toward the questioners, giving the image of a politician who wants to bridge the gap between himself and the public.

In any case, non-verbal communication by essence is highly difficult to influence. Since it is mainly subjective, the interpretation of the message it conveys can vary considerably according to the different recipients, much more so than in cases of verbal communication. The political discourse found in a verbal communication is relatively precise: it makes use of words, a language, thereby limiting the possible interpretations. On the other hand, non-verbal communication is related to a much less perceivable discourse, thus more hazardous to decipher, hence the increasing difficulty in controlling the decoding process. In fact, as for the substance of the communication itself, deciphering the unconscious elements of non-verbal communication is a direct consequence of the individual interpretation made by each viewer. When present, favorable or unfavorable prejudice can thus provoke a completely contrary interpretation to the non-verbal communication.

Despite the resulting difficulty of dealing with the problem, communication advisors systematically do what they can to remedy the most obvious defects of this sort in their politician clients. The growing importance of such a task has led to the development of genuine training in audiovisual media.

5.1.2   Media training arising from the difficulties of using the audiovisual media

It is practically impossible for today's politician to make an audiovisual presentation without appropriate media training, as communication consultants commonly call it. The earliest example of media training dates from the first use of audiovisual media for purposes of political communication. We have mentioned how, during his 1952 American presidential campaign, General Eisenhower was advised not to read his speeches, not only for the sake of more effective communication, but also to avoid bending down and showing his bald pate while lowering his head in order to read the words on the paper as the teleprompter did not yet exist.

Subsequently, politicians systematically undertook media training, following the brilliant example set by Kennedy himself in 1960. When he became president, Richard Nixon would spend two days rehearsing before each of his press conferences. Some politicians spend even more time rehearsing for each of their main television appearances. The record may be held by a French politician, the many-times cabinet minister: François Leotard. He is said to have spent an entire month rehearsing his first important TV appearance in the mid-1980s!

This training is very often carried out with the help of actual TV news anchormen, who give politicians the benefit of their experience – usually for a princely sum. During these training sessions, the politicians are mercilessly "put on the hot seat," both for the form and content of their presentations. Most news anchormen have at one time or another taken part in these media training sessions,[18] though many television networks now often forbid their employees from doing it under contract for obvious ethical reasons.

We shall make a distinction between:

- formal training, directly linked to the elements concerning non-verbal communication we have just exposed;
- training in substance.

5.1.2.1 *Formal training*
5.1.2.1.1 Presentation   As a first step, communication advisors systematically review the politician's overall presentation, from their physical appearance to their clothes.

THE POLITICIAN'S PHYSICAL APPEARANCE   Communication consultants often suggest changing the politician's physical appearance as far as possible. Generally, alterations are intended to limit the risk of the politician appearing too different from the average individual, and, in particular, from the average politician. It would be too long and tedious to cite the names of all the politicians who have submitted to this process. Let us simply say that alterations in physical presentation have been known to lead to plastic surgery, or, even more frequently, cosmetic dentistry. In the United States alone, one loses count of the number of candidates who have undergone surgery prior to a campaign to acquire a more "assertive" chin or reduce an "exaggerated" nose. For instance, before trying to make a bid for the American presidential race, in 1991, former Ku Klux Klan leader David Duke underwent plastic surgery for major facial changes, including a more impressive chin.

In some cases, this "battle of looks" can even allow a politician to take the lead by imposing certain physical traits, which then become components of his audiovisual image. Ronald Reagan's near-permanent tan is a good example of this kind, as is the large moustache of the former Polish President Lech Walesa, or the wine stain birthmark on Mikhail Gorbachev forehead, popularized by cartoonists the world over.

Once long hidden, these extensive changes are now more and more obvious and less and less concealed. For instance, the Italian Prime Minister, Silvio Berlusconi, after having disappeared for three weeks for a stay in a foreign clinic, admitted to the press in 2004 that he went regularly to an American plastic surgery clinic. He even hinted that for him, any politician who could afford it should look his or her best to the voters, which was the reason he went away for a "technical control" (sic).[19]

Finally, let us mention that gender here plays a particular role, since women candidates are put on the spot for their physical appearance (and clothes) much more than men. In fact, gender stereotypes still abound. In 1984, Geraldine Ferraro, the first woman running as a vice-presidential candidate was asked questions about her hairstyle, while Ségolène Royal, running for the French presidency in 2007, was so annoyed by questions on her physical appearance that she sued or threatened to sue journalists who paid too much attention to that. For her part, Hillary Clinton never seems to have reacted to the many unpleasant Internet rumors that she had used Botox to improve her looks when confronting Barack Obama during the 2008 primaries.[20] More recently, in France, *Le Monde*, the serious French daily, ran an article entitled "La metamorphose de Martine Aubry" in which the new décor of the French Socialist Party leader's office, her new "more elaborate" make-up, and her more refined hairstyle were as much discussed as her political abilities.[21]

THE POLITICIAN'S CLOTHES   Communication advisors usually insist on a certain neutrality in a politician's clothes: as they are easily noticed. Politicians generally wear dark blue suits, a matching tie, and, inevitably, a light-blue shirt. This tradition is a consequence of the technical defects of early television. In the late 1960s, when color TV was in its infancy, there were problems with the correct transmission of brighter colors, particularly reds: they usually ran over into the neighboring colors on the television screen, thereby giving the image an aggressive tonality. Conversely, white was forbidden because it was too shiny in contrast to the politician's skin. These defects were so noticeable that Americans came to mock their color television system, NTSC, by nicknaming it "never twice the same color".

Even if the technical quality has improved today, the old habits of communications consultants die hard. In any case, politicians are also often strongly advised to wear clothes that make them look better, or appear more modern, from the current fashion in tie sizes to eyeglasses with trendy frames.

In some cases, the politician's clothes even carry a specific communication message for a campaign. Of course, there is the now classical case of the politician asked by his communication consultant to "improve" the way he dresses allegedly to enhance his image. The results, here, incidentally, may be mistaken: for instance, in France, Lionel Jospin was asked to wear suits designed by Lanvin for the 2002 presidential campaign and never seemed at ease in his new attire. More recently, in 2008, the Republican Party apparently bought new clothing worth US$150,000 for Sarah Palin within a few days of her surprise nomination as John McCain's vice presidential candidate, somewhat contradictory to her positioning as a "no-frills mom."[22]

In other cases, a candidate's dress may be deliberately designed to convey a specific message or suggest the way he (or his team) wants his image to be perceived by the citizen. The best recent example probably comes from Ségolène Royal, the Socialist candidate for the 2007 French presidential election, who deliberately wore plain white skirts and dresses during the campaign, instead of the traditional red or pink colors of Socialist Party. She thus achieved a dual goal: of course, being constantly in white made her immediately distinguishable in crowds, but it was also an obvious metaphor for womanhood and virginity, a clear reference to the fact that she was campaigning to win, trying to evade the usual Socialist Party supporters in order to reach more conservative voters, who were thus reminded of the white dresses worn by Catholic girls in France for their first communion. German Chancellor Angela Merkel has been more successful with her masculine dark suits, choosing to disregard femininity and to promote an image of seriousness and competence.

5.1.2.1.2 Training in "classic" techniques of expression

There is no doubt that the politician must understand and practice the now classic methods for improving delivery of speeches intended for the public, as now taught in the applied linguistic courses in most of universities (semiology, speech acts, propositional logic, etc.).

One of the main components of audiovisual training in this domain is the necessity of discourse-simplification formulated by communication advisors. To begin with, they usually suggest that the politician limit his vocabulary to the common spoken language, about 1,200–2,000 words for most main western languages. He is then given guidance on using only relatively brief sentences to be better understood, and so on.[23]

Thus, most communication consultants attempt to discourage their clients from using obscure words, and try to get them to slow down their delivery, and so on. The politician is also instructed never to cite political opponent(s) by name, or at least to keep it to a strict minimum. This can lead to an abundance of circumlocutions, such as "the incumbent senator", and so on.

Finally, a great effort is made to remedy the politician's deficiencies by teaching him how to give rhythm and accent to his words, a kind of "music," so that they do not merely seem like a string of random notes. But this preparation cannot completely compensate for the physical shortcomings of his non-verbal communication.

5.1.2.1.3 Training in conscious gestures

Just as mothers do with their young children, communication consultants also instruct politicians on how to control of their gestures during a television appearance. For example, pointing a finger at an opponent during a debate, or, worse, at a TV viewer, is systematically discouraged, for instance, because of its overly aggressive connotation. Knowing which camera is operating allows for the use of certain effects, such as looking away from the opponent and directly addressing the camera, in other words, looking at the viewer in the eye, and so on.

We can distinguish two axes of controlling conscious gestures:

- the relationship to the TV viewer;
- the relationship to the speech.

CONTROLLING GESTURES IN RELATIONSHIP TO THE TV VIEWER The first gestural factor that politician can attempt to control is his position and movements in relation to the camera. This is a cardinal element of his non-verbal audiovisual communication manner: the camera eye represents the viewer, who only sees what it transmits, in the same way and from the same viewpoint.

Much of the media training provided by communication consultants is centered on making the politician aware of which camera is filming him at a given moment, to immediately locate the small light, usually red, which indicates which studio camera is actually recording what is being broadcast to the viewers. In this way, the politician can judge how and in which direction to turn and direct his gaze.

This is crucial, as part of the credibility of the message depends on knowing the position of the camera that is recording. In some instances, an eye-to-eye declaration to viewers can give it a durable positive connotation, but will not abide the slightest hesitation. During the 1960 Kennedy-Nixon debate, Kennedy, well trained by his advisors, made a much better impression, indeed seemed more sincere, merely because he virtually never looked at his opponent, but kept his gaze turned toward the camera.[24] Nixon, on the contrary, kept his head turned towards Kennedy while speaking, thus diverting his gaze from the camera eye and the television audience.

Knowing the camera position also allows the politician to improve his physical position and appearance in the eyes of the viewer: there is no point in straightening your back when you are being filmed in close-up, but some gestures when you think you are not on the air can harm your image.

CONTROLLING GESTURES IN RELATIONSHIP WITH THE SPEECH   This second mode of control is much more familiar to politicians, since it is closely bound up with the conventional manner in which verbal discourse is reinforced and punctuated by gestures, as orators have done for ages, or lawyers in court.

We must nevertheless point out that the peculiar nature of the audiovisual media, particularly the predominance given to the close-up, renders the practice of these punctuating effects much less simple, for two reasons:

- many of the usual effects run the risk of not being perceived on the television screen, and must be adapted to it; a good number of politicians have thus taken to enumerating the points of their speech on their fingers while speaking, a visible but measured gesture, which gives their discourse a semblance of scientific method;
- some traditional oratorical effects, like broad gestures, etc., so useful during public meetings, for instance, are discouraged on television, because they seem overwrought and detrimental to the speaker, as the theatrical acting of the movie actors became suddenly outdated once the arrival of the talking picture rendered such emphasis pointless.

5.1.2.2 *Training in substance*

The formal conditioning of politicians also entails an intensive training in matters of substance: the issues which are likely to be treated. Many training sessions is devoted to this aspect. A large team of advisors generally engages in a great deal of preliminary documentation work. They determine the important issues of the time, those most likely to shape the questions of debating opponents or journalists. This training is generally quite effective. American political analysts David Paletz and

Robert Entman have estimated that 90% of the questions were determined in advance by President Ronald Reagan's team of advisors for his regular White House press conferences.[25]

Naturally, they also prepare the answers to be given in public, and, during sessions that resemble dress rehearsals, the politician is taught to respond, in real time, to the more brusque or embarrassing questions.[26] The team also prepares a few powerful "sound bites" intended to remain in the viewers' memory, and politicians are also taught how to seamlessly insert them when speaking in an artificially spontaneous manner.

For example, American political communication specialists still recall the famous formula carefully prepared for Ronald Reagan, speaking with TV viewers, during the second Reagan-Mondale debate in 1984: "I want you to know that I won't make my age an issue of the present campaign. I shall never use as a political argument in my favor the youth and the lack of experience of my adversary." It did cut short any further maneuvers from Walter Mondale on this line![27]

During this type of media training, the politician also learns to condense his speeches, due the brevity of the average item on television newscasts: today, a politician who talks for too long will often be interrupted by the news anchorman in most western countries, certainly in the US in any case. Some observers have empirically established that in recent years, the average length of time allotted to a politician during a television interview to answer the journalist's questions, the so called "soundbite" left to them, was no greater than nine seconds in 1988, as opposed to 43 seconds in 1968.[28]

Certain training methods for audiovisual intervention very much depend on the kind of broadcast the politician takes part in. In the next section we shall concentrate on the most important kinds of broadcasts, with an emphasis, when necessary, on their particularities.

5.2 Principal applications of audiovisual means to political communication

Today, televised debates and talk shows constitute the chief modes of political communication. But a brief appearance in one of the main evening newscasts, a well-designed advertising spot, when and where possible, and various other forms of participation in not overtly political television programs, can also effectively aid the communication process.

It is therefore in the politician's interest to maximize participation in order to give his campaign a useful media showcasing, his appearance in the different categories of broadcasts contributing to an intensification of mass media agenda-setting effects, a phenomenon becoming clearer from year to year, as already mentioned. This explains the changes in the "center stage" for political communication, which naturally varies from year to year. In the United States a few years ago, it would have been essential to be Dan Rather's guest on CBS evening news.[29] Then, of course, Larry King's famous interviews on CNN have had their followers, but their reputation might have been more influential abroad than within the United States. Today, the "leading" path is less clear than before, and since Bill Clinton's 1992 appearance on the *Arsenio Hall Show,* televised talk shows have focused the attention of politicians and their advisors. Oprah Winfrey and now Ellen DeGeneres and other similar TV hosts have become essential for campaigning politicians' televised appearances and are regarded as important as regular newscasts in the eyes of political communication advisors. Of course, for national elections the world over, debates between the leading candidates are an additional and crucial tool.

We shall now discuss the main types of politician appearances on television, after first examining the difficult question of access to television.

5.2.1   The problem of access to audiovisual media

The answer to this question varies in different countries, depending on whether or not the candidate is authorized to pay for access to the media during the electoral campaign.

In the United States, like in many western countries, candidates can legally buy airtime on television, either for short spots or longer broadcasts. Since the Radio Act of 1927 and the Communication Act of 1934, the US Federal Communication Commission (FCC), the broadcast regulatory body, has enforced the Equal Time Rule. According to this rule, not in fact a real law, but a ruling handed down by the FCC, all radio and television broadcasters are obliged to grant all politicians equal access to their airwaves, which is the broadcast equivalent of "most favored nation status" in international law. As soon as airtime is sold to one politician, all others must be able to obtain the same amount of time and programming slots, provided they can afford it. Of course, the main problem here is that no money implies no television ads. The only limitation of the Equal Time Rule has been set by the Commission on Presidential Debates. To settle the question of the presence of "non-partisan," independent or third party candidates during presidential election debates, the Commission has granted networks organizing debates the right to restrict the choice of participants to the main politicians, namely those who are given at least 15% of intended votes by the surveys.[30]

In some other countries such as France, the problem is quite different: paid television and radio networks access for politicians is forbidden by law. Since the first modern campaign for presidential elections in 1965, a 1964 decree granted official candidates free airtime on public-owned radio and television channels. Based on the same principles as the Equal Time Rule, this regulation, still more or less in force today, though slightly modified from election to election, organizes election campaign broadcasts on the public networks. It stipulates free access to the public media for all officially registered candidates in the presidential elections, who are entitled to equal time in special broadcasts, during the final two weeks before polling; to avoid any favoritism, a lottery determines the candidates' order of appearance. The French television regulatory board, the Conseil Superieur de l'Audiovisuel (CSA), is now in charge of supervising the process.

Today, in many countries, the "Equal Time Rule" and similar rules are sometimes contested, particularly by network owners or operators when the number of marginal politicians competing for office is too great, causing them to view these programs as a burden. On the other hand, "independent" candidates as well as small or new political parties (like the Green parties in Europe) often complain that most of the free airtime is given to "mainstream" candidates and political parties already represented in their respective parliaments, but there does not seem to be a better solution.[31]

In some cases, anyway, even in democracies, access to television is not completely guaranteed, notably for independent candidates, or politicians not from the main parties. We have mentioned that non-partisan candidates have thus no access to the American "decisive" televised debates if the Commission on Presidential Debates does not feel they are able to win, and in many countries, the time allocated to political parties for campaigning on television is based on the number of members of parliament, quite an obstacle for new political parties, for instance.

5.2.2 Televised debates

Today, the audiovisual debate is increasingly regarded as the keystone of the election campaign, with the decisive debate between the two, sometimes three, candidates still in the running on the eve of election day. This is common not only in France, Brazil, or the US, but in virtually every democratic nation in the world.[32]

The televised debate can be one of the key events by which the outcome of the campaign is determined and played out, with the drawback of reducing the politician to something of a poker player: he could lose all on a single deal, and maybe for reasons of form, such as being out of sorts on that particular day. For example, Richard Nixon was handicapped by a knee inflammation on the day of his first televised debate with John Kennedy.

As most follow-up press commentaries clearly tend to concentrate not on the issues debated but on who "won," the decisive debate then becomes too often just another detail of the "horse race story" perfunctorily indulged in by the principal media. For this reason, politicians take the utmost care in preparing for these debates, the only time during the campaign when they appear publicly without having more or less complete control of the situation.

The timing is in two stages:

- first, negotiation on the technical organization of the debate;
- second, controlling in real time how the show is shot and transmitted.

5.2.2.1 *Negotiating the technical conditions of televised debates*[33]
All the technical aspects of television broadcasting, framing, editing, and even sound, can have considerable influence on a communication, by injecting other factors, without the candidate being the wiser. A low camera angle can thus be

auspicious, making the politician appear higher than his interlocutor, but can just as well turn to his disadvantage, if this angle shows up a poorly shaped chin; the nuances of sound recording can unhappily accentuate a somewhat too high-pitched masculine voice, or attenuate an overly deep one, and so on.

A good option available to politicians concerned about limiting the hazards of audiovisual communication is to seek the help of a television director who knows how to film them to their best advantage and who represents them in these negotiations. This is the case in most countries for most major candidates in important television debates.

At first, the director working with a politician usually meets his counterpart(s) employed by the other debating politicians, and the official director assigned by the sponsoring network, to work out the general format and conditions of the debate. These negotiations are normally concluded by a formal written agreement.[34] These preparations are very thorough and can go into great detail:

- establishing the time limits and conditions for speaking;
- determining the decor for the broadcast;
- agreeing the range of shots the director can use;
- deciding which editing techniques are authorized.

5.2.2.1.1 Taking the floor and dealing with interruptions The first steps in technical discussions always involve the following questions. Can the participants interrupt one another? Must they take turns to answer to identical questions asked by journalists, or can they address each other directly?

Determining these modalities involves a delicate balance between the "bearing" of the broadcast and the risks the participants agree to take. Responding individually to the questions of journalists present in the studio affords the inestimable advantage of running fewer risks, since journalists tend to be less aggressive than their opponents. Agreeing to short response time limits is another way of preventing risks, since it avoids in-depth answers to possible critical questions from journalists or to opponents' remarks and thus allows the politician to save face. But, on the other hand, the debate inevitably becomes dull for viewers, since it seems more like a series of monologues. And boredom can seriously weaken the effectiveness of a communication. For example, the 1988 American presidential debates were generally regarded as boring, whereas the combative presence of Ross Perot between Bill Clinton and George Bush in 1992 greatly helped the debates.[35]

Conversely, the possibility of direct engagements between participants makes for a livelier debate and a better-paced broadcast, while making things more risky for the politicians. This explains the now customary system of decisive debates with politicians being queried by journalists politely in turn, disregarding the risk of boredom for the audience.

5.2.2.1.2 The decor The way the studio is arranged can make a difference in the way viewers assess the candidates. It should be neutral in relation to the politicians, both intrinsically and with regard to placement: a piece of furniture can detract from a politician of too slight, or too heavy, a build; similarly, certain colors in the decor can put certain participants at a disadvantage, and so on. The comfort and preferences of the candidates are also taken into account, which can at times make the preparations for a debate look like the long quarrels between Kasparov and Karpov about their respective armchairs before their many world chess championships.

5.2.2.1.3 The filming The filming of the debate, the framing of shots, and so on, can in themselves be vectors of an involuntary non-verbal communication which might prove detrimental to the candidate's image. When, for example, the opponents are markedly dissimilar in stature, a wide-angle shot can be harmful to one or the other, due to the involuntary consequences of this comparison on the viewer.

Certain physical traits can also be unfavorably emphasized by certain shots, or, conversely, played down by them. In this sense, politicians are no different from movie stars who always insist on being photographed looking their best. Other similar details play the same kind of role (shots increasing the visibility of a muscular twitch, etc.).

5.2.2.1.4 Authorized editing techniques The interpretation of a candidate's speech can be completely transformed by certain kinds of editing techniques. An insert shot of an opponent's dubious expression while the speaker is putting forward an idea can sometimes be enough to negate its impact.[36] For this reason, during the preparations for the debate, the candidates' advisors often demand that insert shots should not be authorized during the broadcast (which does not help its pace). Directors assisting the politicians must then considerably limit the "authorized" editing alternatives in order to reduce risks of that kind.

Limiting the director's editing range in this way furthermore harms the technical quality of televised debates, which are often reduced to a monotonous sequence of fixed shots of the participants, which in turn affects the attention of viewers, unconsciously bored by the dull filming.

An unwilling demonstration of the efficiency, so to speak, of these protective measures was made on the occasion of the first debate between John Kerry and George W. Bush for the 2004 US presidential campaign, when media and politicians were initially surprised to see in the journalists' comments very different interpretations of the outcome of the debate for the two politicians. The explanation was quickly found: on its own program, the network hosting the debate had kept to the word the editing "rules" agreed upon, but had mistakenly sent to the other networks transmitting the debate all the images shot by all the cameras on the set, thus making them do their own editing – which they did. George W. Bush was thus at disadvantage in the eyes of the audience of these other networks since some images were shown in which he was obviously embarrassed by some questions, when he did not think that the program was live.

5.2.2.2 Broadcast control

While the debate is on the air, the role of the director assisting his candidate is to ensure personally, alongside the resident director, that the actual technical direction of the broadcast conforms exactly to what has been formally agreed on. Respect of kind of shots used, absence of inserts, level and quality of the sound transmission, are thus under constant supervision and verification.

In some cases, the actual direction of the televised debate is almost entirely under the direct supervision of the directors hired by the candidates, the resident director only retaining a mere technical function. Some preparatory agreements might even stipulate that the assistants to the rival politicians, and not the resident director, are the ones to decide on shot changes when their own client is on the screen.

5.2.3   Televised newscasts

At first glance, it might seem that the candidate exercises little control over his appearances in ordinary televised newscasts. In fact, he does have opportunities to intervene actively, but which paradoxically creates more problems of content than of form.

5.2.3.1 Intervention in the form of newscast participation

First, participating in regular televised newscasts does not in appearance depend on the politician himself: he is invited to do so by the network news desk, which usually tries to be as neutral as possible, if only to maintain its credibility in the public eye. But in fact, as we already mentioned, in many instances, journalists, both from television and other media, are virtually obliged to grant coverage to events once they seem to have any importance, even if they are in fact pseudo-events staged by a politician's communication team.

Similarly, controlling the technical conditions of his participation in the newscast seems beyond the average politician's reach. Invited on a newscast set, or filmed on campaign by an independent team of reporters, the politician will not always appear to his best advantage.

But, concretely, to a certain extent, he is able to influence the form of his appearance itself. He can naturally, on one hand, make good use of his audiovisual media training, and, in particular, he might have benefited from a run-through of the questions likely to be asked. On the other hand, the communication team, in a subtler manner, can exert a direct influence on the conditions of the newscast's direction. For example, during his 1980 presidential campaign, Ronald Reagan's campaign team systematically placed at the disposal of television news cameramen a platform specially equipped for their material during his electoral meetings. All the cameramen made use of it, because it was convenient, not realizing that the platform was unusually close to the stage, thus giving on the television screens the sensation that the crowd which came to hear Ronald Reagan was quite large: only its front rows, inevitably filled, were visible on screen.[37]

Similarly, we have already mentioned that during the 2007 French presidential campaign, Nicolas Sarkozy's campaign team let the television journalists following him to use free of charge the extremely favorable images taken by a camera on a

Louma crane during his rallies, thus limiting the risk of having negative images on the air.

5.2.3.2 Difficulty of steering issues

The possibilities open to the politician for influencing the contents of a televised newscast remain on the whole relatively few, especially with regard to the way the newscast deals with the words and deeds of the politician, in his absence. This can lead to substantial distortions in their retransmission, which he is powerless to avoid. Consciously or not, in their televised newscasts, journalists in fact operate more of a theatricalization of politics rather than a faithful retransmission.

For this reason, politicians often discover to their dismay that TV newscasts rarely or poorly relay the issues that constitute the basis of their communication campaigns. A number of North American political analysts have noted that, despite what one might think, even the televised political commercials deal much more with the real political issues of the campaign than TV news programs, which tend to deal more with aspects of peripheral political significance: the politician's personality and private life.[38] We have also already mentioned that even more so than others, television journalists, because of the short time at their disposal, devote much of it to more "visible" news items, such as the latest poll results, the "horse race story," which supplant items that revolve more around political issues.

Another problem is that frequently, journalists tend to devote greater coverage to a politician when he alters his views on some issue or another, changes which often harm the positive effect of the political communication, by prejudicially creating a feeling of instability.

Even worse for politicians, journalists will always treat every time a politician falters as a major event. This was particularly obvious in the 2008 US presidential campaign when Sarah Palin was suddenly pushed to front stage by her nomination as the vice presidential Republican candidate. Her lack of knowledge of John McCain's program, her naïve phrasing, her blind willingness to repeat in her statements what she was told by the Republican Party Campaign, her hesitations when interviewed by CBS evening news anchorwoman Katie Couric, the cost of her clothes, and so on, the governor of Alaska could not get away with very little. In France, a year earlier, the same difficulties incidentally struck Ségolène Royal, when the local media laughed at some of her slips of the tongue or her inability to answer specific questions during her bid for the French presidency.[39]

Along the same lines, the fact that journalists pay more and more attention in their reports to campaign strategy, treating that as news, whereas it was virtually ignored in the past and did not come to the attention of the general audience, clearly hinders politicians whose smallest campaign decisions are scrutinized with new consequences. For instance, the choice of US presidential candidates not to seriously campaign in some states, either because they consider them clearly lost, or because they feel that the media will give them a hard time, can have consequences for some voters who feel abandoned or betrayed, not to mention the blow to local activist morale.

While the televised newscast remains one of the preferred conduits for the agenda-setting effect in political communication, it participates in the process in a quite unpredictable way: the candidate may often be in the spotlight at an inconvenient time, or see some of his ideas being relayed at an inopportune moment; and, conversely, will be unable to obtain the relay of his communication easily when he wants to.

5.2.4   Political commercials

The United States is the best example of intensive use of political commercials. The great freedom enjoyed by American radio and television earned them rapid development, and the enforcement of Section 315 of the Communication Act, 1935 has guaranteed complete freedom as regards their contents, with, of course, the minor restrictions imposed by the aforementioned FCC rulings. Whether for national or local elections, no politician will deprive himself of political commercials. Consequently, a major part of election campaign finances are invested in them. In 2008, Barack Obama alone, refusing federal funding which would have diminished the number of ads he could fund, allegedly spent more than US$200 million on primary and general election ads, overwhelming McCain and the Republican party who spent merely half of that, not counting the other primary candidates earlier in the year.[40] The new January 21, 2010 Supreme Court ruling, *Citizens United v. Federal Election Commission* even allows corporations to fund unlimited political advertising, as long as they act in their own name and are not giving money directly to the candidate they support.[41] Although the use of ads presents many advantages, it can also have treacherous consequences.

5.2.4.1   *Advantages of political commercials*
North American political marketing specialists quickly discovered that brief political commercials have a greater advantage over longer paid broadcasts: they do not allow enough time for the viewer's attention to lapse, nor, of course, to flip to another channel. Ads enjoy this advantage of leaving their mark, so to speak, on viewers who might not otherwise have tuned in knowingly to a political communication.

In the early 1960s, American politicians hesitated between short ads and broadcasts of a longer format. Their hesitations vanished once surveys established that nearly one third of a network's regular audience at a given time either switched to another channel of turned their TV sets off when their usual program was preceded by a thirty-minute (or more) political broadcast, whereas a commercial running five minutes (or less) only led to an audience loss of 5 to 10% (and this at a time when the remote control was not in widespread use!).[42]

In the United States, political commercials have become all the more favored by politicians in that they have inherited broader capacities of the advertising spot. This allows for any number of variations, including the most aggressive, as we have described in Chapter 1: American communication consultants, just like their counterparts in commercial advertising, do not hesitate to use comparative or negative advertising, which can sometimes lead to excesses.

Contrary to common belief, although television is a mass medium, commercials still have targeting possibilities. They can be scheduled during certain regular broadcasts that have a more particular audience than the general prime time audience. Since the example set in 1960 by John Kennedy, addressing Spanish-speaking TV viewers in their own language, many ads intended for ethnic minorities have also been produced in the United States.

These targeting possibilities have even been enhanced in recent years by two factors: the rise of cable television, and the appearance of the Internet. The rise of cable television, first, has created opportunities to target viewers much more precisely, by deciding to broadcast spots specifically intended for very specialized television channels that fit the targeting. Second, the appearance of the Internet has provided a new way to test ads, and particularly a new ad with specific political stands, in order to check its compatibility with the voters. If popular among web surfers, it may then be shown on terrestrial television.[43] Finally, it should be said that political marketing specialists have made the empirical observation that ads appear to be much more effective in reinforcing already established viewpoints favorable to politicians rather than causing a change of opinion among unsympathetic viewers.

5.2.4.2   The dangers of political commercials

The first obvious danger of the political commercial resides in their excessive use. A simple accumulation of effective 30-second spots in order to impose a "name" as a political figure will prove to be too artificial and runs a dual risk:

- the politician might in the future turn out to be "inexistent" in reality, if his personality fails to correspond to his image as presented in his ads; this is the "Ottinger syndrome" which we described in Chapter 2 of this volume; the character portrayed in ads playacts at being a politician, in a way, but is not really a politician, or, at least, not the politician described by the commercial;
- the substance of the political field itself will end up being cramped by the weak ability of TV commercials to convey complex or fundamental political messages.

But the main danger seems to be in the so-called "negative spots," aggressive attacks on opposing politicians that have risen in popularity in recent years in countries like the United States. By mainly attacking the candidate's personality, they have reduced the coherence of the campaigns and of the issues that should be raised. In recent decades, negative spots on people have noticeably tended to replace negative spots regarding the issues. The problem has been even greater in the United States due to the unintended effects of the 2002 legislative reform, as indicated in Chapter 1, since "527 Groups" now play an important part in the spread of negative spots to the detriment of issues. When John Kerry was finally forced in 2004 to spend time and money to try and confirm that he was not the fake hero portrayed by some pro-Bush 527 Groups, the quality of political communication fell by the wayside.

Surprisingly, so-called "negative" spots do not systematically appear more effective. For instance the British Labour Party's now famous 1992 spot on the inadequacies of the National Health Service (*Jennifer's Ear*) did not prevent the Conservative Party, from winning, even if it undoubtedly put this issue on the political and media agenda and is remembered in the United Kingdom.[44] Also, negative spots can backfire against their author, as happened in October 2008, when John McCain's campaign began to appear as solely made up of negative spots, to no avail.[45] Attacking your opponent might in that case only increase sympathy for him if you end up making him look like a victim and you look like the aggressor.

Observers are divided as to the long term effects of contrary and negative spots, as already mentioned, some believing that they might turn voters away from politicians and therefore politics, and enforce cynicism about the whole democratic process.[46] But it must be admitted that unfavorable or negative ads may sometimes carry the politician's message more effectively. Ronald Reagan's victory against the incumbent president, Jimmy Carter, was helped by an astute spot "Democrats for Reagan" showing Senator Edward Kennedy shouting "No more Jimmy Carter" during the early Democratic primaries, which helped him carry the votes of soft democratic voters. And one of the most effective spots of Barack Obama's winning 2008 campaign, "Vote different" was also a negative spot parodying the notorious 1984 Apple Corporation spot mocking Microsoft, "Think Different": there, Hillary Clinton was compared with "Big Brother." In cases like these, negative spots convey content in a more or less subtle way, and even more so than many newscasts and journalists' reports which are often too focused on the "*horse race story.*"

Altogether, many scholars concur that on the whole negative ads seem to diminish political participation by turning away potential voters disgusted with politicians and politics by these attacks. Therefore, one might question the adequacy of the free ride that Section 315 of the Communications Act gives them,[47] and by the freedom given to 527 Groups to add their frequently aggressive spots to those of the candidates' campaigns.

5.2.5 Non-directly political television programs

Politicians today are often prevailed upon by their communication advisors to take part in non-directly political programs, just as leaders in the past have attended the circus or sports events. In this way, the candidate claims to be close to the recipients of his communication by providing them with elements that enforce a better sense of identification, and thus permit a better penetration of the messages, or that, at least, is what they hope.

There are three kinds of such activities:

- participation in indirect political broadcasts;
- participation in programs featuring the private aspects of politicians' lives;
- participation in pure entertainment programs.

5.2.5.1 *Participation in indirect political broadcasts*

In recent years, most politicians in the western hemisphere have increasingly agreed to be regular guests on " societal" television talk shows, which do not revolve mainly around political issues. The most famous recent example is Bill Clinton's appearance on Arsenio Hall's famous talk show during which he played the saxophone wearing dark glasses. This practice is now quite widespread. James Carville, Bill Clinton's campaign manager in 1992, arranged several similar non-political talk show appearances for the future president, as a way of reaching out to the less politically-minded swing voters, even going so far as to forego conventional interviews with political journalists in favor of staged meetings with ordinary citizens, as in a 90-minute special broadcast on MTV in which he fielded questions from several young people.[48] Another example we have already previously mentioned is Arnold Schwarzenegger winning the 2003 election for governor of California which was nearly exclusively based on participation in these programs, short-circuiting newscasts and political broadcasts. It can also be noted that that even a politician who did not regularly appear on talk shows, such as John McCain, announced his 2008 presidential candidacy on the *Late Night with David Letterman*.[49]

The growth of cable television has made these occasions more prolific, which allow politicians to direct their communication towards a particular carefully targeted "niche," whether it be sports, culture, or industrial pollution. Twenty-four hour news networks, first CNN, now Fox News, Bloomberg and the like, have been systematically cultivating societal talk shows which reach a fairly limited number of viewers, of course, but who are efficient opinion relays in their respective fields of interest. In 2008, a record number of campaigning politicians took part in mostly late night talk shows, those hosted by Oprah Winfrey, Ellen DeGeneres, Jay Leno, and David Letterman probably being the most influential, along with those hosted on CNN by Larry King for more select audiences.

These societal talk shows and televised debates carry another positive aspect by presenting the politician in a less constrained framework than the purely political programs. They may also allow him to reach targeted recipients who are not directly interested by politics, but by current social issues, which thus constitute an effective tool for a conquest campaign. Oprah Winfrey's influential talk show support for Barack Obama throughout the 2008 campaign was thus a great help to his communication campaign.

5.2.5.2 *Audiovisual exhibition representing the "private life" of politicians*

The logic behind the increasing participation in non-directly political broadcasts was bound to encourage television networks to be no longer satisfied with circumstantial revelations of aspects of a politician's "private life," but to begin systematically devoting entire programs to it, playing on the desire of politicians on the way to appear more accessible to voters. In some countries, such as the United States, where moral standards are quite strict, television broadcasts were as much seen as investigations into certain aspects of the private lives of politicians competing for public office, as for the public response to any of these inquiries. Bill Clinton's famous appearance with his wife, Hillary, to make a public confession of past adulterous behavior (and that all was now forgiven) is a radical example of this.

The recent increased personalization of the political campaigns has led to a growth in television programs dedicated purely to exhibiting the private side, if not the private life, of prominent politicians, similar to their growing exposure in the printed press magazines. This even continues now when politicians hold office. Recently, two of the most well-known spouses of world heads of state, Michelle Obama in the US and Carla Bruni-Sarkozy in France, have thus been featured on special television programs that have gone further in this exposure of the "intimacy" of politicians and their families. Here, the image-building of candidates and politicians takes a new meaning by willingly encompassing a part of the private sphere which he consents to make public in a previously unimaginable way.

5.2.5.3   Participation in pure entertainment programs

Finally, the quest for swing voters has led politicians to agree to appear on pure entertainment television shows. Of course, there are limits to this transformation of politicians into public entertainers in a new kind of television political show. If politicians make too many personal appearances on entertainment shows, people might think that they are not, after all, as entertaining as professional entertainers, a point well caricatured by the Tim Robbins movie *Bob Roberts*. Should all politicians be able to hit a punch ball as well as Barack Obama did when he arrived on Ellen DeGeneres' stage, and then also be able to dance well enough with her, to convince voters that their personality, if not their program, is a reason enough to cast their vote for them?

The mirror is even sometimes reversed when in some cases, artists and athletes convey political messages on behalf of politicians, as Michael J. Fox did for the 2006 Democratic Congressional campaign, or the soccer players enlisted by the Spanish Prime Minister José Luis Zapatero did in the campaign to vote "yes" in the 2005 referendum on the European Constitution.

Politicians should thus not be surprised when the process goes on without them, and when they are caricatured by puppets,[50] or when entertainment shows poke fun at them, in the same way as celebrity magazines publish unauthorized pictures of them. Tina Fey might not have caricatured Sarah Palin so scathingly and repeatedly on *Saturday Night Live* several weeks in a row in 2008[51] and Hillary Clinton might have not been such a target for late night syndicated television shows during the primaries[52] if Bill Clinton had not played the saxophone for Arsenio Hall in 1992.

***

The expansion and particularities of the use of the audiovisual media provide one of the explanations for the diminishing role of political parties and the loss of content clearly endured by modern political communication. First, the personalizing effect for politicians induced by audiovisual communication means reduces considerably the role of the political party in two ways:

- the political party is rendered useless as a springboard for rising politicians; once the latter are blessed with a audiovisual charisma, it allows them direct access to broadcast media;
- the political party is no longer indispensable as a transmission belt between politicians and activists and volunteers; the former can directly and even more rapidly address their supporters via the audiovisual media.

But the modes of audiovisual action also involve a major drawback: a considerable loss of substance in the political communication. First, because the quality of the communication as mediated by it strongly devalues the content of political discourse. This is something we must stress. In order to exist, the televised political message can sometimes do without a real political discourse, especially if the politician has audiovisual charisma. Moreover, this loss of substance also occurs because the political communication campaign today too often tends to restrict itself to a handful of decisive debates between major political leaders, debates that are no longer intended to loudly assert a political program, but simply to win a debate, or at least appear to win it. In this respect, the decisive debate is thus enjoyed by TV viewers as the modern form of the ancient Roman circus: secretly, the viewers hope to see a politician's spectacular triumph, and a similarly spectacular defeat, to be able to say "I was there!" The substance of political discourse and of the issues it raises thus becomes quite secondary. The deficiencies or inadequacies of a political discourse may thus remain camouflaged to a large extent.

This process is certainly one of the reasons behind the surprisingly good electoral showing of a former Polish migrant, Stanislaw Tyminski, during Poland's first free presidential elections since the Second World War, or the election as president of Peru in 1990 of a previously unknown Japanese-Peruvian, Alberto Fujimori, who never set out a real government program during his campaign.[53]

At this level, the use of the audiovisual media in modern political communication looks undoubtedly like a modern version of double-or-nothing game shows on these same networks. Even when he believes that extensive media training has put the odds in his favor, the candidate remains at the mercy of subsequent journalistic commentary, which could ultimately declare him the loser, and which the TV viewer may not have seen in the same way at the time. But the worst will probably come from journalists who will view a video recording of a debate, and who might exaggerate some previously unnoticed part of the broadcast: an awkward word taken out of context in this way, and sometimes not even noticed by most of the audience at the time, can later be blown up out of proportion in the press or newscasts.

Although the politician must be extremely well prepared for the indispensable use of audiovisual media, he will need a great deal of perseverance if he is also to maintain a political communication of real substance. The "ideal" of the "communicating/telegenic" politician tends to lead him, willingly or not, to a kind of unnatural anonymity: his consultants will always insist he should try to approximate the "model politician," controlled in his movements to the point of immobility, invariably dressed in blue, promoting a reassuring and banal discourse, elements which are supposed to guarantee the lowest rejection rate among TV viewers, though at the same time he will be compelled to expose parts of his private life to the media in some other non-political programs in order to reach undecided voters at the risk of being overwhelmed by celebrity overtones in his campaign, what we call "peopolization."

Notes

1 For more details, see Chapter 1.
2 See Blumler, Cayrol et al. 1978; despite the surge of the Internet, recent surveys for France, for instance, show that television is still the dominant medium for political communication – but not always the most trusted – as in a 2007 *CEVIPOF* Barometer, quoted in Thierry Vedel 2007.
3 Debates also took place afterwards, for the 2009 parliamentary elections.
4 Or three in a few cases, see Table 1.1.
5 Nielsen Institute data, from http://blog.nielsen.com/ (last accessed December 2, 2010.
6 See Note 5 above.
7 See McCombs and Shaw 1972, and McCombs, *The Agenda-setting Approach*, Nimmo and Sanders 1981; during the following years, the acceleration of media consumption and the multiplication of the media have considerably shortened the length of the formation of the agenda-setting effect: in 1989/90, the whole liberalization phenomena in Eastern Europe was greatly helped by the repeated coverage in European media of the political disobedience phenomenon in East Germany. The flight of many citizens from that country to the Western Europe, particularly Austria, when the border between this country and Hungary was left open, was in particular increased by huge coverage by the media, the agenda-setting effect being produced there within a very short lapse of time. In fact, the "agenda-setting effect" is mainly a "shifted duplication" of the communication process: the message is repeated, modified more or less, by several new media differing from the initial one, and with a chronological shift. The increased reiteration of these shifted duplications in the case of extremely well covered events, as those in Eastern Europe in 1989/90, explains the acceleration of the agenda-setting effect in that case (on shifted duplication, see Maarek 1986).
8 See Paletz and Entman 1981.
9 On non-verbal communication, see Maarek 1989; Calbris 2003, and more specifically regarding Canadian politicians, Giasson 2006.
10 Like movie stars, prominent politicians are known to use frequently the same makeup artist from year to year – with a subtle note of superstition, as was the case for French President Jacques Chirac: he kept the same makeup artist in his service for many years after having hired her for the first time in 1985, when he won an important televised debate facing the then Socialist Prime Minister, Laurent Fabius.
11 In particular, see the results of research conducted by an American team of political analysts led by Roger Masters, in R. Masters, "Emotional and cognitive responses to televised images of political leaders: mass media and political thought," 1985, and the same authors' "Happy warriors, leaders' facial displays, viewers, emotions and political support," in *American Journal of Political Science* (2), 32, 1988, see also Maarek 1989.
12 Past prejudices apparently play a good deal on this kind of non-verbal communication effect, unfavorable biases tending to provoke unfavorable effects and vice versa.

13 See Daniel J. Benjamin and Jess M. Shapiro, "*Thin-Slice Forecasts of Gubernatorial Elections*", NBER Working Papers series, WP 12660, November 2006.

14 On this point, see Ramirez and Rolot 1988.

15 Including a trembling leg, when visible to the viewer, as was the case with (future) French president François Mitterrand during his climactic debate with Valéry Giscard d'Estaing in the 1974 presidential race.

16 See M.C. Banwart, K. Winfrey, and J.M. Schnoebelen in Sheckels 2009.

17 On audiovisual charisma, see also Maarek 2007. []

18 They can be paid from US$20 to US$50,000 for a two-day session.

19 *Le Point*, April 19, 2004.

20 The most aggressive gender attack on Hillary Clinton has probably been the sale in some shops of "Hillary Nutcrackers": a Hillary Clinton doll with stainless steel dented thighs (able to crack nuts) … (Nelson 2010).

21 *Le Monde*, February 11, 2010.

22 See for instance *The Washington Post*, October 23, 2008, summing up the information on the Alaska governor's makeover, which was first revealed by the political news web site http://www.politico.com/ (last accessed December 2, 2010).

23 See in particular Jean Marie Cotteret, Claude Emeri, Jacques Gerstlé and R. Moreau, *Giscard d'Estaing-Mitterrand, 54,774 mots pour convaincre*, an extensive analysis of the vocabulary used by the two candidates during the decisive debate of the 1974 French presidential campaign. It demonstrates how the vocabulary employed by the future victor was probably better perceived by the general public and put together in his favor.

24 The Democrats were even able to edit some political spots straight from clips extracted from the debate, which showed Kennedy looking directly into the camera lens, just as if he had been alone.

25 See Paletz and Entman 1981.

26 This, again, can shed doubt on the ethics and objectivity of the journalist who would later be interviewing a candidate with whom he has worked earlier during one of these media training sessions.

27 In 1980, another powerful soundbite delivered by Ronald Reagan was in the midst of the debate with Carter, "Are you better off now than you were four years ago," a soundbite incidentally echoed by Bill Clinton in his opening statement during the first 1996 debate.

28 See Daniel C. Hallin 1989, "Sound bite news: television coverage of elections, 1968–1988", UCSD.

29 Dan Rather succeeded, though somewhat less successfully, the prestigious Walter Cronkite upon his retirement. The latter virtually invented the concept of television news "anchorman," which set an example the world over.

30 The Commission also demands that enough ballots in enough states to allow a win include the candidates' names, and of course that they legally qualify to become president; see http://www.debates.org/ (last accessed December 2, 2010).

31 For the 1992 US presidential election, for example, independent candidate Ross Perot, who bought a great deal of television time, at one point was denied access to the final decisive debate, but his participation was finally accepted because of his significant progress in the surveys.

32 As we mentioned earlier, most countries holding free elections now hold televised debates between the main competitors on the eve of polling day, thus often giving a good sign of their level of freedom of speech: Canada started in 1968, France in 1974, Brazil in 1989, right after the end of the military dictatorship, Germany in 2002 and the United

Kingdom in 2010; even troubled Ivory Coast held a debate on November 25, 2010 for its Presidential election, etc.

33   Most of what follows concerns televised debates, particularly the decisive television debate(s) in election campaigns. Appearances on "regular" political shows or talk shows leave less technical latitude for modifying shooting conditions: being a guest among others, the politician has to be content with the program's customary broadcast conditions.

34   For instance, a 32-page agreement was drawn up at the end of the negotiations between John Kerry's and George W. Bush's advisors in 2004; it included very detailed specifications, such as the exact size of the desks of the candidates (1.27 m), the number of persons allowed on the behalf of the candidates in the control room (one each), to the prohibition of moving away from behind their respective desks. See the complete agreement in Appendix 1.

35   For the first time, one of the 1992 debates was also different and more attractive to viewers since journalists were replaced by 209 alleged representatives of America's undecided citizens. A similar format of "town hall meetings," questioning by "average" Americans has been used for later US presidential elections, usually for the second "decisive" debate.

36   Meaning a shot of the debating politician who is not currently speaking, inserted in the middle of a shot of the speaker.

37   In the same line of ideas, the borderline of formal intervention in a newscast appearance was zealously crossed in 1990 by a French Minister, Olivier Stirn, who paid some unemployed people to attend a political meeting he had organized – he had to resign from office when this was disclosed to the press by one of the people he hired. Oddly enough, another French Minister, Luc Chatel, had the same mishap in the summer of 2009, when a visit to a supermarket followed by journalists was understood to have been set up with actors impersonating current employees.

38   In particular see Garrett J. O'Keefe and L. Erwin Atwood, "Communication and election campaigns," in Nimmo and Sanders (1981). The same research was carried out for the 1992 British parliamentary election campaign by Martin Harrison, (University of Keele), who revealed that only 10% of the political newscasts of BBC and ITV dealt directly with what the candidates were actually saying (in "Television and the election," unpublished paper given during a panel on *The 1992 British Elections*, November 20 and 21, 1992, AFSP, Paris.

39   She was even tricked by an imitator who had her say on the phone that France might be better off without Corsica (the birthplace of Napoleon) and its problems.

40   In the final days of October, Obama's campaign was apparently spending about US$3.5 million a day (from www.politico.com (last accessed December 2, 2010), October 14, 2008). Like Ross Perot in 1992, Obama even spent some US$ 1 million each for 30-minute time slots.

41   In many other democracies, candidates are barred from buying airtime. They are usually granted some free broadcasting within specific electoral programs (see Kaid and Holt-Bacha 1995).

42   For the first time in his years of political campaigning, in 1992 Ross Perot did revert to an intensive use of longer broadcasts (usually 30 minutes) to expose his views on politics and economics, and even his life story (two half-hour broadcasts, beginning with his childhood); but this exception probably was due to the fact that he had been absent from the media for some time, and wanted, therefore, to make up for lost time by saturating the media in every way possible, and at any cost.

43 So-called "vapor" ads may also play a similar testing role: not meant to be broadcast and publicly viewed, they are sent to unknowing journalists, in order to get their comments in their papers or newscasts, and sometimes taken to broader audiences if the comments are deemed exceptionally favorable. But the method presents risks, because it may provoke journalists' anger at being misled (see West 2010).

44 *Jennifer's Ear* showed two little girls suffering from the same acute hearing problem requiring surgery; the girl from a poor family, due to the long delays of the British National Health Service, lost a whole school year and remained in a terrible physical and psychological condition, while the girl from a well-off family went immediately to surgery and was cured within a few days with no side-effects thanks to her family's money which enabled her to be treated in a private clinic.

45 Neither did McCain's earlier attempts during the primaries to link him to harsh statements made by his former pastor, Jeremiah Wright really appear to have harmed Barack Obama.

46 Again, the best reference against negativity is probably Ansolabehere and Iyengar 1993 and 1995; see also Patterson 2003. For another viewpoint, see in particular a politician's opinion, Senator Tom Daschle's plea for negativity (in his foreword for Geer 2006), and of course, Geer 2006 itself.

47 See for instance Ansolabehere and Iyengar 1993 and 1995, though all researchers agree (see D.V. Shah et al. 2007).

48 His influence was later to be felt when Clinton became president in similar refusals to initially hold traditional press conferences, which were again supplanted by phone or live-television "meetings" with "representatives" of the citizens.

49 Anyway, these "late night" shows used in such a way by the politicians seem to be regarded differently by viewers than the rest of their day-time counterparts: a recent study found a connection between exposure to late-night comedies and increased attention to the political campaigns (see Feldman and Goldthwaite Young, 2008).

50 Puppet-show political satires now make fun of political figures in many countries, following the trend set by the United Kingdom's famous *Spitting Image*, Former French President François Mitterrand was seen as a frog in *"Le Bébête Show"* on the commercial TV network TF1, and Polish President Lech Walesa as a noisy lion in the Polish television's *"Zoo,"* etc.

51 This was in fact not a first for *Saturday Night Live*. During the 1976 presidential run, Chevy Chase extensively caricatured incumbent President Gerald Ford, a man prone to embarrassing incidents, as one might remember. Later, among other caricatures, the show even had Bill Clinton reading erotic novels or directly questioning George Bush, Jr.'s intelligence.

52 The Center for Media and Public Affairs (CMPA), had been doing a survey of the five more popular late night shows and found that Hillary Clinton was, the election candidate who inspired the most jokes, with a total of 562. John McCain was the butt of 549 and Barack Obama 382 (see http://www.cmpa.com/media_room_press_1.htm (last accessed December 2, 2010).

53 His political career ended in being blamed for corruption, and he fled first to Japan before being extradited to Peru to serve a prison sentence.

6

Direct marketing methods

In the United States, it is often surprising to realize how well some interest groups, such as the Moral Majority, have managed to be heard. As recently as in the 1980s, one of their many protest and intimidation campaigns resulted in measures against a rap music group, after many similar threats were directed at some of Madonna's songs, notably her big hit "Like a Virgin." Even more recently, the Telecommunications Act, 1996 has made the installation of the anti-violence chip, the V-Chip, mandatory in American television sets after a powerful lobbying campaign, not to mention the frequent petitions to limit the freedom of the Internet. Political lobbies of all kinds have gained a second wind in the US thanks to a combination of communication techniques and means grouped under the generic term of "direct marketing."

Over the past several years, political marketing specialists have come to the conclusion that the deluge of messages conveyed over unidirectional or indirect mass communication channels has finally made them superfluous. Instead of creating the desired agenda-setting effect, the accumulation of unidirectional messages has often produced merely a series of overlapping communications interfering with each other, just like the problem of the "Larsen effect", the audio feedback, well known to concert-hall sound technicians (a microphone placed right in front of a loudspeaker does not amplify the sound, but instead produces a strident whistle). In any case, it is hardly possible to remedy fully the unidirectional aspect of the communication process, or the distance between the communicator and the audience, inherent to the use of certain media: however well targeted, and however well in tune they are to opinion feedback, the improvements can only be imperfect palliatives.

Campaign Communication and Political Marketing, First Edition. Philippe J. Maarek.
© 2011 Philippe J. Maarek. Published 2011 by Blackwell Publishing Ltd.

Political marketing has thus adapted a new set of tools developed by commercial marketing methods, referred to by the general term "direct marketing," or "marketing one-to-one." What all these tools have in common is to allow, separately or cumulatively:

- a return to bidirectional political communication, or at least, a simulation of bidirectionality;
- a re-establishment of the direct link between the politician and the recipient, or at least a simulation of a direct link;
- lower demand on the communication recipient, being a "push" medium which comes straight to him rather than a "*pull*" medium.

Some of the tools, such as the mail or the telephone, have been around for quite a long time, but had never before been used in such a rigorous and systematic way to relay a political message. Others, for instance, videos or direct marketing through television, have been employed from the start for the purposes of political communication. We shall not consider specifically in this chapter some uses of the Internet which relate to direct marketing, but are linked to the Web, such as direct electronic mailing (also known as spam): they present peculiarities which differentiate them from what is commonly understood as "direct marketing" and will be addressed in Chapter 7.

6.1   Direct marketing rediscovers traditional media

On realizing the limits of mass communication media, political marketing specialists discovered that some of the "traditional" media, though able to reach a quantitatively narrower audience, ensured greater quality in the communication process through the restoration of some degree of bidirectionality and better targeting. They then undertook to rationalize the use of these media to remedy their mediocre scope: an effective medium, but limited in the number of possible recipients, that could thus be employed by increasing that number considerably.

6.1.1   Direct mail, or mailings: re-establishing a direct link

Just as it is impossible for the politician to have direct verbal contact with the entire population, or at least the widest audience possible, he obviously cannot write directly to every citizen. Until recently, it was, of course, possible for him to send "generic" letters, but their effect was very similar to that of the partisan press directly sent to the homes of the addressees. There is very little difference between a partisan paper and a "tract" received in the mail announcing a political program. Both suffer from the same weakness: they are perceived as one more piece of "junk" mail. Direct mail, by taking the addressee out of anonymity, is completely different from this kind of mail.

6.1.1.1   Direct marketing: a well-suited tool for political communication
6.1.1.1.1 The principles of direct mail   The sales marketing professionals have long known how to turn progress in modern computing to their best advantage. They have endowed direct mail with an apparent personalization of the content as well as the form, with respect to the recipient of the communication.

PERSONALIZATION OF THE ISSUE CONTENT   To avoid sending the same kind of letter to every recipient of the message, it is today possible to enter data into a computer memory containing the name, address, and profession if known, of every recipient to whom a mailing is destined, as well as other data directly relevant to him. The campaign organization therefore has at its disposal the components of what is called a "personalized letter," to be included in a mailing. Sometimes, knowledge of personal information, provided consciously or not by the recipient (such as date of birth or the amount of luxury goods purchased), even serves to add a somewhat "personal" note.

The communication process can achieve much greater impact thanks to this form of "personalization." A sophisticated computer system will even compose letters in real time based on a common core (the "main" message), with additional paragraphs selected according to the individual recipient (the "personalization process"). The recipient's geographic or sociologic characteristics can, for instance, be taken into account this way. The suburban dweller will read in his letter a paragraph dedicated to commuting problems, while the computer will automatically insert a different paragraph on pollution intended for the metropolitan inhabitant, and so on.

Personalization of the content can thus be quite extensive, which explains the keen interest of commercial marketing specialists in direct marketing by mail. It also explains why our mailboxes sometimes overflow.[1]

PERSONALIZATION OF THE FORM   Progress in computer technology and the quality of laser printing now allow personalization of the form, at least in appearance. Today it is possible to construct "personalized letters" as quickly as undifferentiated ones.

On the one hand, personalization provides a means of individually addressing each recipient. His name can be printed in the very body of the letter, together with more personal data available if it exists on file. Furthermore, personalization can also be achieved in the way the letter itself is laid out. Today's laser printers can produce a very convincing facsimile of the politician's signature (quite often using blue ink to imitate the pen). Some electronically-traced marks can mimic handwritten ones (words underlined with irregular lines drawn on purpose in a different color from the main text, etc.). Detailed "recipes" for formal personalization of mailings have been developed, and direct marketing specialists regularly pick up on and imitate their counterparts' new techniques. Moreover, not only has it become possible to improve the implication level of the recipient, but a further degree of sophistication can also be achieved that involves obtaining feedback, by encouraging the recipients to write back in answer to the personalized letter they received.

Here again, marketers have designed now tried and true methods of increasing response rates. For instance, the recipient is frequently asked to tear off coupons or response stickers and affix them to his own reply in order to compensate the effort and constraint of answering by a game-like task. The effort of responding can also be pleasantly simplified for the recipient by enclosing a pre-paid envelope. He can even be prompted to answer by an instilled sense of guilt: it is an established fact that the response rate is higher if real postage stamps are sent to the recipient, rather than the usual pre-printed postage-paid envelopes, because he feels morally compelled to answer.[2]

6.1.1.1.2 Direct mail: a technique suited to political communication Direct mail thus allows the political message to reach very precise targets, to send each target the most personally tailored texts, and to implicate the recipients much more than in the case of non-personalized generic letters. The guidelines for personalizing form and content meet the requirement of re-establishing a direct link with the recipient, or at least in appearance. This process alone sufficiently demonstrates how well-suited direct mail is to modern political communication. But its particular suitability is all the more valuable because it is a means of communication that can easily relay complex messages (programs, etc.), for which most other media do not do so well:

- contrary to what one might expect, commercial marketing specialists have gained the empirical knowledge that letters should be long and detailed, whatever the product or the service promoted, because the consumer expects a visible effort of explanation even if he does not read the entire text; when this rule is applied to political marketing, the complex message is given the space it needs;
- the sales marketer's "recipes" that guide the visual presentation of a letter's strong points (post-scriptum, sentences underlined "by hand," etc.), are quite useful in emphasizing the essential messages of the current political campaign, particularly slogans.

Let us add, finally, that in the case of communication beyond the framework of election campaigns, in many countries the mailings from incumbent politicians can be sent directly from their parliamentary offices. The envelope containing the message thus displays the official parliamentary heading, thereby increasing its effectiveness by conferring a higher status on the letter enclosed: not everyone gets a chance to receive a letter from a congressman or member of parliament. In that case, the politician can even profit from the franking privileges of his office, if any, which is a non-negligible advantage. For instance, American congressmen have been using, and abusing, for years the franking privilege granted them when they are writing to their constituents: between 1980 and 1988, the franking paid to the US Post Office by Congress amounted to more than US$150 million.[3]

6.1.1.2   The different uses of direct mail

Political marketing does not use mailings simply to convey campaign messages. Several other possible uses of this medium have been found. Mailings are now common for three main objectives:

- to test various options open for the future campaign;
- as one of the vectors of the political communication campaign, naturally;
- to solicit financial donations from recipients.

6.1.1.2.1 Testing components of the communication campaign   We have already mentioned this possible use of direct mail, as a means of gaining knowledge of the field before the actual communication campaign. In the United States, this method was employed as early as Eisenhower's 1952 presidential election campaign. Unsure as to how to translate their candidate's political popularity concretely into a specific program,[4] Eisenhower's Republican advisors hit on the idea of sending out ten standard letters to ten groups of 10,000 voters raising ten different campaign issues, to ascertain which topic was most clearly associated with the figure of Ike. In accordance with the response results, it was then decided to play up his part in the Korean War and in the pacification process to come.

Employing direct mail to test the main elements of the campaign (particularly key issues) is all the more positive for political communication as the reliability of the process is quite high: an answer in writing to a letter received implicates the recipient of the message much more than a simple verbal response to a poll-taker. Unfortunately for the politician, using direct mail for field analysis incurs much higher expenses than standard surveying tools, so they generally content themselves with ordinary opinion polls.

6.1.1.2.2 Conveying the campaign message itself   This naturally remains the main use of direct mail. For reasons we have just explained, mailings enable politicians to convey complex messages much better than many other media, and in particular much better than the indirect or unidirectional mass media, starting with the audiovisual ones. Mailings are, therefore, choice instruments.

But the appalling cost of direct mail makes it quite difficult to use systematically as a principal campaigning tool.[5] For that reason, it is mainly used in the context of local communication campaigns. In such cases, costs are lower in absolute value, and above all, the quality of contact it generates compensates its financial drawbacks:

- the politician is sure to reach precisely the intended recipients of his communication;
- he can capitalize on this communication by combining it with more traditional means (canvassing, meetings, etc.). Direct mail then satisfies a dual purpose, since it not only relays the political message, but also announces an upcoming communication and motivates its future participants.

6.1.1.2.3 The (increasing) use of direct mail for campaign (and political party) fundraising Just as charities and religious organizations have done, Western political parties were quick to understand that direct mail is an extremely profitable source of funding. Today, a substantial part of small donations to politicians comes via this means.

Mailings are particularly well suited to fundraising in their form as well as substance. As to substance, they enable funds to be obtained from the recipients while requesting only a minimal effort: recipients are no longer required to leave the comfort of their own home in order to help a politician (since they are reached through their mailboxes). As to the question of form, technically, mailings are a very flexible communication tool. A well-designed mailing campaign can influence the recipients without their knowledge. For instance, campaign treasurers are well aware that it is generally better to use "poor quality" paper for their mailings when they are seeking financial help. It gives the recipient the feeling that the campaign is really short of money and truly needs their help! Using recycled paper and pointing out the fact in the text is another means commonly used by direct mail when addressing ecology-sensitive targets.

In the United States, mailings have become one of the main financing methods for political parties. It is estimated that since the mid-1980s at least US$1 billion are channeled each year to parties or political action committees from 14 million donors as a result of such soliciting.[6]

The Republicans were the first to develop this method of finance, and have used it systematically: as early as 1964, in Barry Goldwater's campaign, 12 million letters were mailed. This mailing brought in nearly US$5 million, and, especially, generated for the party a list of sympathizers prepared to reach into their pockets.[7] Later, the list of contributors who donated US$50 or more was systematically exploited not only during election years, but at least once a year (and the number of donors has tripled, as far as we know). Renewed and computerized in the mid-1970s by Tennessee Senator Bill Brock, this direct soliciting process enabled the Republicans to receive US$200 million in donations in 1983–1984, three times more than the Democrats at the time. Only with Bill Clinton's re-election campaign in 1996 did the Democrats again start to raise more money for campaigns than the Republicans, and then again in 2008 with Barack Obama.

6.1.1.3 The disadvantages of direct mail

Integrating direct mail into the campaign process can present both financial and material disadvantages, not counting the legal problems in the countries where personal data are specifically protected by law.

6.1.1.3.1 The high cost of mailings The chief disadvantage of this method is its cost. First, there are the postal fees to consider, which have become quite high, even if the mail is pre-sorted. The price of printing the actual mailings is also high: computers and laser printers are still costly to purchase and operate.

The greatest expense is purchasing, or, most often, renting, an address list. Political campaigns obviously cannot limit their mailings to lists of registered voters, which are free everywhere in the world, or nearly so. These lists are not sufficiently precise: in many countries, citizens register only once in a lifetime, unless they move to another town, and the occupation listed is the one held at that time, sometimes decades before. This means that the quality of direct mail is closely related to the "quality" of the lists employed. Commercial marketers often say that direct mail is only as good as the list of addresses it uses. It is essential to buy or rent up-to-date address lists containing the main socio-cultural criteria useful in the political communication process. Thus, political parties keep their lists of former donors jealously secret; these form, so to speak, their most valuable commercial asset.

This explains the tenacious advantage the United States Republican party has long had over its Democratic rivals in the field of direct marketing: Republicans have systematically taken advantage of the famous list of those who contributed US$50 and more obtained in 1964 during Senator Goldwater's campaign, which unknowingly helped several campaigns in the following years. For the 2006 congressional elections, the Republican National Committee is said to have spent about US$68 million in order to rebuild a large and reliable databank of its potential supporters.[8] Indeed, the quality of mailings closely depends on the quality of the personal data about the recipients. Specialists always stipulate that direct marketing by mail is only as good as the list of addresses it can bring into play.

Due to this combination of expenses, direct mail is a tool that politicians must use with consideration caution: especially when used to obtain financial contributions, the cost of the mailing can sometimes exceed the amount of funding it brings in, as some politicians or charities have learned by experience.

6.1.1.3.2 The break-down of local relays of political communication

The second drawback of direct mail is similar to the one inherent in many media commonly used by modern political communication. Since this communication process occurs without the help of the usual go-betweens, local activists and volunteers, they become less useful, and this demobilizes them. Incorporating direct mail in a political communication campaign can thus be difficult, and creates major disadvantages of this nature.

The diversion of the fundraising circuits further exacerbates the consequence of demobilization among volunteers and activists in the field. As the following two figures indicated clearly, the use of direct mail excludes them from the fundraising process: activists are no longer the intermediaries thanks to whom political parties obtain finance, but, on the contrary, are now often obliged to request funding from the central campaign organization in order to finance their own activities. This creates a dependency among activists on the campaign organization, a very demobilizing loss of autonomy.

As a partial remedy to this loss of responsibility among activists and volunteers, it is sometimes possible to attempt to involve the field organization with the direct mail operation. This can be done by contacting the activists about it in order to have them reinforce it and at the same time to give them some responsibility – gratifying as such – in the process. One might for instance ask field volunteers and activists to

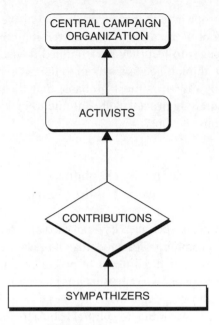

Figure 6.1 The traditional fundraising circuit.

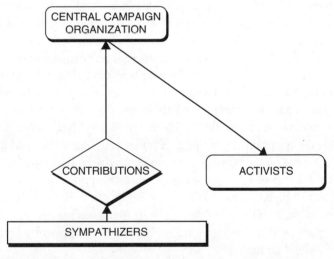

Figure 6.2 The "diversion" of the fundraising circuit caused by direct mail.

write in support to a dozen of their friends or relatives to explain why they have decided to help the candidate and that a direct mailing is soon going to reach them.[9]

Thanks to direct mail, it then becomes possible to re-establish a rather efficient direct link between the politician and the recipient of the message. But this process cannot be universally employed: it must be used in moderation, because of the high operating cost as well as the weakening of the substance of the field organization it causes.

We must also point out here that some researchers have quoted direct mail as being one of the causes of the increase in voter abstention, particularly in the United States: citizens are thought to feel they have fulfilled their civic duty by sending a check, and thus do not think it necessary to go to the polls. This theory lacks complete proof, and, in any case, it is most probable that the potential usefulness of direct mail in the fundraising process will continue to make it an essential tool in modern political communication.

6.1.2   Direct marketing by telephone, or phone marketing: re-discovering bidirectionality

Here again, modern marketing specialists have polished the use of a traditional medium to mold it into a broader communication tool than it previously had been. Some firms have specialized in maintaining hired teams of phone operators trained to promote products of all sorts by telephone surveys using lists taken from the phone book.

In terms of political subjects, phone marketing has evolved in different ways in the main democratic countries, according to cultural habits. In many European countries people are not used to openly formulating their political opinions, or even their sympathies, over the phone; the lack of a long-standing tradition of primary elections may explain this reluctance. In the United States, for instance, the immediate refusal rate of polling by phone generally varies between 25 to 35%. Hesitations, or a refusal to answer certain questions, can add another 20% subsequent loss, leaving a total of around 50% useful answers. In European countries like France, phone marketing specialists expect an immediate refusal rate of up to 80%. This explains why, at the present time, in some countries, phone marketing is rarely employed to convey political messages per se. Instead it is used to conduct surveys or barometers that are shorter or more expeditious than the ones still based on the traditional method of face-to-face interviews.

In any case, the telephone marketing response rate increases considerably when the person called has already shown a previous interest in participating in this kind of process, or has expressed a sympathy toward the politician who sponsors the campaign. For instance, phone marketing is often much easier to use for regular surveys operating with the same panel, when its members have accepted in advance to be polled by phone (but their answers are then somewhat distorted with regard to the "average" individual replies).

Even if telephone marketing is not always practical to carry out, political communication specialists have demonstrated some interest in this renewed medium, as it presents significant and original advantages.

6.1.2.1   *The advantages of phone marketing*
6.1.2.1.1 Personalizing the communication process   The high degree of personalization in the communication process is obvious. This medium benefits from the highest degree possible of personalization: the person is called at home and addressed by name. From a psycho-sociological point of view, being called by your name constitutes as such a gratifying factor, thus introduced to the communication process.

Consequently, a well-designed phone marketing campaign can only be based on lists of names, and not on phone numbers dialed at random. Similarly, just like in the case of direct mail, its impact will be much stronger if a quality address list is used: it allows for more precise targeting of the respondents and greater personalization of the communication process, instead of having as a sole criterion the address found in the directory next to the phone number.

6.1.2.1.2 Re-establishing bidirectionality   Re-establishing bidirectionality, or at least a semblance of bidirectionality, also improves the quality of the communication process. The person called can respond with questions of his own, even if the person who calls him is of course not the politician himself, but an employee or a sympathizer who reads prepared answers and is told not to engage in a real political discussion: it would take too much time, and it would run the risk of an unsatisfying result.

Bidirectionality is not complete, then, but in any event, the respondent is reached in person by a "genuine" interlocutor, which lends considerable force to the communication, thanks to the direct link thus established.

6.1.2.1.3 A swift and effective operation   This is the third advantage of phone marketing in relation to other direct marketing methods. This advantage is twofold, swiftness being combined here with greater efficacy.

As for speed, most other direct marketing methods demand a minimal time lapse before the recipient can be reached: delays due to the slowness of mail, for instance. Phone marketing provides a means of reaching respondents almost immediately; all that is required is an adequately large team of phone operators.

Moreover, the method is more productive, at least in the short term. Other direct marketing means often demand a voluntary effort on the part of the recipient of the communication (written answer to the letter). This is not the case for the people reached by phone: their only effort is to pick up the receiver, and to listen. Without any doubt, the operation can be conducted with greater efficacy.

6.1.2.2 *The drawbacks of phone marketing*

Aside from culture-specific difficulties met in some countries, two factors make the use of this medium difficult:

- financial and staff costs;
- the high level of skill required.

6.1.2.2.1 The high cost of telephone marketing   The high price of telephone marketing is the primary reason restricting its widespread use in the area of political communication. Because of the large number of operators required, it implies either:

- a heavy financial outlay, in the case of paid staff (especially when specialized telephone marketing companies are hired);
- or a vast number of activists and sympathizers (who must also be trained).

In the first instance, frequent in countries where political activism has declined, contracting out to specialized telephone marketing firms is prohibitive: reaching 500 persons might entail an outlay of up to US$50,000.

In the second case, help from a large network of activists can be a means to reduce this expense to the mere cost of a local telephone call. But the activist structure has then to be evenly established throughout the area to be reached by the companies' campaign. When the campaign is planned on a national scale, very few parties or politicians benefit from such an extensive network. Moreover, activists participating in the telephone campaign should be specially trained, due the skills involved in telephone marketing.

6.1.2.2.2 The high level of skill of telephone marketing   Cost is not the only obstacle encountered when using telephone marketing. Contrary to what one might expect, successful use of this medium requires considerable training.

In making a telephone marketing contact, care must be taken not to dissatisfy the respondent. This obliges the operator to reach a balance between two rather contradictory requirements:

- giving the respondent the feeling that the communication process is truly bidirectional, that he is a true interlocutor;
- getting a message across to him, without giving him the chance to formulate questions in return. There is a great risk of the operators being unable to answer the question, or that their answer might simply not satisfy the respondent, producing an effect contrary to the one sought.

These difficulties illustrate why telephone marketing can only be used for rather straightforward messages, and that it is unwise to enlist the help of activists who have not been previously trained. They must contradict a natural habit and become accustomed to the idea that they should attempt to persuade the respondents in view of convincing them, but that their only task is to convey a message.

Because of this high level of skill, "telephone chains" are rarely used, especially if one considers the high level of distortion the initial message undergoes as it is relayed. Whenever a politician does have a geographically well-distributed and strong network of activists, he might ask them to form telephone chains by asking them to convey his message by directly calling people among their friends or relations, asking the latter to do the same, and so on (exactly as might be done with direct mail). But since verbal communication is much less precise than the written word, it has been acknowledged that in this case, a message can prove quite difficult to convey in this fashion. Consciously or not, each relay modifies the content in conveying it, to the extent that in the end it may hardly be intelligible, or scarcely resemble the original message. Usually, distortion reaches an unacceptable level after only two or three relays, as certain political action groups in the United States who tried to put telephone chains into action have found out.

Because of these difficulties, telephone marketing is very often used in conjunction with another medium. For instance it is often combined with direct mail: the telephone operator initiates the contact by mentioning a letter sent previously, and pursues the conversation depending on the respondent's reaction. A telephone chain can also be co-ordinated with proximity or direct contact media, such as campaign rallies: once the message is conveyed by telephone, the operator can reply to the respondent's possible questions by saying that the latter will certainly get an answer at the upcoming meeting.

When combined with electoral meetings or rallies, telephone marketing can be doubly effective. Of course it allows a politician's message to be relayed, but it can also increase meeting attendance by motivating portions of the public that would normally not attend it if they had not received a call. Thus, telephone marketing is now often used when politicians go on the campaign circuit or hold rallies. It is a means of reaching a small number of people two or three days before a politician's arrival, to inform them of it or provide details of the event. Phone marketing is a particularly useful tool for local political communication. Mayors, for instance, can personally telephone some of their constituents on a regular basis.

6.1.2.2.3 Substitutes for telephone marketing

As surprising as it may seem, in some cases, to avoid the considerable expense of telephone marketing, here, the telephone is still used as the preferred means of communication, but the process is inverted. Several telephone numbers are advertised; by dialing them, the caller can be in touch either with a team of activists and sympathizers, or with telephone operators from a direct marketing firm, or even with a set of answering machines capable of responding simultaneously to a given number of callers by playing a previously recorded message. The lack of personalization of the latter process is usually compensated by recording the politician's voice, who thus addresses the caller "directly."

The advantage of this method is to permit a relative individualization of the calls. Several different telephone numbers can be advertised that correspond to the different targets one wishes to reach – farmers, students, and so on, so as to deliver a particular message intended for each. The widespread development of toll-free numbers granting a free telephone call from anywhere in a country has considerably encouraged this method, as it has long been demonstrated in North America. Using this system, the politician or his supporting committee naturally has to pay for the call, but it incurs less expense than hiring telephone operators and paying for calls made to people who do not listen to the message.

The major drawback of the system is of course that it is in fact similar to a different, and moreover, less effective medium. First, the medium is different. The bidirectionality of communication by telephone disappears: the caller has no true interlocutor, but only listens to a magnetic tape that plays for a minute or two and invariably conveys the same message to the caller, even if he calls a number of times. As a medium, the process is closer to radio than the telephone. As for its effectiveness, since answering machines have to be reached by the caller, this requires an act of will by the caller to make the call himself. As a rule then, only the "interested" public will be exposed to the message: they will be the only ones to call the telephone number advertised or sent by mail.

In order to remedy this particular problem, computerized telephone systems have been devised. They call telephone subscribers – either at random from directory listings, or in a more calculated manner, using previously established files – and play the respondent a recorded message when he lifts the receiver. In a more "human" version of this method, volunteer phone operators simply explain to the persons called that they are going to put be put through to a taped message from the politician. But whatever the case, the first – and major – drawback mentioned remains: the communication process is still unidirectional.

Altogether, telephone marketing is undoubtedly one of the more interesting instruments "re-discovered" by direct marketing methods, but it remains mainly suited to conveying short messages, and is preferably combined with other more direct media, such as meetings and rallies. In any event, the swiftness with which the operation can be carried out makes it indispensable in some cases

6.2   The use of audiovisual media for direct marketing

Political communication did not only reconsider existing media, revitalizing them with the help of technical progress. It also quickly learned specific uses for the audiovisual media. Video, radio and television are also used by political marketing in several new ways, more in the line of direct marketing than their usual unidirectional form of communication.

6.2.1   Direct marketing by television or radio

The basic principle is simple: to collect immediate telephone donations from the audience via a switchboard in response to live broadcast appeals for contributions. This involves the guest participation of various celebrities to promote the importance of a "cause" or political personalities. Generally, the program mixes variety show entertainment fundraising appeals.

This method has been exploited for years in the United States; it started with telethons sponsoring research against muscular dystrophy, and was expanded to back a large variety of political and social causes.[10] Evening-long election campaign telethons have been part of the array of common political communication tools for years, since buying television or radio airtime is authorized in that country, as we mentioned in Chapter 1.

More so than political parties, the main practitioners of this technique are the famous "televangelists," whose "churches" amass millions of dollars through their "preach and collect" television shows. With the aid of computers, any person who dials the telephone number that flashes across the TV screen during the broadcasts is filed and henceforth always within their grasp. Some preachers, like Jerry Falwell, the former head of the Moral Majority lobby, or Pat Robertson, whose 700 Club television became notorious, have thus managed to win fame along with financial support.[11]

Politicians also have been holding telethons since 1976, when Jimmy Carter managed to collect more than US$300,000 during a five-hour telethon endorsed by a professional baseball player and a number of other stars. Twenty years later, Bill Clinton retraced the same steps by seeking the help of another baseball player for a very profitable telethon during his 1996 re-election campaign.

Of course, direct marketing by television or radio exists in some form even when fundraising is not the main aim of the program. In such cases, a politician is to some extent "made available" to the radio or television show audience by answering questions directly phoned in (usually after the switchboard operator has screened them to avoid any unwelcome incidents). Telephone numbers are then given out so that members of the audience can call in and have the "guest" politician answer his listeners. This method is often used by politicians in their constituencies, in which case it serves two aims, since it becomes both a personal communication means for the politician, and also a means of institutional communication (since the constituents can address their problems to their elected representative). In any case, the political communication aspect usually takes precedence whenever election time approaches.

6.2.2   Videos

The circulation of videotape cassettes at first, now DVDs,[12] has grown into an important means of communication for political marketing, even though the costs of this method can soar in the event that a sophisticated production involving a full professional crew is called for.

These are generally used for two quite different purposes:

- internal circulation within the campaign organization, among sympathizers and activists, or inside the party;
- external circulation, during meetings and rallies.

6.2.2.1   *Circulating videos inside campaign organizations or political parties*
In this context, the aim of circulating videos is twofold: the reinforcement of unity among the supporters of the political campaign, and the dissemination of communication models.

As to the first goal, videos help reinforce the activists' and volunteers' sense of loyalty to the politician. Since the latter cannot meet each of them in person, he instead communicates with them through taped images shown during meetings in which attendance is limited so as to strengthen the group's sense of cohesion. This tactic often proves quite gratifying, and strongly increases the psychological mobilization of the campaign organization, particularly of sympathizers and activists in the field.

Regarding the second goal, certain types of videos are intended to give activists precise indications on the politician's program and ideas. They provide a basis for future discussions with the general public so the activists can conduct the campaign in the most effective manner. Thus, videos are scripted to contain the components of the communication campaign, or at least, the main points to be disseminated.

In some cases, videos can be even more explicitly instructional, giving activists precise guidelines as to how the campaign should be relayed. This method is quite common in the United States, where one finds, for instance, the circulation of videos dramatizing canvassing techniques: actors impersonate the sympathizers to demonstrate how they should react depending on the reactions of the people they call on.

6.2.2.2   Videos intended for election meetings and rallies

These can fulfill two different aims: to simply convey a message, or as a visual aid for the proceedings of the meeting.

Videos from the first category are usually intended for "closed circle" meetings as well as large-scale rallies. To some extent, they serve as a substitute for direct communication if the politician cannot attend the meeting in person. In such cases, he addresses the participants, seemingly delivering a message directly to their attention, even to the point of claiming it has been recorded especially for the occasion.

Here, sympathizers who come and look at these videos will hopefully relay stronger opinions due to the gratifying idea that they were addressed almost directly: the video is designed to indicate that the politician has recorded a specific, narrowly targeted message with them in mind. In fact it is easy to achieve that goal adding various statements, depending on the various targets decided, to a longer core speech. Afterwards, the different versions of the recording can be sent out according to the content corresponding to the intended target.

In the second case, videos can serve the hosts of the meeting as a springboard for opening the proceedings, or to introduce points of discussion to help the meeting progress. Shown early in the proceedings, they are used to condition the audience's mood, pending the appearance or the speeches of the main politicians invited. They prepare the participants psychologically before the arrival of the politician, somewhat like a start-up band does for the band featured at a rock concert.

* * *

Direct marketing is probably one of the most useful tools for political communication. But politicians and political parties must use it with the utmost caution. It was introduced to re-establish a direct link with the recipients of the communication and re-motivate citizens who have been alienated from collective concerns due to excessive use of unidirectional and indirect means of communication, particularly mass media. But the efficacy of many media employed by direct marketing is somewhat detrimental to the cohesion of campaign organizations, and to traditional activist and sympathizer structures. In some cases, contrary to the intended goals, direct marketing can even weaken political participation of the target public.

Of course, the risk of demobilizing "traditional" activist and sympathizer structures can easily be compensated by involving them in the direct marketing campaign. But this option is all too often overlooked.

The decline of political participation caused by the increase in direct marketing is more volatile, and perhaps more difficult to avoid. Surveys show that the bonds established between political parties and those to whom their communication is addressed appear to be more transient than those established by traditional means of political communication.[13] The citizen, reached at his own home, and performing his political action from there, sometimes tends to feel that he has already performed his civic duty by mail, and gets less involved later: he might not even think it necessary to go to the polls on election day.

This phenomenon is even stronger now that direct marketing uses the Internet among its tools, as we shall see in Chapter 7. The Internet audience is also reached at home without making any real effort, with the same consequence of little involvement in politics and even actual political participation.

Direct marketing has to be reconciled with the traditional components of political communication to avoid any long-term damage to the latter in exchange for temporary improvement in the short term. A viable solution would probably be to launch the direct marketing campaign after the initial political communication campaign. This should be done particularly during a politician's mandate, to keep those who responded or contributed financially during the campaign informed of the enacted policies and their results. But the high cost of such contact renewal tends to prohibit a more generalized use.

One can also point out that the common element of many direct marketing instruments, radio and television being notable exceptions, is the use of address lists of potential respondents. But a significant minority of citizens, and voters, will never be reached through this channel: the "social non-participants," meaning persons who are not listed by mail-order organizations, do not subscribe to a newspaper or have never answered a mail request, and so on. Since direct marketing, political or not, is nearly always based on the circulation of such lists, this removes social non-participants from the potential targets of direct marketing. On the other hand, people who figure on several lists are over-solicited, and may be tired of being so.

Direct marketing presents an even more insidious risk for the normal functioning of the political sphere: it gives considerable leeway to the organization making use of it, meaning political party headquarters or political action committees. The power of influence it gives to the respondent to such appeals is much weaker than what it would be by going through traditional channels of political activism, within which the relatively democratic process allows action to acquire greater significance. This phenomenon also explains the transient nature of the fruits of direct marketing: since an individual feels unable to exert a direct influence on the organization that has made contact with him through this medium, the recruit soon grows weary of the appeal, or turns to other new and more enticing ones that reach him in a similar manner.

Finally, some North American surveys show that direct marketing is particularly effective in mobilizing individuals who display "aggressive" or "extremist" political behavior, probably because it allows them the relative anonymity of the post, in contrast, for instance, to open participation in meetings.

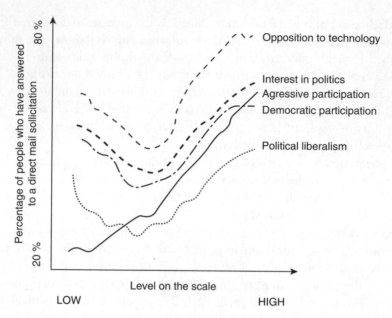

Figure 6.3 Political opinions and responsiveness to direct marketing.

This phenomenon was clearly shown by political analyst R. Kenneth Godwin in a survey conducted in 1987. He sent out a questionnaire to 5,000 people who had previously responded favorably to at least one appeal from one of the five main environmental interest groups that primarily use direct marketing (1,000 for each group). Figure 6.3 (above) shows his findings.

It is not surprising to observe that the efficiency of direct marketing appears greater for individuals showing little interest in political participation, or in democratic partici-pation (the progression is significant, as it starts at a very low point). Likewise, one finds the same progression among people strongly interested in politics: the progression is also logical, since they are, of course, interested in the political appeals they receive. But it is curious to note that this survey did not find this inverted bell curve to apply to the "aggressive political behavior" category. This may explain the success of certain relatively aggressive or conservative pressure groups mentioned in the Introduction, direct marketing seeming to have served them well as a catalyst, so to speak.

Notes

1 This has led to excessive solicitation and exasperation of the addressees, who cannot help but diminish the effectiveness of the contact.
2 In the United Kingdom, *Reader's Digest* has sometimes in the past taken the refinement so far as to send strips of different-colored postage stamps to reinforce the effect.
3 See Godwin 1988. The figure seems to be now even higher, over US$30 million a year for the two chambers (see http://www.c-span.org/questions/weekly22.asp (last accessed December 2, 2010).

4   His previous political positioning had been so vague that the Democrats had also tried to get the former supreme commander of Allied forces in Europe as their candidate in the same election.

5   In 1988, for instance, French President François Mitterrand, in his bid for re-election, decided not to send his "Letter to all the French" ("Lettre à tous les Français") directly to each voter as he had originally planned, as it would have cost an additional 50% of the entire amount spent during the whole campaign! He therefore had to be content with publishing it as an advertisement in the main daily papers.

6   This figure gave the title to Godwin's 1988, *One Billion Dollars of Influence*, a book that provided the figures we quote in these two paragraphs.

7   The very first mailing brought in 221,000 contributions (which corresponds to a 1.84% response rate).

8   *Le Monde*, November 9, 2006.

9   Activists and volunteers might even be asked to initiate by themselves a more personal mailing to some of their acquaintances. The efficacy of such a process, which is somewhat akin to superstitious "chain letters," could occasionally be better than that of "industrialized" direct mail: in this case, activists and sympathizers in theory relay the political message without inaccuracies or any loss of information, unlike the "usual" opinion relays, which insert distortions in the communication process caused by their own chance interpretations. This particular mechanism also saves on expenses: the addresses given or used by activists and sympathizers are as free as their letters. But the loss of "quality" of the process is blatant: the contents of the letters, here not monitored at all, might lead to mishaps, and conquest communication is rare in that way, since activists are usually writing to people with similar opinions. So the result is often disappointing.

10 Some countries, such as France, do not allow telethons for political causes, only for charitable purposes.

11 On the subject of televangelism, see J.K. Hadden and A. Shupe 1988.

12 Which are now sometimes replaced by direct links sent to sympathizers or activists allowing them to stream or download the videos, but used in a similar way as tapes and DVDs.

13 See in particular Godwin 1988.

7

The growing importance
of the Internet

We have seen previously that political communication has not only used traditional media, but also invented new ways of using them thanks to technical progress, following the example set by commercial marketing. In the same way, politicians have now brought the Internet into their service.

Indeed, the Internet has become today a huge rumor mill, in two ways:

- "Traditional" media, and particularly journalists, have started to surf the Internet in order to update the information they convey in their newscasts or newspapers. While the Internet is theoretically a rather "slow" medium – you have to wait until the Net surfers get to your web site or your blog in the hope that your messages will reach them – this allows a possible acceleration of their diffusion when they are picked up by the more traditional media.
- The evolution of the Internet with its growing interactivity (the so-called "Web 2.0," with its blogs and "social networks") has somehow changed its nature: from a "pull" medium, meaning that the recipient must get out and reach the information, it is becoming a "push" medium, where the information arrives to the recipient without any effort on his part – which strongly enhances the speed of message penetration among potential recipients.

Both phenomena, which occur simultaneously, have built up the Internet as a new and indisputable tool for political communication. Everyone is now aware of the Internet's role in Barack Obama's 2008 successful presidential campaign, but we have already mentioned its importance in giving Howard Dean national stature in the 2004 campaign, not counting many other examples in other countries. For instance in France, socialist leader Ségolène Royal probably won the "primaries"

Campaign Communication and Political Marketing, First Edition. Philippe J. Maarek.
© 2011 Philippe J. Maarek. Published 2011 by Blackwell Publishing Ltd.

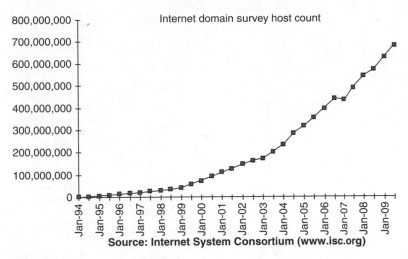

Figure 7.1 The exponential growth in the number of Internet web sites.

within the Socialist Party thanks to a clever use of Internet blogging, and then made constant use of the Internet and its new modes during the ensuing 2007 presidential campaign, even though this same tool sometimes seriously worked to her detriment when some of her private statements or communication misfortunes where exaggerated here.

There can be no hesitation about including the Internet as a major world medium today. We have already seen in Chapter 1 of this book that the penetration of the Internet in households has accelerated considerably in recent years, peaking in the whole of North America with three households out of four being connected (and even a little more in the United States alone).

Not only is the number of persons connected growing. Mere consideration of "web sites" shows a similar exponential growth of the data available on the Internet all around the world, at a range of only a few clicks on the mouse. In July 2009, it was estimated that there were 700 million web sites around the world, about twice as many as there were in 2005 (see Figure 7.1 above).

The expansion of the Internet is not only quantitative, but also qualitative: the Internet keeps being improved daily, notably in order to be more useful for paying services, leading to new marketing methods that are also very useful for political marketing.

7.1 The multiple aspects of the Internet

Internet versatility certainly makes it a very peculiar medium because of its multiple facets, so to speak, its rather different possibilities of use, which can be visualized in Figure 7.2: eight different kinds of communication are possible with the Internet, and the Web surfer may switch from one to the other almost instantly, with a simple click of the mouse.

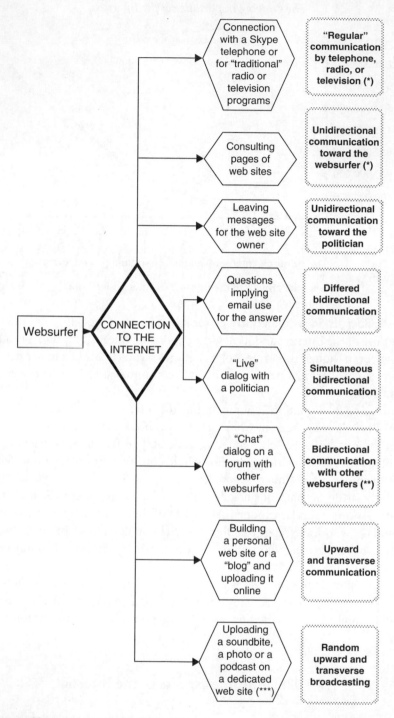

Figure 7.2   The Internet: a versatile medium.

* Monitoring connections in these cases provides indirect (and involuntary) feedback – pages consulted, for how long, which programs watched, etc.

** In the case of "public" forums, a similar feedback is allowed by monitoring the forum (and/or moderating)

*** Dedicated web sites such as *Facebook*, *YouTube*, etc.

These eight categories may be reordered into three groups. The first, now known as Web 1.0, includes all the "initial" uses of the Internet, which are roughly the same as a traditional computer network – and used to be those of the French precursor of the Internet, Minitel.[1] The second category, what is now called Web 2.0, relates to the new and more interactive uses of the Internet. Finally, we shall add a third category of Internet use, which is increasingly growing, and which in a way makes the Internet transparent, invisible, since it is used as a "virtual conduit," so to speak, exactly as do airwaves, or phone wires.

In fact, there is no real demarcation line between these groups from the standpoint of communication science. Technical progress is plainly responsible for the development of the Internet and its evolution, mostly the improvement of bandwidth and the miniaturization of computer power. These technical advances have endowed the Internet with much more interactivity, so that any connected individual anywhere in the world not only has quicker access to the Web, for downloading information, but may also easily become an instant uploader of information.

7.1.1   Web 1.0: improved targeting and versatility

This is the initial way of using the Internet, which has already been in existence in governments or big company computer networks for some time now:

7.1.1.1   *Consulting a web site*

When an individual only consults the information put up on a web site, the Internet is used as a unidirectional medium, but with two advantagespoints than most other unidirectional media for effective political communication.

First, the surfer unwillingly provides the politician with feedback to the extent that web site monitoring is organized. Political marketing specialists are helped here because it is easy to monitor what specific parts of the web site are accessed the most, not only page by page but also the time they spend reading them, and so on. This provides feedback that recipients of Internet communication give without even being aware of it, and which gives significant information on the quality of communication – a fact first discovered by commercial marketing and now used in political communication. For instance, when John McCain was running in the 2000 primaries (which George W. Bush finally won), he was seen at the time to be a more serious contestant than expected when observers discovered that people connecting to his web site spent about ten times longer on it than his Republican opponent's web site.

Second, and this soon sparked an interest among political communication specialists, the Internet provides what is probably the best possible targeting: the connected surfer only retrieves messages he is interested in. Targeting could not be better: it is not done by the communicator of the message in light of what he thinks the interests of the target audience are, but by the user himself. The interactive process of clicking on a link or not depending on the surfer's interests allows him to choose only those messages and information he wants to consult. This is self-targeting at its best.

7.1.1.2   *Posting messages*

Posting messages is a second possibility, with three variations, which all include a more or less high degree of bidirectionality – a first in a medium which may instantly reach millions of communication recipients:

(i)   Activists or sympathizers (and sometimes people who do not agree) can send messages to the central campaign organization's e-mail account without the stress, expenses, and staff needed to simply use the phone or putting a letter in the letter box. In short, this is e-mail feedback.

(ii) Furthermore, the Internet allows actual time-deferred bidirectional communication, when a question requires an answer and the answer is given.

(iii) This bidirectional communication becomes simultaneous when the answer is immediately possible, such as when a live dialog or chat is organized online with a politician at a previously set time.

7.1.1.3   *Interactivity among recipients*

The third use of Web 1.0 is interactivity among recipients, here again something rather unobtainable with other media used by political communication to reach large audiences: the Internet allows bidirectional transversal communication.

This is for instance the case if the web site enables different users to communicate together in real time (*chat* between users, *live* forums) or deferred in time (other forums). This incidentally also allows for vertical communication (if these communications are monitored by the host – the politician).

7.1.2   Web 2.0: from interactivity to "social" media

These are the more recent ways of using the Internet that have been made possible thanks to rapid improvement in both hardware and software. As for hardware, Web 2.0 would not exist without the enormous and continuous increase of bandwidth and without skyrocketing computer capabilities and miniaturization. As for software, the simplification of operating systems and specific applications has enabled users to easily become transmitters without demanding any computing skills from them.

7.1.2.1   *Becoming a provider of online information*

The net surfer may now easily upload his own Internet web site online thanks to the improved accessibility of computer software. Particularly, and even more easily than for a "proper" web site, he may now maintain his own blog online, without any particular technical knowledge, or even any layout abilities, using templates put at his disposal.

These blogs are built on a tacitly codified principle that makes interactivity easy. The blogger directly addresses his visitors in his posts, usually in a rather personal way, which seems to establish direct communication with the other surfers. To increase interactivity, blogs always include at least two boosters:

- a forum allowing other surfers to react to the messages posted;
- "links" toward other "friendly" blogs, or just those deemed interesting.

The blogger may use his own provider facilities or the data storage offered by dedicated web sites that help him build up blogs[2], and often host them, usually for free, at least as long as the blog remains reasonable in size and flow of visitors.

An even easier model of social networking has been created by web sites like *MySpace, Facebook* and *LinkedIn*,[3] which are in fact an Internet variation of personal ads found in newspapers, but where the initial form to fill out when you become a user records personal details of your life (*MySpace, Facebook*) or more professional data (*LinkedIn*).[4] These allow net surfers to find each other more easily, via a search by center of interest, an interactive method now frequently used by politicians. Most of the time, the social network algorithms in fact present their members with potential "friends" according to the personal data they have logged in their profile.

Another type of social medium is *Twitter*, a kind of permanent personal journal that the user puts online regularly, since messages must be shorter than 140 characters.[5] Outside of this seemingly permanent link with the message author, *Twitter* includes a technical innovation that considerably accelerates diffusion: the user may decide to post his message on the Internet, but may also send it via SMS to the other subscribers' cell phones, a possibility widely used for the first time by Barack Obama during the 2008 US presidential campaign.[6]

7.1.2.2   *From online video sharing to becoming a web broadcaster*

The net surfer may also put short sound bites or videoclips directly online on dedicated web sites which he does not have to maintain himself, such as *YouTube* or *DailyMotion*,[7] which of course have a more random transversal diffusion. He simply has to register with them – for free – and upload his soundbites or clips to them.

The "popularity" of the clips puts them on the top of the lists visible to the surfers, and may thus become another way to influence political campaigns if clever spots are sent in by the politician's team (or discreetly helped to do so by "friends"). Sometimes, this spontaneous surge may be even more openly organized: for instance, during the 2004 American presidential campaign, for the sake of a "contest," the independent political group *MoveOn.org* managed within a few days to get dozens of anonymous people to send online on *YouTube* "home made" ads attacking incumbent President Bush.[8]

Online video sharing is just a first step. If a surfer produces more elaborate clips and in sufficient number, that person can virtually become a broadcaster by creating small radio or television clips distributed for free over the Internet (so-called podcasts, which may be accessed via iTunes).[9] Here the communication happens randomly, since other Web surfers will need to "find" the podcast, or to click on links to it situated on friendly web sites and/or blogs. Nevertheless, altogether, the speed of this kind of diffusion, the videoclip equivalent to word-of-mouth, is stupefying.

All these new uses of the Internet are gaining in importance because of the increased convergence of electronic media. Since the example set in 2007 by the iPhone, "smart" phones are taking a greater and greater share of cell phones sales. They are directly able to surf on the Internet, becoming a sort of simplified portable computer permanently connected to the Web. Dedicated iPhone software is even given away for free on the so-called iTunes Store by *Twitter* and the like in order to access these Internet services more easily than by using the "general" Internet software delivered with the smart phones.

Also, the enormous number of these phones that can now take pictures or record a few minutes of film and instantly upload them on these web sites now offers unlimited possibilities for ascending political communication. Many press agencies or news network now air footage of unplanned events that happened to be filmed and then sent (or sold) to them by chance passers-by owning such phones.

7.1.3   The Internet as a virtual conduit for other media

A third possible use of the Internet now exists, though there is little awareness of it. When a surfer is connected with a powerful enough connection (ADSL, cable or 3 G for cell phones), the large bandwidth allows him to use the Internet as a simple conduit for other media that are using it, exactly as they would use a cable or a satellite in order to transmit communication.

It is now for instance possible to make phone calls with an Internet connection, on the mode created initially by *Skype*, and now taken up by many Internet providers around the world, using the computer as a classical phone receiver – and with now dedicated phone receivers connected to the computer, making the Internet event more "transparent," so to speak.

It is also now possible to listen to radio or to watch television live over the Internet, whether through direct transmission, or a transmission passing through the broadcasters' own Internet web sites. But here, there is no interaction with the recipient; the Internet is just a new easier-to-use "conduit," without the technical and financial limitations of "ordinary" television.

In this third case, the nature of the Internet changes completely: it is just a new way to transmit other previously existing media, phone, radio or television.[10] But it may also be used to broadcast special dedicated "Internet TV channels," specially put together by campaign organizations or pressure groups. For instance, during his winning 2007 presidential campaign, French President Nicolas Sarkozy ran a permanent live feed on the Web, NSTV.com (for "Nicolas Sarkozy Television") which followed him hour by hour, and became quite popular. He has since been imitated by many politicians all around the world, and shorter clips are even appearing on the first dedicated iApps put up by some politicians for the iPhone.

Finally, we must remember that these three different ways of using the Internet imply that the recipient of the communication needs to voluntarily seek a connection and look for them, which is theoretically a strong limitation to the diffusion of information.[11] This makes the Internet more of a pull medium, contrasting it with technology that allows the message to arrive to the recipient without any effort on his part (telephone call, mail in the mailbox, and so on). Also, some socio-cultural sections of the population have little or no access to the Internet, and some social strata are "resistant" to a medium that requires the use of a keyboard to communicate (older people for instance). Of course, we should also add the problem of reaching those who have a problem with a medium that requires the ability to read and write with ease.

On the other hand, once equipped, the relatively low cost of Internet use, through basic subscriptions available all around the world, is a more positive factor.[12] Also, Web 2.0 is a considerable acceleration factor for the dissemination of political communication, similar to word-of-mouth. Here, the Internet was well understood by people wanting to help Barack Obama's campaign: some playful *YouTube* videos like the *Obama Girl* spot or *Obama's Baby* were hits of his 2008 presidential campaign, much more than most of his own speeches[13].

But one must be very attentive to the fact that, like word-of-mouth indeed, communication from blog to blog or within Internet social networks cannot be controlled, and may easily harm the campaigning politician (though some marketing specialists are of the opinion that even negative communication may have a positive effect).

Quite frequently, the ineffective sides of campaigns and political communication will be conveyed instead of political messages. The low-cut dress worn only once by Angela Merkel in 2008 had much more impact on the Web than any of her political statements, and Ségolène Royal's slip of the tongue on the Great Wall of China was the cause of nearly 1 million mostly ironic Google quotations in a single week in 2007.[14]

7.2 The main kinds of Internet use for political communication

There are three main categories of Internet use for political communication:

- institutional
- political campaigning
- lobbying and promoting "marginal" political parties

7.2.1 Institutional uses of the Internet: from the official party web site to political *spam*

The core of this category is obviously constituted by "traditional" political parties' web sites. We are of course excluding here, as already mentioned in our introduction, the permanent or semi-permanent web site established by government (ministries, and so on.), local government (town halls) and public services (health services, and so on.). Here, the politician is supposed to give way to a more "neutral" communication, designed to support his political actions, of course, but not directly to promote him or his party.

Today, all "traditional" political parties all around the world have established a permanent web site – or nearly. In most cases, these web sites present the main elements of their program, and are obviously complemented during the campaigns by pages on the candidate(s) chosen by the party and/or by links to the latter's own campaign web sites. These party web sites play a particularly important part in campaigns in redirecting the net surfers to the local politicians currently campaigning during parliamentary elections.[15]

These web sites now often include forums, or are linked to a party blog, in order to satisfy the interaction needs of net surfers wishing to leave their opinion, or simply looking for other surfers' points of view. In these cases, net surfer participation is usually "moderated" in order to avoid overly aggressive or defamatory statements.

In recent years, in many countries, some political parties have tried to increase their activist base by using the Internet in a less traditional way by sending out unsolicited spam, incidentally with not negligible effects.[16] Though the method is not traditional, we are still here in the same category of institutional use of the Internet. Even if these unsolicited e-mails or other new methods of unwillingly reaching the recipient through the Internet are not quite "orthodox," they do have a positive effect on political socialization: political parties without any doubt benefit from them to increase their ground support, and it does push into action a good number of previously unknown activists.

So political parties have found in the Internet a very positive way to rebuild a link with their local activists or sympathizers that was damaged by the audiovisual mass media. While the initial ways of using the Internet ("plain" web sites) have not changed much in that respect, the new interactive ways of Web 2.0 have been quite an effective tool helping to put political parties back in touch with modern society.

7.2.2   Using the Internet during election campaigns

With the spread of the Internet in the United States as well as in most democratic countries, its use for electoral campaigning is now taken for granted. In the United States, the March 27, 2006 ruling of the Federal Election Commission paved the way for political communication on the Internet by allowing it nearly unlimited freedom, exempting most Internet uses from legal campaign expenditure rules.[17] Even if web sites remain the backbone of campaigning, despite their flaws, political marketing has developed other means of reaching the voters.

7.2.2.1   Campaign web sites
During political campaigns, the mainstay of Internet tools is still the candidate's web site (or party web site for parliamentary elections). It constitutes the intersection where all the various categories of net surfers aim to reach. A typical campaign web site is usually composed of at least three categories of content:

7.2.2.1.1 Information for the outside visitor
Most often are found:

- a biography (and photographs) of the candidate and more or less detailed information on his close family and relatives, depending on the degree of personalization of his campaign;
- a more or less detailed program, with a notably a clear outline of its main themes and slogans;
- elements of the current campaign (short accounts of the last campaign efforts of the candidate, some of his speeches, including photos and short clips of his more recent rallies, or television interviews, samples of canvassing, and so on, with in some cases, live Internet video transmissions of high points in his campaign, announced in advance);
- the campaign schedule, specifying places and times of forthcoming trips, meetings, rallies, and so on. planned for the candidates (or for the fellow politicians supporting him);
- a forum (usually moderated), possibly with a link to a blog of the candidate existing separately;
- a mailbox to ask specific questions to the politician and get answers (in fact mostly written by dedicated campaign staff);
- forms allowing the user to make direct donations to help the candidate (this was even the mandatory opening page on John McCain's web site in the fall of 2008, when he was in search of funding);
- video archives of television and Internet ads (if any);
- links to other friendly web sites or blogs, or to subscribe to electronic newsletters, mailing lists, and so on.

Of course, here, imagination is only limited by the technical capacities of the Internet. For instance, some politicians have cleverly played on its interactivity, following the example set by the 2004 George W. Bush campaign, which had devised a "Kerry Gas Tax Calculator" which Web surfers could use to assess how much the new gas tax advocated by John Kerry would personally cost them.

7.2.2.1.2 Information and downloading platform for the press
A second category of data is intended for journalists. They can find more detailed information on the campaign, high definition photographs of the campaign to download for their articles, schedules of specific appointments of the candidates with the press (press conferences, "photo-calls"), and so on.

In some cases, following commercial marketing practices, journalists must first send in a request to the campaign press officer for a personal login. This is generally a way of discreetly finding out which journalists visit the web site, which pages they looked for, and what they downloaded. The fact that some information (but not other information) is put on the press web-platform may also be a way of attempting to manipulate journalists who are in too great a hurry to check elsewhere the true significance of what seems to be given so readily to him to fill his newspaper columns. Here, the apparent privilege may be misleading.

In any event, these parts of the web site, and the web site contents as a whole, are a tremendous accelerator of media coverage for the candidate. They enable news media that are even short of cash and not able to send a reporter on the campaign trail, to fill in daily reports of the campaign from afar with enough information. This implies, of course, the risk of using only biased news, since it emanates from the candidate, but that is the journalist's problem to sort out, while the candidate will benefit from much more significant coverage.

7.2.2.1.3 Information and downloading platform for the activists   A last part of the web site, finally, is usually dedicated to the activists. They find messages specifically intended for them, and, most usefully, campaign material to download: samples and templates of posters, leaflets, where they just need to include a minimal amount of data specific to their own use (address of the local campaign headquarters, schedule of the next meeting, etc.).

Here, a password might be necessary for access, rather in order to limit the bandwidth needed for hosting the web site, though whenever it is possible, another choice should be made to leave some of this part open to any visitor to accommodate unregistered or isolated sympathizers who want to help the candidate.

Activists also find here directions in order to build their local blog and useful links to campaign elements they may include in them (clickable "banners," etc.). Exactly like in the non-political sector, they may even get templates in order to put a personal blog online thanks to the campaigning politician's web site.

Somehow, the Internet seems to be a very good way of multiplying the number of activists: since visitors to candidate web sites are usually rather favorable to the candidate, some may more easily be persuaded to concretely help him and become "active activists" so to speak, rather than passive supporters. Here, social media also greatly concur to that effect, and altogether, the Internet has thus been molding a new generation of activists, a fact blatantly demonstrated by Barack Obama's 2008 presidential run.

Since a "good" 'campaign web site needs to be updated constantly, in order not to lose the attention of returning visitors, professionally maintaining a campaign web site is a demanding task. This obviously means human and thus financial cost.

7.2.2.2   Other kinds of Internet use for a campaign by the candidates
7.2.2.2.1 Upstream   The first known use of the Internet to promote a politician's candidacy before the campaign and to make it credible is probably owed to Jesse Ventura, the former wrestler. He became governor of Minnesota in 1998 as an independent candidate of Ross Perot Reform Party thanks to a "virtual" campaign on the Web, and also after an intensive e-mailing of political messages to all the lists of e-mail addresses located in the state his team could get a hold of.[18]

Howard Dean's petitioning campaign on the Internet in 2003–2004 to support his bid to run for the US presidency has definitely proved that this medium may, alone, enable a person to stand as a candidate, but not yet get him elected. Howard Dean's Internet campaign in any event allowed him to become a political leader of national stature and to compete in the first 2004 primaries. This upbeat promotional campaign was staged on an innovation: after an unheard use of one of the first social networking web sites, *Meetup.com*, his team conceived the first cross-utilization of a web site (www.deanforamerica.com) and an interactive blog (www.blogforamerica.com): the web site included interactive parts that directed visitors to the blog, and other Web 2.0 interactive uses.[19] Even the form of his Internet campaign was quite creative, as when he used a baseball bat to encourage donations: the bat changed color as funds poured in, until it was entirely colored red when the goal, another million dollars in fundraising, was achieved.

Two years later, a similar promotional use of the Internet upstream thanks to a blog, *Désirs d'avenir,* helped French Socialist politician Ségolène Royal, prior to the 2007 French presidential campaign. Her blog had been her main communication tool during the months before the socialist "primaries," and contributed considerably to establishing her as a more popular candidate than her main opponents, and also gave her the possibility of overcoming her main rival in the future election, Nicolas Sarkozy, which did not happen.

These examples, among others, clearly indicate that a politician may now declare his candidacy over the Internet, and that as long as it is well relayed by the other media, the Internet seems now to be at least as efficient as an audiovisual mass medium, and in any event easier to use, since here, there is no need to seek the invitations of newscasters and program hosts.

7.2.2.2.2 During the campaign

- maintaining "internal" communication among campaign staff

During the campaign, sending out newsletters or shorter messages directed to the activists' e-mail lists and maintaining specific closed forums with password access for them, builds an internal communication network similar to Intranet in companies or administrations networks. It has become a useful means of fostering the cohesion and the efficiency of a campaign organization, especially when the field organization is scattered over a wide area.

When there is a forum, and/or a directory, the main advantage of the system is to allow bidirectional communication (even multi-directional in some instances) and nearly simultaneous replies, without the delays, and expense, involved in waiting for an available phone line when the activists need help. New messages can be sent from headquarters to field organization activists and sympathizers, campaign participants can report their experiences instantly, or make requests of the central campaign organization faster than by telephone.

- maintaining the "buzz"

Most of the communication techniques developed by commercial marketing for the Internet may be used during the campaign, and we certainly have not seen the end of it. Today, all politicians have to accept more or less willingly to put online a now mandatory blog, to *twitter* (now already a verb) and generally to employ the techniques of so-called *e-Marketing,* in order to maintain a high level of attention among potential voters. Politicians should also regularly send out newsletters, and also shorter direct marketing e-mails to extensive mailing lists formed at least by the surfers who registered on the campaign web site, not counting the many other possible sources. The Internet may also be used for televised telethons, and so on.

During the campaign, politicians and their supporters are also secretly battling in order to manage to be more "visible" on the Internet than their opponents by using tricks well-known in *e-Marketing,* among which:

- buying well chosen *keywords* on search engines – mainly Google at the moment, obviously in order to reroute net surfers to their own web sites;
- faking existing web sites in order to trick overly distracted web surfers and send them messages in favor of the candidate, even if this was not in the logic of the surfer search;
- multiplying "friendly" blogs in order to increase the Internet *buzz*, which not only allows more categories of net surfers to be reached, but also to dupe the search engines, since artificial cross-linking of these blogs will improve the ranking of them in the eyes of the surfers undertaking a search; in fact, many of these blogs are directly managed by the campaign team or by party activists asked to help by opening their own blogs;
- buying ads on other non-political and even commercial web sites, in countries where it is allowed, thus allowing for excellent targeting, if the locations and the web sites are well chosen;[20]
- using social network web sites to disseminate communication without linking it openly to the politician in order to produce a better effect, such as having activists put online a positive clip on *YouTube*; here Barack Obama's 2008 campaign was particularly efficient, with nearly 38 million viewers as of today for the two most popular clips of the kind, the song "Yes We Can," where friendly artists were singing in parallel of some extracts of his March 18, 2008 speech "A more perfect union" and the funny parody "Obama girl,"[21] and so on.

7.2.3   Lobbies and "marginal" political parties on the Internet

Another consequence of the two main characteristics of the Internet is that lobbies and "marginal" political parties have been quickly rejuvenated:

- first, as already mentioned, it is now extremely easy to create a personal web site or a blog, which may then be consulted from anywhere around the world, making it very easy for small groups of people, and even individuals, to be present on the Net; the technique is now elementary, and it is very easy to be hosted by a provider, even if it sometimes means finding a provider in another country, for instance to expose political ideas that are illegal at home;

- second, the thoroughness of the search engines, which index the millions of pages of the Net (notably Google, obviously), have now made it easy to find web sites and blogs promoting any political idea (or any kind of idea, in fact), however far-fetched.

These two factors alone explain why the presence of lobbies and "marginal" political parties on the Internet have increased exponentially. Whether you support the ban on genetically modified food or defend a social habit not really accepted in most countries, the Internet nearly always allows you to find in a few seconds that you are not alone, and then helps you contact other people who share your views. This facilitates considerably the constitution of all kinds of social and political groups. It probably explains why some "non-traditional" political parties, such as environmental parties and lobbies, have been much better known by more people in recent years. The "established" political parties – watched by the main news media – are no longer the only paths to the citizen.

The first massive international political action on the Internet can be said to have taken place in the summer of 1995. Thousands of people were asking the then newly elected French President, Jacques Chirac, to halt nuclear bomb tests in the South Pacific. The rise of similar Internet political actions was apparent in 1999–2000, with the protest against the liberalization of world commerce, or during the Bosnian and Kosovo conflicts, when many e-mails from all sides seeking support were sent all around the world as long as it was possible.[22]

The appearance of blogs, with their increased ease of use, and the new individual possibilities of diffusing images and online videos (or peer-to-peer videos), have further accelerated Internet access for lobbies and "marginal" political parties. This was particularly proven by the negative result of the referendum on the European Constitution in France in 2005. While most of the main media and political parties were campaigning in vain for a positive vote, the majority of the informal Internet, blogs and forums, were full of negative contents, thus clearly helping the "no" vote which finally won. The same phenomenon is currently happening in Spain, where Basque and Catalan separatists' word-of-mouth clearly dominates the Web and plays a strong part in the local public sphere.

One of the consequences of this phenomenon has been to endanger politicians' communication, since any citizen can now upload his attacks on the Web almost instantaneously through short editorials on blogs or forums, or even images of some clips he might have "stolen" with his cell phone, another example of technical progress allowing this development.[23]

Finally, we have already mentioned that "traditional" media often echo these new voices as soon as they seem to be "heard" on the Net through popularity counts. Election campaigns have of course become a privileged opportunity for the appearance of such lobbies on the Internet, which know that the time is more propitious and that they might then find a stronger echo to their messages.

Therefore, an Internet information watch by the campaign staff is now compulsory, with hour-by-hour supervision, in order to sort out true and false rumors and to try and deviate the manipulative maneuvers on the candidate and his campaign, whether they come from an unpleasant opponent or lobby. Sometimes, possibly harmful information (true or false, that is not the point here) may even suddenly be spread more or less inadvertently by some blogger unaware of the consequences of his online activities. In 2008, the many spontaneous recordings or Tina Fey's six (!) caricatures of Sarah Palin on *Saturday Night Live* sent to *YouTube* by many web surfers for instance considerably helped to damage her reputation by transforming them from a temporary event into a continuous process, as would not have been the case when television was not so liable to be sliced into short clips and shared on the Web.

***

Within less than two decades, the Internet has without any doubt become one of the more active tools of modern political communication. Thanks to its ridiculously low access cost and its increased technical progress, it has been multiplying the available sources of information and thereby increasing the necessity for politicians to be aware of what is happening on this medium and to be present.

Nevertheless, it is apparently not yet as central a medium for campaigns as television: unlike the Internet, television is transmitted to nearly all homes, and requires no learning and effort other than buying a television set once and for all (or nearly so), except of course paying a yearly tax in some countries. Also, though its capacities for more effective political communication are considerable, the fact remains that the Internet is mostly a *pull* medium: a surfer usually has to seek political information rather than receive it effortlessly. This limits the penetration of the political message, except if "classical" media relay it when the Internet *buzz* becomes very strong.

This probably constitutes one of the main explanations for the fact that direct penetration of the political message for conquest campaigns through the Internet is not really operative. A recent study has demonstrated that while politicians and their webmasters design their web sites thinking they will reach undecided voters and "voters in general," the reality is quite different: in fact, they mostly reached the "highly engaged voters."[24] So here, "direct" political communication (politicians' web sites), seems much less effective to win new voters than "indirect" means (blogging, social networks, etc.)

Anyway, though it does not always mean better penetration of the political communication among the voters, the Internet has already taken a prominent place within campaigns thanks to its efficiency in fundraising. Howard Dean in 2004, then Barack Obama in 2008, have proven that huge amounts of money were easily obtainable thanks to the Internet. Of course, some of these donations might have been collected by the campaigns without the Internet, but it's obviously only partly the case, particularly for smaller donations, which keep arriving in significantly strong numbers on the Internet.[25]

Finally, the ever more rapid technical progress of cell phones has been promoting them more and more as another means of conveying political information and communication, as newly found quasi-permanent Internet relays. This evolution started in Asia, notably in South Korea, where the number of cell phones per inhabitant is the world's highest, and where the first political campaign through short text messages (SMS, used in a similar way to spam on the Internet), happened as soon as 2001 for the mayoral election in Seoul. We can expect more in the years to come with regard to this rapid evolution. Barack Obama had well understood this when he used *Twitter* for his 2008 campaign, since this network allows *push* SMS messages to people who are part of the same "community," and, incidentally, his White House has then been doing the same, and will certainly soon be imitated everywhere by every politician and political party in the world.

On most cell phones, SMSs have been followed by messages conveying images or short clips (MMS). Now, after the Japanese specific I-Mode network, and Wap, "smart" phones, like the iPhone, almost equivalent to miniature computers, attest to a new step of media convergence, with their direct Internet access either through Edge and the now faster 3G, or even through WiFi (not counting their proprietary iApps). The appearance of Apple's iPhone and its huge worldwide success has shown particularly that the Internet is indeed becoming a permanent process through media convergence. Some politicians have quickly started to disseminate their own "iApps," little pieces of software available for iPhone users, so that they can access their communication even quicker. Already on October 22, 2009, French Industry Minister and Mayor of Nice, Christian Estrosi, was circulating a very thorough image-building iApp, and Angelica Araujo, a Mexican candidate for the Mérida mayoral election, is apparently the first politician to construct an iApp directly used for a campaign, followed a little later by Valerie Pecresse, a French politician competing for the Paris region seat in local elections in early 2010.[26] We can guess that these are the first of a long series.

Notes

1   In the 1980s the French Government Telecommunications Office gave every telephone subscriber a small computer terminal, called the Minitel, which provided access to hundreds of different services ranging from home banking to telephone sex, usually without any prior subscription. Because the Minitel terminal was initially supplied at no cost, more than 5 million terminals were at one point installed in homes and offices throughout France. But the system became obsolete, especially when the Internet started to develop, because it was a closed system (a contract had to be signed with the government telecom subsidiary to open a service) and also because of its technical shortcomings: the so-called *Videotex* norm it was built on only allowed a speed of 1.2K, whereas broadband Internet transmits at a speed about 25,000 times faster (30 megabytes), and about 100,000 times faster via optical fiber (100/120 megabytes).

2   One of the best-known and easy-to-use blogging websites is Wordpress, at http://wordpress.com/.

3   http://www.facebook.com/, http://www.myspace.com/, and http://www.linkedin.com/.
4   Their membership is now huge: Facebook has for instance reached 500 million members in December 2010 (in *Le Monde*, December 31, 2010).
5   http://twitter.com/.
6   When elected, Barack Obama also became the first US president to use Twitter as one of his means of communication.
7   http://www.youtube.com/ (last accessed December 2, 2010) and http://www.dailymotion.com/us (last accessed December 2, 2010).
8   Devine, in Semiatin 2008.
9   Podcasts were thus named by computer firm Apple, because there were originally only meant to be downloaded to iPods", which the company had invented and which quickly dominated the world market of portable mini music players. iTunes software, for both Macs and PCs, enables users to download music and videos to iPods.
10 In fact, from the beginning of the Internet or nearly so, when activists download campaign templates to use as posters, leaflets, etc., they are using the Internet as they would have previously used a fax machine or the mail.
11 Except of course in the case of the dreaded "spam" that floods e-mail inboxes or the invasive advertising "pop ups" unwillingly obtained when consulting certain website pages.
12 Europe is for once here in a better position than North America for high speed Internet equipment. The United States was the first to disseminate the Internet on a broad scale, so the first equipment was the slow one existing at the time, while the few years' delay in the equipment of most European countries enabled European Internet users to buy high speed equipment right from the start.
13 The *Obama Girl* clip, "I have a crush on Obama" has been viewed on *YouTube* during the campaign about 10 million times, and reached 17 million surfers.
14 In Maarek 2007a.
15 This is often done thanks to a "clickable" map of the country leading the voter to the local candidate's web pages, or at least to a page giving his contact details him or those of his team.
16 For example, the future French President Nicolas Sarkozy notoriously introduced the first broad scale political spam campaign in France in 2006: 1.5 million e-mails were sent off, with a return figure estimated to be somewhat lower, and of course presenting the advantage of costing very little. The expenses were mostly the rental of customer files of two mail-order book specialists and the marketing consultant's fee.
17 see Appendix 1 and www.fec.gov (last accessed December 2, 2010)
18 Jesse Ventura was also helped by clever radio and television spots devised by the well-known political consultant Bill (William) Hillsman, notably parodying the hip tones of the *Shaft* score for a radio spot.
19 Even if Dean's Internet campaign was bold, effective and successful (for fundraising at least), his initial decision to spend the money raised immediately was a disaster, since he started the primaries with a debt of US$1.2 million, while being the candidate who had raised the most money the previous months (Wayne 2008). On the Howard Dean campaign, see for instance M. Cornfield 2004, and on his web campaign particularly, see K. Foot and S.M. Scheider 2006.
20 For instance, families can be reached by inserting an ad about a family-friendly part of the political program of the candidate on an informative web site dedicated to children's

education, or on a commercial website specialized in selling children's goods, etc. (on that point, see for instance Lynda Lee Kaid in A.P. Williams and J.C. Tedesco 2006).

21 Using *YouTube* to host campaign ads and videos gives a twofold benefit: first, the hosting then becomes free, and second, *YouTube* users who might not have looked for these films if they had been hosted on a politician's campaign web site then have a chance to watch them thanks to *YouTube's* elaborate linking system. Barack Obama's 2008 campaign allegedly thus got 14.5 million free hours of Internet broadcasting, so to speak. See Denton (2009), 20.

22 See for instance Jim Walch (1999) with the explicit title *In the Net, an Internet Guide for Activists*.

23 In 2009, images taken by the cell phone of a young Iranian woman, Neda Agha-Soltan, peacefully demonstrating in the street for freedom of speech, and being brutally killed by the militia, gave rise to many blogs being placed online. These have, accordingly, been much more powerful than the demonstrations themselves to convince people of the brutality of the ruling regime. Less dramatic, but also powerful, has been the surge in Italy of the so-called "violet" protest movement, mainly operating through the Internet, and born from opposition to Silvio Berlusconi there, when it seemed that "traditional" opposition parties were not able to block some very questionable actions. Altogether, these examples show that also after being elected, the governing politician must now deal very carefully with the Internet – but this problem is outside the scope of the present book.

24 See J.N. Druckman, M.J. Kifer, and M. Parkin 2009.

25 On Internet fundraising, see for, example, R.G. Boatright, in Semiatin 2008.

26 Government communication soon followed, incidentally: the White House only beat the French Government by nine days with its official *iApp*, *White House* on January 20, 2010, while the French one, amicably called *Gouv* (for "Gouvernement" – (Government)) arrived on iPhone screens on January 29.

Part IV

The actual running of election campaigns

The previous chapters dealt with political communication under any circumstances, whether during the image-making process or the election campaign. Chapters 8 and 9 concentrate on situations in which the politician actually campaigns for office:

- the candidate will have to set up and operate a rather large-scale organization to assist him;
- in the particular case of local communication campaigns, the candidate will encounter specific problems, but will also have more convenient modes of communication at his disposal.

8

Structure and organization of the campaign

Because of its complexity, a political communication campaign must be backed by a well-designed infrastructure and an ad hoc staff called upon to fulfill any number of tasks. In political communication, even the most obviously trivial decision multiplies the categories of people and types of tasks to accomplish. The latter involves all the activities of political marketing: designing and supervising every stage of the campaign; planning and organizing a politician's campaign trail; initiating and overseeing the fundraising processes; co-ordinating the activities from top to bottom, in other words, the politician and his or her closest advisors on the one hand, the team of field activists and volunteers,[1] on the other; following the campaigns of the other politicians in the running and countering their moves, just as one would do at a football or hockey match; assuming all real activities inherent in the media chosen to convey the message, from designing the poster graphics to the actual distribution of leaflets in mailboxes; keeping blogs and social networks running by leading discussion forums and increasing linkage to friendly web sites, and so on.

The organization that must be set up may be quite large, and as complex as that of the small company, which in fact it is. As in any private company, this entity, commonly called the "campaign organization," may suffer from dispersals of energy: a poor configuration may result in poor communication choices, both in terms of content as well as form (prohibitively costly choices, for instance). As with any private company, too, part of a campaign team's energy and resources will be spent simply in maintaining its own structure: money allocated to the organization headquarters; fundraising campaigns conducted to cover the overheads of the campaign organization itself, and so on.

Campaign Communication and Political Marketing, First Edition. Philippe J. Maarek.
© 2011 Philippe J. Maarek. Published 2011 by Blackwell Publishing Ltd.

The campaign organization must also face psycho-sociological handicaps to a greater extent than an ordinary organization or company, and this for a number of reasons:

- First, its lack of a past history prevents it from being able to draw instantly on stock solutions adopted during previous activities, as in the case of ordinary firms, where, for instance, regular staff turnover enables new employees to benefit from pre-established work habits.[2]
- Second, its temporary nature, since a campaign organization exists, at best, only for the duration of the election race. The staff must deal with the discrepancy between the extent of the workload they have come together to undertake and its brief life span (with the exception of staff who are considering a longer term collaboration with the politician once he is elected).[3]
- Furthermore, the management style of a campaign organization has the psychological bearing of Russian roulette because of its probable lack of future. Obviously, since the objective is to get the politician elected, there are by definition many more losing than winning campaigns. As election day draws nearer the stress increases, since losing the race will irremediably bring the enterprise to a negative conclusion for most of the competing teams. This stress is comparable to that of a motion picture unit starting a movie with the awareness that the odds are nine in ten (if ten candidates are running) that his work will be for nothing, since the producer runs away with the cash after having destroyed whatever footage has already been shot.
- Last, the discrepancy between the highly tedious nature of most of the tasks to be performed and the aims of the campaign creates in the participant a much greater psychological tension than for the employee of an ordinary firm (where it is much bearable, since, however wearisome the work may be, it still brings definite and immediate rewards in the form of wages). Members of the campaign organization are much more anonymous performers than planners, especially since a great part of the campaign planning is out of their hands, either because it arises directly from decisions made by the politician and his closest advisors, or because it is contracted to outside consultants.

Several of these drawbacks easily explain, in retrospect, the undeniable advantage incumbent politicians have over their novice opponents in matters of political communication. Barring, naturally, a blatant mistake committed during their mandate, outside the psychological advantage granted by a previous win, incumbent politicians benefit simultaneously from:

- better funding, if only because of an existing list of previous donors, who can be approached again for new campaign contributions;
- an earlier reputation, which need only be revamped or developed, a much easier task than building one from scratch;

- finally, from a "memory" of past campaigns, which remedies the common drawbacks of a lack and the brief duration of the campaign organization; in this respect, the presence of former participants in a previously successful election, either field activists or insiders who have since joined the incumbent politician's team, is the most favorable factor in the new race.

This last point partly explains the relative durability of the two major parties in the United States over the decades, if not centuries: once the primaries are won, the candidate appointed by the Democratic or Republican Party benefits from an organization that has cut its teeth on the campaigns his predecessor conducted a mere two or three years before. Of course, new sympathizers are attracted by the candidate's personal charisma alone, but their lack of previous "political communication memory" is compensated by the presence of this more experienced group of supporters.

8.1 The campaign set up

At the start, the politician is faced with two primordial decisions, on which the harmony of his team's activities depends:

- the appointment of two key positions: campaign manager and field coordinator;
- the choice of management style.

8.1.1 The appointment of the two key position holders

The campaign manager and the field co-ordinator occupy the two key posts in the political communication campaign. Of course, we could add a third post: the person in charge of fundraising and the finance sector (usually called the campaign treasurer). But since political communication is the subject at hand, the post of campaign treasurer is not a key position in that regard and we take for granted his skill and efficiency.

Both the campaign manager and the field co-ordinator should be endowed simultaneously with talents we generally take to be contradictory. As the interface of the campaign organization, they must be able to command as well as to discuss, to be both war leaders and diplomats. Their job is all the more difficult since they must work without any safety net, so to speak. As mentioned earlier, they do not have the benefit of previous work habits: by nature, most people who devote themselves to a political communication campaign have been brought together recently, for a limited time, and may never meet again.

The candidate's team of direct advisors, sometimes known as his "cabinet," is not included in the campaign organization chart, for it is generally constituted before the campaign and will remain as such afterwards. But since a "cabinet" member often exerts a direct influence over the politician's political communication decisions, we will virtually consider the cabinet members and the candidate himself as a unit: when we mention the politician or candidate in this chapter, we are referring to the candidate and/or his close advisors. Though we do no dissociate the cabinet from the candidate himself, as they form the core of the decision-making process, we should mention that problems of coordination and even disagreement among the candidate's direct advisors, or between the campaign organization and some cabinet members, are known to crop up to further complicate matters.

8.1.1.1 The campaign manager

The candidate almost always personally chooses the campaign manager, due to the nature of his responsibilities, of course, but also because the campaign manager is a person who can be trusted. The campaign manager must establish a direct working relationship with the candidate and is delegated extensive powers. This delegation is necessary because of the considerable amount of traveling that the candidate must do in the course of the campaign. He is usually expected to tour his whole constituency, which can be the whole country. In the meantime, the campaign organization requires leadership and decisions cannot wait for the candidate's periodic return.

This implies a perfect understanding between the two people and that there should be nothing which overshadows their relationship. The campaign manager is usually one of the rare figures in the campaign organization staff connected with the politician's cabinet. He is notably in charge of co-ordinating the politician's campaign schedule with his other duties and even of providing the candidate with minimal leisure time. One cabinet member is usually placed in charge of his personal agenda, in agreement with the campaign manager.

The influence of the campaign manager is considerable.[4] He hires or accepts the help of all the main members of the campaign organization, he manages them, settles their conflicts and co-ordinates them. The campaign manager is usually also the one who decides on the management style of the organization.

A campaign manager's tasks are threefold:

- leading and managing the campaign as a whole, and also in a large part the central campaign organization;
- managing and co-ordinating the entire campaign team, which include both volunteers enlisted for its duration, and regular party members supporting the candidate and relaying his campaign in the field;
- co-ordinating and supervising links with all outside organizations, from advertising agencies to ordinary suppliers.

Altogether, this explains why the campaign manager plays a key role in a successful campaign, and why a politician should always be very careful in choosing a campaign manager, since they will have to work together for the whole campaign. In fact, dismissing a campaign manager in the course of the campaign generally has more negative effects than keeping the person in post even if everything does not go as planned: the morale of the other staff members, often appointed by the campaign manager, will usually be adversely affected by his dismissal, and it is usually a bad omen for a campaign.

In the 2004 US presidential campaign, John Kerry was wise enough, in the light of Howard Dean's bold initial Internet campaign, to dismiss his campaign manager, Jim Jordan. This happened almost at the at the beginning of the campaign, in November 2003, and he was replaced by veteran Democratic staffer Mary Beth Cahill, thus avoiding the difficulties this would inevitably cause had been it been done later. John McCain also did the same thing relatively early in his campaign by replacing Terry Nelson with Rick Davis in July 2007. On the contrary, keen observers already knew that Hillary Clinton's campaign was at real risk, and would not make an easy run in February 2008, when just after the loss of four primaries to Barack Obama, her campaign manager, Patti Solis Doyle, resigned (and was replaced by an old time collaborator, her former chief of staff Maggie Williams).

The campaign manager's role is so important that any weakness is always a bad omen. For instance, in France a year before, when Ségolène Royal chose to divide the job between two persons (both politicians, incidentally, not "technicians," as is ordinarily the case), this very unusual decision was liable to lead to difficulties in running her campaign – which indeed happened.

8.1.1.2   The field co-ordinator

The responsibility of the field co-ordinator is also very important. He is posted at the intersection of three categories of players from widely contrasting backgrounds and with very different methods. The field co-ordinator's job is to try to ensure they work together:

- the regular activists and party members, sometimes far removed from the candidate's ideas, and whose competence in the area of modern political marketing is not always much greater than that of the sympathizers, although they often perceive it to be the contrary;
- the sympathizers, who have to be allocated to supporting committees to create minimal cohesion and professionalism among these forces, are often inexperienced and ill-prepared for a communication operation;
- the central campaign organization, which conveys sometimes unclear, even contradictory ideas, especially if it is hampered by a poorly managed vertical structure.

The task of the field co-ordinator is all the more difficult because each of the above-mentioned categories naturally tends to maintain an uneasy coexistence with the others:

- The central campaign organization is resented by activists and sympathizers for the reigning aura of professionalism it enjoys. They are also envious of the campaign organization's closeness to the candidate.
- Activists and sympathizers are often underestimated by the central organization, because of their supposed lack of professionalism.

- Old-time activists and party members and newly-arrived sympathizers, tacitly reproach one another the varying lengths of their respective commitments. This happens especially when activists have watched their favorite candidate campaign internally for party nomination be dismissed in favor of another, and must then work with the sympathizers of the winning candidate.[5]

Obviously the field co-ordinator should then be endowed with strong human resource management abilities. Well aware of that question, Barack Obama, for instance, chose to hire a former labor organizer, Temo Figueroa, himself the son of a farm organizer.

Unlike the campaign manager, the field co-ordinator might not have direct access to the politician. But he must work in close conjunction with the campaign manager, as he acts as the latter's main relay by which to gauge the performance of the campaign and follow-up on decisions implemented. Thus, he is usually chosen and approved by the campaign manager.

8.1.2   Choosing the management style

There are two main management styles, which involve either a horizontal or vertical division of tasks.

8.1.2.1   *Horizontal task division*
In this case, team members are less and less specialized as one approaches the top of the organization, that is the candidate. At each level, whatever the decision, it is a much as possible a collective one, which ensures a better synergy among the participants (see Figure 8.1).

The obvious advantage of horizontal task division lies in that it allows no important campaign decision to be taken without the consent of the main staff, at every level. A sluggish decision-making process, and a considerable inertia, constitutes its major drawback, as each decision must be discussed by all the members on the decision-making level.

8.1.2.2   *Vertical task division*
A vertical task division is often preferred because more efficient in the short term: the "first circle" of campaign planners remains relatively small, and the tasks are distributed almost immediately according to their nature (see Figure 8.2).

Another common means of vertical task division is a breakdown according to the different types of targets identified by the campaign. One group might be in charge of communications with young people, another with women, a third group with the working class or upper classes, and so on. Sometimes, a small number of precisely defined "vertical" sectors are combined with a horizontal structure: if, for example, the preliminary surveys identify a certain category of the population as a specific target, a particular department might be set up (see Figure 8.3).

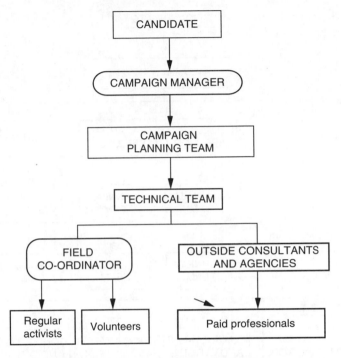

Figure 8.1 Horizontal task division in a campaign organization.

Theoretically, the vertical management style has greater appeal, because on a task-by-task basis things can be accomplished more swiftly and with greater efficiency. But three weaknesses in this type of organization impede its smooth running:

- The need to change management styles in mid-course, so to speak, once the action is implemented in the field: here, the structure is always horizontal, as activists and sympathizers are hardly specialized. This can cause considerable trouble in coordinating the central campaign planners and the agents in the field.
- The lack of synergy among different actions, since each team is working in its own area without really paying heed to the other organization members. Moreover, overspecialized team members develop a strong tendency to overestimate the importance of their own task in relation to the whole campaign; this can lead to serious mistakes.
- Increased campaign costs, both because vertical division creates more structural redundancy and because each sector will generally try to increase its budget to the detriment of the others, as each views its role in the campaign as the more important.

Because of these problems, vertical division should only be considered if the candidate has both an excellent campaign manager and field co-ordinator. In this case, vertical division can prove highly efficient.

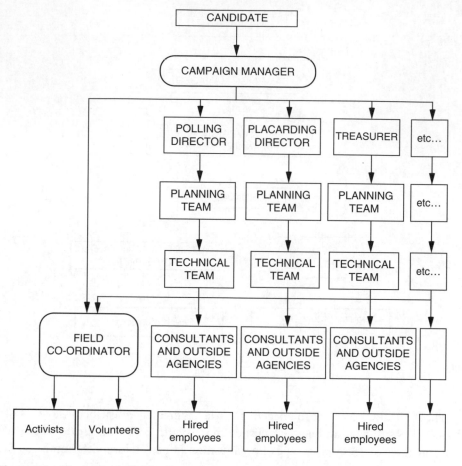

Figure 8.2   Vertical task division in a campaign organization.

In any case, one must keep in mind that the choice of general management style is quite often put to the test during the actual course of the campaign. The immediate reaction required in response to all kinds of political events frequently disrupts the decision-making process, much faster than changes that can occur in commercial marketing (in which campaigns to promote new products are planned months in advance, with few surprises when they are launched). Most political analysts who have studied a campaign, or have taken part in one, know that there are many cases when certain decisions, even crucial ones, are not made in accordance with the established division of tasks, but are made by the highest person in the hierarchy physically present at headquarters at the time the decision has been taken. In general, a political communication campaign has no time to lose. This explains why the higher-ranking the staff member, the more hours he tends to put in at campaign headquarters. If a senior staff member wants to avoid major decisions concerning his sector of activity from being taken while absent, he must be physically present.[6]

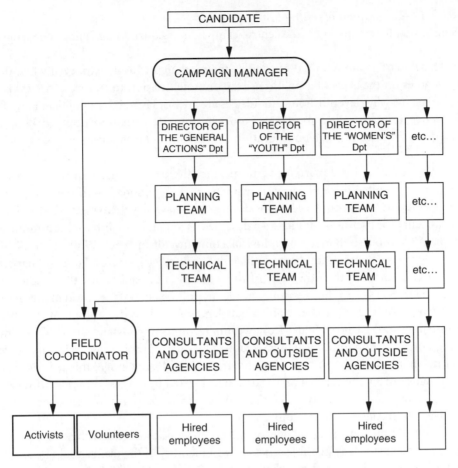

Figure 8.3 Combined division of tasks in a campaign organization.

8.2 Establishing campaign headquarters

The highly mundane task of setting up a campaign infrastructure is an essential step in guaranteeing a properly run campaign organization, and involves problems related to its nature and purpose. We will distinguish between problems of location and other material concerns.

8.2.1 The location of campaign organization premises

As with any organization in charge of communication operations, the campaign staff has to be as open to the outside world as possible. The choice of premises for campaign organization headquarters must be consistent with this objective, to prevent internal rumors and gossip from taking precedence over what is going on outside. The geographical location of the campaign organization should reflect this openness, while fostering a productive and synergetic work environment for the entire staff.

8.2.1.1   *The location of central headquarters*

The search for premises for the central campaign organization is quite a challenge:

- headquarters are required as soon as the campaign is underway, even when this comes on the heels of a politician's last-minute decision to run for office (which explains why eleventh-hour candidacies are are not favored by a politician's staff);
- since it is materially impossible to move headquarters in mid-campaign, because of its short duration, a poor location choice cannot be changed.

But the choice of headquarters is crucial, since the true efficiency of the campaign organization often depends on it. It will have to accommodate staff members with very different backgrounds, skills, and roles, who have never worked together. This means that the premises should be so designed as to maximize internal communication, much more so than for an industrial company, for instance. While it is possible for a company to maintain its head office in London, Paris or New York and have its factories located on the other side of the globe, it is unrealistic for the candidate's speechwriters to be in the city center, while his polling analysts are located out in the suburbs.[7] Political researcher Xandra Kayden, who followed a number of political campaigns in the United States from within, recounts one instance in which a campaign organization found itself handicapped by such a problem: its offices had been set up in a building with two wings separated by a large garage; this led to severe problems during the campaign, because staff located in the two different wings did not communicate properly, since they could not be bothered to cross the garage between both sides of the building.[8]

Unity within central campaign organization's headquarters is thus essential in order to create the best possible synergy: each member of the team should be able to know immediately, if need be, what the other is doing. Good internal communication is all the more important when the tasks to accomplish increase in complexity, as we have noted in previous chapters. In the frame of an electoral campaign, even an efficient Intranet network cannot replace direct contact.

Furthermore, the premises should be centrally located and easily accessible by road and public transportation: there is no advantage in having vast premises if they are located at more than an hour by car from the nearest printer's or television studio. Expenses involved in the setting up of campaign organization headquarters are therefore a major budget item. Candidates who enjoy established political party support thus have a genuine advantage, since they usually have free use of its headquarters, unless, and this is sometimes the case, they feel that the ostensible association might harm their image.

8.2.1.2   *Decentralized campaign premises*

Looking for a location for the central campaign organization is not all. While he is on campaign, the candidate needs a strong network of decentralized campaign premises throughout his constituency, especially in the case of a large-scale election, a national campaign, in particular. First of all, these premises must obviously be of service to the field personnel working for the campaign. They meet there, plan operations, liaise with the central campaign organization, design their own texts and leaflets tailored to the local situation, and so on. But decentralized premises are also useful for the communication campaign because they help relay it in two other ways:

- Local sympathizers can easily pick up leaflets, badges, and stickers there, and this proximity allows sympathizers wishing to join the campaign team to do so easily.
- Decentralized premises not only give the campaign greater visibility but also take on a symbolic dimension to the anonymous passer-by, by anchoring the candidate's presence in the citizen's everyday environment, thus suggesting the politician's concern for even the remotest community. To this end, even if there are not enough sympathizers to receive visitors on a daily basis, the very existence of a local office, even if it is often closed, is enough to fulfill that role. Trade unions the world over long ago provided empirical proof as to the utility of this visual relay function of decentralized premises.

8.2.2   Equipment

The technical equipment does not have to constitute a large expense item in the campaign budget, since professional communication consultants usually provide this as part of their services. Other equipment required by the team is generally rented, since the job is limited in time and will be finished by a specific date, namely election day.

The main difficulty is probably the speed with which equipment must be set up and become operational. This means that the campaign organization has to obtain all at once a long list of articles which any ordinary enterprise would acquire over a long period of time: from pencil sharpeners to delivery vans, from a large platform of networked computers to immediately operative fast Internet connections, and every item must be available immediately.

It should be noted that today's campaign organizations tend to make systematic use of personal computers, since costs have dropped and they are doubly productive. First, personal computers allow better capitalization on human resources; they can, for instance, be used for simple simulations or analyses, such as exploiting survey results and compiling address lists on that basis. But computers also offer the advantage of improving internal communication within the campaign organization if they are networked, forming a so-called Intranet network: even remotely located campaign staff members may then be reached instantly by the campaign organization and vice versa. Free telephone through the Internet (with Skype and similar) adds even more interest to having such a network immediately available.

8.3   The problem of finance

8.3.1   The cost and financing of political campaigning

The high cost of modern political marketing can easily be imagined in light of what we have mentioned in previous chapters. To take only two examples among thousands of others: organizing a 5,000 person meeting in a marquee can cost up to US$200,000, and a direct mail campaign can amount to a US$1 million or more, depending on the number of recipients. It is no surprise, then, to discover that the total cost of the 2008 American Democratic Convention was allegedly above US$100 million, more than three times what it was for Bill Clinton's nomination in 1992 (about US$30 million). Altogether, according to the US Federal Election Commission, Barack Obama spent US$730 million for the 2008 presidential campaign compared with the US$333 million spent by John McCain, a much less effective fundraiser.[9]

Moreover, only the bills actually paid are reported in the campaign finances, and not the real costs. For example, the wide range of benefits in kind granted by business executives and sympathetic patrons are usually not reported, for good reason, in the official campaign figures. How can one be sure that a printer or an advertising firm that produced a commercial spot did not undercharge, and their bills reflect the true cost of the job? Nor is there any way to completely itemize in the campaign books the free trips made in private planes of generous patrons, and so on.[10]

We will not deal here with the question of campaign financing in its entirety which overlaps with that of political party financing: this topic is, and always has been, a source of difficulty in every country in the world. Often obscured, or not clearly and effectively regulated by law, the subject as much deserves the scrutiny of a political analyst as of a detective. Even the federal financing of presidential candidates in the United States, although reformed in 2002, is not an entirely satisfactory system and has not prevented a considerable increase in campaign expenditure. Incidentally, the Supreme Court decisions seem to revoke the efforts of Congress to regulate the amount of money spent on political campaigns. As mentioned it earlier, its January 21, 2010 ruling, *Citizens United v. Federal Election Commission*, has reversed the former Supreme Court ruling prohibiting corporations from using their own money to help a candidate during campaigns. So, added to its *Buckley v. Valeo* former ruling, which allows unlimited spending from candidates' own pockets, this seems to encourage a further increase of campaign expenditure.

However, certain peculiarities of campaign finances should be brought to light. Although theoretically located further away from communication activities, for which it supplies the necessary funds, the financial department of the campaign organization in fact plays a substantial role in them. Its two main activities have an influence on the campaigning process:

- fundraising;
- financial management.

8.3.2   Fundraising

The prohibitive cost of campaigns makes the incorporation of a direct fundraising component into the campaign organization a necessity. The purpose, then, is not to persuade solicited individuals to vote for the candidate – a fairly foregone conclusion by virtue of the fact that they are on the list – but rather and more prosaically to contribute financial, or, possibly, material support. Today, it has become completely illusory to attempt to start any political marketing process without considering the question of fundraising. A specific fundraising campaign is nearly always organized, either as part of the ordinary campaign, or parallel to it.

Certain activities of the communication campaign might be adjusted to serve a dual purpose: to convince specific target groups or strengthen their approval of the candidate, and at the same time encourage the target groups to make contributions. This explains why citizens who are staunch supporters of the politician should never be completely neglected: if their vote is bound to be positive, their financial support is not always guaranteed, and it is worth trying to secure it.

Several members of the campaign organization are specifically assigned to this task, and have to follow closely every communication decision to ascertain whether a fundraising aspect can be added to it. They should also instigate new drives, if necessary.

Two traditional instruments of political marketing are particularly suited to this simultaneous fundraising process:

- closed-circle meetings, dinners or banquets;
- direct person-to-person contacts, among acquaintances if possible, and particularly, privileged direct contacts between the candidate and substantial donors.

As for newer political marketing tools, direct mail and now the Internet are used more and more frequently in many countries to replenish political party and campaign coffers, as we described in Chapter 7, telephone marketing being more or less effective depending on the country, used more in North America than in Southern Europe, for instance. We have also noted that the expansion of this practice leads inevitably to greater professionalism, but also increases the anonymity of the fundraising process: the local party treasurer or devoted sympathizer whose knack for finding important donors was appreciated has been replaced either by anonymous telephone operators, or by "direct" mail, and e-mail, anonymously produced by computer.

The increased role of direct mail in the fundraising circuit has more fundamental consequences. Since it often leads to contracting out the technical aspects of fundraising, politicians, or the political sphere as such, can thereby lose part of their autonomy, as happened years ago in the United States: a direct mail specialist, Richard A. Viguerie, has held for many years the purse strings to a substantial share of Republican Party finances, thanks to four floors of computers in Virginia, for the exclusive use of conservative parties, individuals or political action committees.

As for the Internet, it has quickly become a preferred means of fundraising. More and more political parties, and politicians campaigning all around the world, have put online specific Web pages or even sometimes annoying popup windows ena-bling sympathizers to manifest their support with donations, with secure links for credit card use. Political spam eliciting donations is also on the rise. This has enabled numerous "small" donations to be collected that would probably never have been raised by other methods, since it is so easy to give money to help your favorite party or candidate with a credit card number without having to leave the comfort of your own home. The example of efficient Internet fundraising was set in 2003, when Howard Dean, by his astute use of web sites and blogs, allegedly raised nearly US$30 million during the last six months of that year.[11] We have also already shown how successful Barack Obama's 2008 Internet fundraising campaign has been.

Thus fundraising does have a direct influence on the political communication campaigns, modifying them to integrate it as a specific dimension of their activity. Furthermore, campaign organizations must also pay particular attention to the management of their finances.

8.3.3   Financial management

Managing campaign finances has direct repercussions on the progress of campaign activities. Each marketing decision has financial consequences: design costs, com-mercial airtime for television spots, travel expenses, and so on.

In many countries, the management of campaign funds, by a department led by a "treasurer" or "campaign treasurer," poses three kinds of problems, some rather standard and others derived from the particular nature of election campaigns:

- income has to be "smoothed out";
- campaign organization expenses must be controlled;
- laws and regulations overseeing campaign or party financing must be complied with.

8.3.3.1   "Smoothing" the income

Managing the campaign finances requires a certain degree of financial acrobatics, because of the inevitable time lag between the moment expenses are incurred for campaign activities and the day when donations and public funding are called in.

This time lag is unavoidable for two reasons:

- a major portion of the campaign income is provided by donations and support generated by the campaign in action; it follows that at the very least, the funds required to launch the campaign must be advanced;
- in countries where the state partially reimburses campaign expenditures, and if the candidate or the political party meets the legal requirements to benefit from such a refund, the money is almost always paid out according to the results of the election, and usually only if the party or candidate has obtained a minimum

percentage of the vote (or seats). The Federal Republic of Germany was the first and for a long time the only nation to have taken this shortcoming into account, by ruling (Law of 24 July 1967) that public campaign financing was to be awarded from the start to the parties already represented in parliament, in proportion to their previous representation. But this does not solve the problem of new parties not represented in parliament, or of candidates running for office for the first time, or on an independent ticket. Further legislation and rulings, such as France's law of 15 January 1990, have partly replicated this system, while correcting this problem: a portion of the funding is often allocated according to previous representation in parliament, and another portion according to the election outcome, which for the treasurer again raises the problem of having to wait for the state funds.

Thus, election campaign finances are by nature unbalanced and need considerable "smoothing" which must often depend on the ability of the treasurer or the candidate himself, to organize all types of expenditure with delayed payment facilities. A friendly printer or advertising spot producer who only bills the candidate at the end of the campaign gives a cash advance as tangible as a direct financial contribution, and can thus provide true financial support that escapes legislation. This gives a clear advantage to a candidate, treasurer or other leading campaign organization member with well-kept address books and a friendly banker granting low interest rates on the remainder of the overdraft.

Because campaign finances must be smoothed out whenever possible, as long as the campaign does not get off to too bumpy a start due to a belated candidacy, major donors are usually solicited well in advance: their contributions will help launch the campaign quickly and effectively, in itself an initiator of a steady flow of contributions in turn. Early fundraising also allows time, if necessary, to go back to the initial donors during the campaign run to request renewed support.

Naturally, for a campaign treasurer, the ideal situation would be to find a ready cash reserve supplied by a previous campaigns. Logically, an election campaign should be prepared by regular fundraising campaigns among known sympathizers of the politician or party. In the United States, ever since Carlton Ketchum led such a preliminary campaign in 1937, the Republican Party has organized fundraising campaigns annually, whether an election year or not. As mentioned previously, this has been done through direct mail since the Barry Goldwater campaign in 1964.

8.3.3.2 *Keeping expenses under control*

Managing the campaign finances has direct implications for its evolution. Each marketing decision has financial consequences: cost of creative development, cost of ad space, of transportation, and so on. Maintaining a good communication campaign thus clearly depends on a good financial manager. If he is overly optimistic, he can lead the candidate or party to ruin at the end of the campaign by putting it too heavily in debt. If he is too pessimistic, he can have money left towards the end of the campaign, but it will be too late to spend it, since prime airtime for television spots, or the best billboard locations will no longer be available (the worst case being in countries where campaigns make wide use of televised commercials, since the best slots are sometimes reserved a year in advance, as for the Super Bowl football championship). Controlling expenditures includes both a quantitative and qualitative aspect.

8.3.3.2.1 Quantitatively regulating expenditures   Just as a finance minister in a government has a direct influence over a substantial part of political action through his power to deny funding to such or such a ministry (unless he receives a deliberate injunction to allocate it more money), the financial management of a campaign can have consequences once a choice is made, if only through admonitions to limit expenditures, when viewed as excessive with respect to the anticipated effect. Like commercial marketing, where the cost of each customer contact is closely calculated, a good campaign treasurer has to intervene to control excessive expenditures. But he must do so with a full knowledge of the campaign needs, and not simply with the aim of keeping his accounts in the black. A candidate who loses an election will never thank a treasurer who has withheld money until the end without spending it: that would mean that the campaign did not use all the means at its disposal, perhaps resulting in the defeat.

Quantitative campaign finance management is even harder in the case of two-round elections, common in many countries, from France to Brazil, for instance, notably for presidential elections. Limiting campaign expenditures too zealously during the first round of voting in order to keep enough for the second round may lead to not achieving a good enough result to remain in the running. Conversely, being able to reach the second round when all funds have already been spent in order to get there will be an obvious handicap, except if the treasurer has put money away for that purpose or is able to raise money instantly or almost so, usually by cultivating banks sympathetic to the campaign.

8.3.3.2.2 Qualitatively regulating expenditures   Sound financial management also frequently involves adjusting decisions of the campaign team in a more dynamic direction. Like any other kind of organization some expenses often appear irreducible: certain staff salaries, travel expenses, and the like.

Here, this phenomenon is particularly striking since the sums involved are large ones from a relative standpoint (a staff salary as the employee perceives it, for example) but low in absolute value, in relation to the global budget of the campaign. If it is necessary to tighten spending, the organization will more willingly trim campaign expenditures, which are much greater in absolute value, but not so much in relative value. It will notably limit the budgets earmarked for media advertising, for instance: if the amount saved is equal, it is psychologically much easier for the organization to reduce the money spent on commercials than the salary of a hundred paid staff members. Thus good financial management of a campaign paradoxically requires making choices that may appear more prodigal.

That means that the campaign organization will have to put its treasurer in a position of being able to fulfill his task of controlling expenditure properly by informing him systematically of all decisions made, just as it does for other main department managers. A treasurer who would see his role as merely that of an accountant in charge of entering donations on one side and signing checks on the other, only making sure that accounts are balanced, would not be a good campaign treasurer.

8.3.3.3   Complying with the law

In many democratic countries, campaign financing over the years has been the object of increasingly detailed and restrictive regulations, for three reasons:

- the growing amounts spent by candidates for office, closely linked to the increasingly sophisticated means used for communication campaigns;
- the correlative increase of inevitable financial scandals, notably caused by loopholes in previous regulations (or by the absence of regulation);
- the desire to achieve a balance, to the extent that this is possible, between major parties and smaller parties, or at least to obtain minimal representation of minority parties.

Usually, these laws and regulations strike some kind of balance between various kinds of rulings:

- The public funding of parties or candidates for office, in proportion either to their previous election results, or a combination of the two criteria.
- The obligation to keep accurate records, with penalties ranging from being disqualified for public funding to being disqualified from standing for election for one year (in France since 1990).
- Limitation of the amounts an individual or a company can donate to a single party or candidate for office (or on a yearly basis). In some countries, such as the United States, this limitation can be circumvented if a politician receives funds through political action committees[12], or if they decline the financial help of the state. The best known examples of the kind have been billionaire Ross Perot in 1992, spending nearly US$40 million only in the last month of the campaign, when he re-entered the race on October 1,[13] some of George W. Bush campaigns, and more recently Barack Obama, when he refused to take federal funding for the actual campaign (not the primaries) in June 2008, when he realized that this would prevent him from being able to spend the huge amount of donations he had already received and he thought he would still be able to collect.[14] Of course, today, the January 21, 2010 Supreme Court decision "*Citizens United v. Federal Election Commission*" will change considerably the balance of the system, since it allows unlimited corporate spending to support "independent" political groups during campaigns.

Although they may provide considerable financial aid to political parties or candidates, most of these regulations nevertheless can cause problems for the campaign treasurer, who is often obliged to keep meticulous records, supposedly to eliminate slush funds.

Of course, one should add to these regulations another kind of state support: regulations giving free access, or access with favorable financial conditions, to the main media, which is the case in most democratic nations, usually under the strict control of an independent Commission, such as the Federal Communication Commission in the United States, the Political Broadcast Committee in the United Kingdom, or the Conseil Supérieur de l'Audiovisuel in France. In the United States, for instance, the Federal regulation allows the candidate either to pay the networks the lowest going rate for advertising spots, or to buy longer slots just by compensating the amount corresponding to the financial loss of the commercials already booked at the same time.

8.4   The staff

At the start of the present chapter we examined the role of two key players in any political communication campaign: the campaign manager and the field co-ordinator. These two individuals are at the node of the two main categories of personnel: the central organization staff and those working in the field, generally covering the entire constituency. They have final responsibility for most of the hiring of personnel and the recruitment of volunteer help.

Nevertheless, the choice of campaign staff is not left entirely to their discretion, nor does it always result in the most desirable team. First, naturally, because of the expense involved: no campaign can afford to hire professionals for each sector of activity connected with it. One must therefore make do with the activists and sympathizers who offer their services. Moreover, the hiring of staff can be just as objective (choosing the most qualified person to fill a specific job) as it can be subjective (special relationships, the obligation to take on people strongly recommended by the politician who wish to "donate" their time, or who have contributed large sums, etc.). But the diversity and complexity of functions frequently demand highly skilled participants.

Three categories of competent personnel can be identified:

- the central campaign organization staff usually group together the most qualified members of the team, whether involved in communication activities, or simply routine tasks;
- outside advertising and public relations agencies or consultants are hired because of the irreplaceable technical and professional assistance they provide;
- decentralized or field personnel, who are much less specialized, form the "foot soldiers" of the campaign forces.

8.4.1   The central campaign organization staff

We will describe their roles independently of how they interact. Those who are specifically involved in political communication tasks, strictly speaking, will receive particular attention. We will then outline the roles of persons assigned to what we group under the term "routine tasks."

8.4.1.1   *Staff directly involved in communication activities*

8.4.1.1.1 Personnel in charge of information research and news monitoring (newswatch) during the campaign   The campaign organization needs number of workers in two main fields to keep the communication process performing at an optimal level:

- far from limiting itself to the data analyzed before the campaign and which was used in designing it, the campaign organization must ensure the constant flow of useful information, to provide a basis on which to effect necessary adjustments to original plans;
- it must pay particular attention to recent developments in the opponents' campaigns, which requires constant information gathering.

CONTINUAL ANALYSIS OF PUBLIC OPINION AND CURRENT EVENTS   This first type of research is identical to the daily activities of news agencies. One or more members of the team must be constantly on the look-out for all varieties of news items: from the sudden announcement of a natural disaster to the publication of new survey results, any information can influence or help the campaign. Furthermore, certain staff members will be specifically assigned to pure documentary research, again exactly as in a news agency, so as to be able to put the information gathered to the most effective use possible.

In recent years, the Internet and particularly blogging and other Web 2.0 practices have considerably complicated news monitoring. Whereas before, one or two staff members were able to put up a summary of the main items on the agenda of the news media every morning, a national campaign in a Western European country or in North America may now require a team of a dozen or more staffers sitting in front of their computers day and night in order to try and keep up with the constant flow of information and rumors circulating on the Net. We have already mentioned how fast campaigning politicians like Sarah Palin in the United States in 2008 or Ségolène Royal in France in 2007 have been victims of demeaning quickly-shot videoclips viewed by millions on *YouTube* and the like.[15]

The campaign organization must sometimes commission its own opinion polls to trace the progress of the campaign in the public eye. This is like the testing of the campaign elements mentioned in Chapter 2. If the results are positive, they must be circulated as soon as possible, not only publicly, to enforce the campaign, but also within the campaign organization itself to improve staff morale.

GATHERING INFORMATION ON OPPONENTS' CAMPAIGNS   Though this type of information is rather closely related to the previous sort, particular attention must be given to each opponent's movements. Tours, speeches and so forth must be observed and analyzed in order to come up with a response to them at the appropriate moment.

There is a temptation to use questionable, if not unlawful, means to obtain information more quickly on an opponent's campaign development. A fairly large team can even be assigned to watch their campaigns, a task not unlike conventional espionage.

This temptation is naturally even stronger when the campaign organization is backing an incumbent, in which case it enjoys certain added advantages. The most notorious example is, of course, the Watergate scandal. The name of this Washington building complex became world-famous overnight in 1973, when campaign staff were caught trespassing on the premises of Democratic party headquarters. The affair finally ended with the resignation of President Nixon.

Though information research and news monitoring is a thankless task, the staff in charge are key ringers of the campaign: they can maintain it on course while avoiding the many unexpected events which might happen. Here damage control is the word.

8.4.1.1.2 The personnel in charge of ensuring campaign continuity for the candidate   During the campaign, the candidate himself has little time to guarantee proper correlation of his speeches and activities, particularly to his many public appearances throughout the constituency. The people in charge of producing any sort of campaign copy must work in close collaboration with campaign organization speechwriters, so that perfect harmony is ensured with the latest campaign developments, whether they are expected or not. Those organizing the candidate's diary also have a part to play here.

PERSONNEL IN CHARGE OF PRODUCING CAMPAIGN COPY   Though not involved in making decisions on major campaign objectives, one or several members of the central organization are placed specifically in charge of producing three types of copy related to the campaign:

- the candidate's platform, and leaflets and brochures reiterating it;
- the candidate's speeches;
- the campaign press releases, in conjunction with the press attaché (we will return to this topic in the next sub-section).

Campaign copywriting does not raise major problems of content: it generally involves writing up decisions made at the planning stage, particularly modeling the different campaign issues according to the audience and the media used to convey the message. On the other hand, writing the dozens, if not the hundreds, of speeches that a candidate may deliver in the course of a campaign is a much more complex matter, since he cannot constantly repeat the same thing, nor can he physically find the time to write them himself.[16] One or more staff members must be assigned to this recurring task.

Long anonymous as ghost writers, speechwriters came out into the open when in 1960 a member of John Kennedy's campaign staff, Theodore (Ted) Sorensen, openly devoted himself to the task, becoming the candidate's, then president's (and later President Johnson's), official speechwriter. In some cases, speechwriters have even sometimes been able to overstep their usual role and slip personal input into a candidate's campaign. Nicolas Sarkozy's speechwriter for his winning French presidential run in 2007, Henri Guaino, is thus notorious for putting into the candidate's mouth his own views in some of the most memorable speeches of the campaign.[17]

In most cases, these speeches clearly do not vary a great deal. Usually, the speechwriter(s) would even prepare some so-called "stock speeches" which can be combined according to the geographical and political specifics of the meetings where the candidate will speak. After a while, once the main issues have been engaged, new speeches merely rehash earlier ones, but must be adapted to changes of location or audience, and incorporate political (or other) events that occur between public appearances. This could appear tedious and repetitive, particularly for the candidate, but such repetition, inevitable in any case, also serves a purpose. The fact that the media pick up on relatively similar elements of the speeches, instead of wearying the audience, reinforces, on the contrary, the agenda-setting effect. The process is identical to the principle of commercial advertising: radio and TV commercials are finally effective even if the audience has stopped paying attention to them. Similarly, constant radio exposure turns a new pop tune into a hit even if it may have sounded indifferent upon its first airing. In the case of an election campaign, we must also emphasize that, in any event, the audience is not the same from one meeting to another; a lack of originality in a new speech is thus less important than the fact that the candidate is personally delivering it in front of a new audience.

The lack of new ideas to be found in most speeches is thus less important than the repetition of main campaign themes, the contact with new audiences, and, finally, cohesion with the campaign's global political marketing plan. Furthermore, it is very difficult for speechwriters to incorporate new issues, since their insertion must be consistent with all the candidate's previous speeches, or with every issue mentioned in his program and his earlier campaign texts, to avoid contradictions that campaign reporters, or political opponents, will be quick to take up. Thus, only speeches intended for special audiences (businessmen and women, industry workers, etc.) differ substantially from other ones.

THE RESEARCH RELATIVE TO THE CANDIDATE'S PERSONAL APPEARANCES IN THE FIELD   Collecting information of this nature depends on close collaboration with the members of the field organization. Each of the candidate's appearances on the campaign trail must be carefully planned in the light of information gathering:

- general data on the place he is to appear, on the main opinion relays the politician might meet;
- knowledge of particular local problems;

- research of any evidence of the candidate's previous local appearance or what might have made an impression (special tax decisions, grants to local businesses, speeches and promises made during a previous visit, and so on).

Though their job can seem obscure and unrewarding, those in charge of research and news watching have a very important role: it is they who ensure that the campaign is kept on track, all the while adapting to local circumstances as closely as possible – searching the local media archives being paramount here.

8.4.1.1.3 Organizing relations with the media   The relationship with the media, particularly with the non-partisan press, is of utmost importance for the communication campaign: the quality of the relationship determines how well the press will participate as a more or less voluntary opinion relay for political communication. To this end, if humanly and financially possible, two types of aid are helpful, and are sometimes performed by a single person (or, less frequently, by a press agency):

- a public relations officer;
- a press attaché.

To co-ordinate information and advertising concerning the candidate, these two main players in media relations often work in collaboration with a "media manager." He is in charge of coordinating their actions with the overall media scheme; an "advertising manager" represents the final side of this department. The structure of the entire press and media department is illustrated in Figure 8.4:

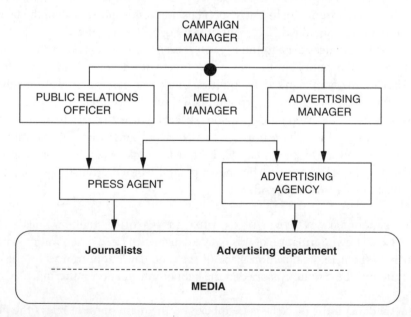

Figure 8.4   The media department of a campaign organization.

Note that the center dot here indicates coordination and dialogue, rather than a hierarchical relationship.

THE PUBLIC RELATIONS OFFICER   The public relations officer stands at the intersection between planning and execution. His particular task is to stage "events" for journalistic coverage, either because they are convinced that these "events" are significant, or simply because competition with the other media obliges them to do so. These "events" are often only staged for the press only, particularly for the television cameras. We will thus refer to them as "pseudo-events." During presidential election campaigns in the United States, it has become common for public relations officers to organize a "pseudo-event" on a daily basis, to fuel the media attention and ensure the constant presence of their candidate.

To this end, the public relations officer must demonstrate a strong imagination and good connections. He should be able to conjure up an inauguration or a visit to an historic or currently popular site, or put on a conference or a competition at a moment's notice. He must also know how to secure the endorsement of respected scholars, popular singers or movie stars. He should also be able to collect an impressive array of signatures for a petition supporting the candidate, and so on. In short, he must as able to devise highly visible "pseudo-events" as well as being able to stage and organize them.[18]

THE PRESS ATTACHÉ   The press attaché works in close liaison with the public relations officer, but is more involved with execution. He must also be very well connected, but in a different way. The press attaché must have a thorough knowledge of the journalistic milieu, and preferably cultivate special relationships with leading reporters, namely those whose presence at and coverage of an event will encourage their fellow journalists to follow suit, in other words, those who act as opinion leaders for their colleagues. This requires great familiarity with the print and audiovisual media and now the Internet, since key reporters can vary depending on the subject matter of a given communication.

The ways in which the press attaché deals with reporters require a certain degree of finesse. They are built on a superficial camaraderie, which often implies an exchange of favors: if a journalist accepts, and sometimes with no illusion as to its real public interest, a press attaché's invitation to cover an "event," he may do so, for example, out of gratitude for or in anticipation of a prompt, exclusive interview with the candidate which the press attaché has arranged or will arrange. Thanks to the press attaché, reporters may similarly be handed a "scoop" or a "leak" that in fact was quite calculated: it is information that the candidate wishes to circulate without it appearing to come directly from him.

When campaign finances permit, the press attaché can promote better relationships with the press when the candidate is on the road, by offering reporters traveling expenses and hotel accommodation, and providing, computers, telex and fax services to campaign reporters. The press attaché for an incumbent politician thereby has an important advantage, since he may be able to offer selected journalists benefits connected to the office (for example, seats on Air Force One, the US presidential plane).

Because of his direct link with the journalists, the press attaché is the only person who knows just how to control the flow of information in the proper proportions.

He might adjust it according to his different interlocutors, so that they choose to relay the message the candidate wishes to convey, rather than highlighting the wrong elements. Intuition and know-how are thus the highly valued practical skills required of a press agent, enabling them to use journalists as opinion relays for the political message without the latter ever feeling manipulated. These points explain why proper campaign cohesion generally calls for a near monopoly of press contacts on the part of the press attaché. Apart from the candidate himself, a very limited number of campaign organization staff will be allowed to speak directly with members of the press, and the fewer the better.

The press attaché's job is also to write press releases, or copy that sums up the crux of the political message; newspapers can then publish this copy as such if they choose to, just as they do with press agency dispatches. This requires good journalistic skills or the help of a professional journalist. Along the same lines, the press attaché also must assemble press kits concerning the candidate. These contain basic facts to supply reporters with a working basis at the start of the campaign (the candidate's biography, position on major issues, quotes or extracts from previous speeches, press clippings, etc.).

From a mere logistical standpoint, the role of the press attaché is also to ensure that the communication arrives on the reporters' desk at the opportune moment. Depending whether they work for a television network, or a daily, weekly or monthly paper, journalists have to meet very different deadlines, sometimes well before the day the publication reaches the newsstand (over a month in advance for most monthly periodicals).[19] On the other hand, some items must sometimes be given to daily newspapers and radio and television journalists ahead of time, along with an "embargo" forbidding them to publish the information before a specific day and time. In this way the premature revelation of a campaign stage can be avoided, while ensuring timely coverage of the event by the entire media.

In some cases, the press attaché will have the delicate task of denying certain journalists access to the information they seek, or to the candidate himself. Sometimes, the reason for this is to avoid relaying the communication through a medium not suited to the campaign media plan (no television appearance before a given date, to reinforce the impact of the first one, for instance). In other cases, it can be a matter of ignoring a particular medium altogether due to its negative connotations, or for any other reason, to avoid downgrading the candidate's image. Finally, such a refusal can be simply to alleviate the candidate's schedule and level of fatigue. In any case, the press attaché must have an unfailing sense of diplomacy: a reporter denied access at a particular moment might very well be solicited the next morning, so he must not be alienated, even when his requests cannot be honored. Here again, compromise and negotiation are the rule.

THE MEDIA MANAGER (AND THE ADVERTISING MANAGER) When the size of the campaign organization permits, a media manager is hired. This person is in charge of choosing precisely which media should be used to convey the campaign message, whereas the press attaché is more concerned with carrying out such decisions.

The media manager works in close conjunction with the campaign manager and the departments or agencies in charge of buying advertising space. This latter department might be headed by an advertising manager, so as to duplicate the free publicity given to the communication by reporters with paid advertising. Communication with the press is thus carefully and thoroughly planned. Long interviews accorded to leading newspapers and magazines by the candidate can be scheduled systematically from the start of the campaign, and so on. In that case, only routine, short press releases are handled solely by the press attaché. A good media manager, working with an advertising manager, can save the campaign treasury a considerable amount of money, by securing free press coverage in the place of costly paid advertisements.

8.4.1.2 *Personnel assigned to routine tasks*

An election campaign involves many kinds of activities, including some very tedious tasks which, though essential, seem apparently quite remote from communication-related activities. For instance, a candidate's road schedule, with one meeting after another, often closely resembles that of a war minister's tour of the front during a conflict. A considerable part of the campaign organization staff is thus engaged in what we refer to here as routine tasks, in contrast to the activities directly connected to communication itself.

These routine tasks can be divided into two areas:

- administrative;
- operational.

8.4.1.2.1 Campaign administration   As surprising as it may seem for an organization with such a short life-span, the campaign organization must have at its disposal a department devoted to its own administration, which consists of:

- a finance department;
- a legal department;
- a human resources department, when the organization is large enough (otherwise it is usually part of the legal department).

THE FINANCE DEPARTMENT   Earlier in this chapter we explained the particularities of a campaign organization's financial activities. They make the campaign treasurer one of the most important members of the campaign staff: he must be able both to find new sources of income and shrewdly manage campaign spending. According to what can be afforded, he must be surrounded by people who can quickly solve the many cost/benefit equations that arise as soon as the use of one instrument for political communication is decided on rather than another. At the same time, the treasurer should have enough influence over the campaign manager and the candidate himself to curb spending if necessary. It should be kept in mind that in most cases the finance department has to prepare various budget forecasts, making "high" and "low" hypotheses, depending on the actual campaign receipts compared with anticipated ones. Because of this dual role, it might be clearer to split the finance department into two divisions:

- one division supervises and controls fundraising activities and the financial management of the funds collected, by negotiating the modalities of the "smoothing" mentioned in the beginning of this chapter;
- the other division controls expenditure.

If possible, fundraising activities should be accompanied by communication with the donors, thus creating a sense of satisfaction that might induce them to renew their support to the politician, now or during a future campaign. It is essential, for example, to send out letters of thanks for all contributions – rather than e-mails, much less gratifying, unless the donation was made on the Web; the computer-generated mail techniques used in direct marketing are an excellent means of personalizing this type of communication.

The finance department should also encourage internal communication within the entire campaign organization team from top to bottom. Everyone, from volunteers to campaign organizers, tends to forget that, in many instances, its activity can also generate income. There is no reason, for example, that a good volunteer, while canvassing, should be content with merely informing citizens orally or with leaflets listing candidate's main positions on certain issues. If a contact seems promising, the canvasser might also solicit financial support. Similarly, at the highest level of the campaign organization, any major communication initiative should be considered from the angle of the income it might bring.

THE LEGAL DEPARTMENT   One or more lawyers are consulted, and are often employed, to advise the campaign organization on two necessary issues:

- the legal aspect of communication operations;
- legislation regulating organizations.

We have mentioned that highly complex legislation often regulates the means of communication which a candidate can employ in a campaign. The legal department must ensure that the campaign respects the main provisions of election laws, which requires thorough knowledge of the many legal texts and precedents applicable to any problems that may arise: from the possible ineligibility of the candidate to the boundaries a slogan cannot overstep to avoid a libel suit. The legal department must also complete the formalities required to file a politician's candidacy in accordance with the law and accomplish all other required formalities within the statutory delays.

Lawyers are also responsible for knowing and accomplishing all formalities necessary to undertake publicity actions, when they exist: in many countries it is mandatory to obtain a permit for a public demonstration, campaign literature needs to be legally registered, and so on. Sometimes, unexpected legal problems may also arise in all kinds of domain, and demand an urgent response.[20]

On a more mundane level, the campaign organization's legal department must also be able to draw up employment contracts for the paid staff of the campaign organization and handle any legal paperwork connected to its material activities, from the rental of office space to the signing of a computer system maintenance contract. When the campaign organization does not have a specific personnel department, the person in charge of the legal department also oversees questions of operational personnel management.

THE PERSONNEL DEPARTMENT   When, on the other hand, the campaign organization is fairly large (as in the case of a national campaign), it may have a personnel department just like any other enterprise.

Its first task then, obviously, is to hire the majority of the staff, with the exception of those individuals handpicked by the campaign management.

The personnel department works in liaison with the other departments to establish which positions the organization will need to fill, according to the objective of the campaign and the media it intends to use. This department may also help to arrange other job placements for certain team members once the campaign is finished.

8.4.1.2.2 Day-to-day campaign operations   It is not our intention to enumerate all the routine tasks for which, as in any private company, the campaign organization must also hire staff. We will mention them briefly, with special emphasis on two categories of functions particular to the candidate's campaign activities, travel schedule and personal safety.

THE CANDIDATE'S "ROAD CREW"   As soon as a communication campaign is involved in the candidate's travel schedule, a special team must be put together to ensure:

- coordination between the politician and the central campaign organization while the latter is on the road;
- an appropriate local welcome for the candidate.

Coordination with the central organization   While on the campaign trail, the candidate requires a large crew. We already know that he must be accompanied by a fair number of assistants in order to be able to respond immediately to any sudden change of political circumstances, such as a unexpected shift in an opponent's campaign. Therefore he always travels with a speechwriter, possibly with one or two private secretaries, and so on.

This requires the best possible co-ordination with the campaign personnel at the central headquarters. A non-stop link to headquarters also serves the important purpose of keeping the candidate in contact with a trustworthy source of information.

When on the road, far from the nerve centers of the campaign, the candidate only has direct access to unreliable information, starting with what can be found in the print, television, or on the Internet. The central campaign organization staff are usually in a much better position to obtain quickly more reliable and accurate information on the many sorts of eventualities.

Excellent co-ordination with the central organization is also vital to the cohesion of the communication campaign itself. The answers given or positions adopted by the candidate on any given event cannot afford to be at variance with press releases that the central organization may issue, thereby causing embarrassment. Generally speaking, the candidate's personal agenda must be widely distributed among the main officials of the campaign organization for ease of location and consultation; also so that they can, if deemed necessary, suggest new communication actions, or modifications to the initial communication plan due to last-minute contingencies. Today, Intranet and electronic agenda-sharing for a limited high ranking campaign staff are extremely useful.

Local preparation for events   In scheduling a candidate's campaign trail, one of the most important figures is the "scout": the person sent ahead to the location the candidate plans to visit. The scout oversees all the logistics of the trip: itinerary, adaptation to the local context, accommodations, local assistance, photo opportunities for the press (and personalities who should be photographed with the candidate for greater credibility among readers of the local newspapers), and so on. During the visit itself, the scout will be constantly posted at the candidate's side to update him in on the repercussions of his previous trip, and to ensure that everything goes according to plan.

In the case of large-scale campaigns, several members of the staff take turns as scouts: one goes ahead to the candidate's next destination, while another accompanies him to the currently scheduled venue, and so on.

SECURITY PERSONNEL   Hiring security personnel for the campaign is a necessity once the candidate has a certain standing. This implies not only ensuring the candidate's physical safety as well as that of other campaign staff but also guarding the campaign material and premises (headquarters in particular).

Physical protection of the candidate and main campaign materials   A minimum number of bodyguards must be hired to prevent any potential danger right from the start of the campaign, especially if the candidate is well known or if for specific reasons (political bent, threats, and so on) caution is warranted. Most often, the people in charge of the candidate's personal security work in close conjunction with the road crew, and those who organize major rallies, meetings and other events.

At first, these precautions might appear somewhat extravagant. Nevertheless, they are not superfluous. Not so long ago, members of certain North American campaigning teams hired henchmen to undermine an opponent's political meetings any way they could, including throwing stink bombs or live mice into the audience![21] So, for other examples of damage to a campaign, we needn't go as far back as the way the Nazis sabotaged meetings of their political adversaries, or to evoke other extreme actions, we can look at recent events such as the assassination of Rajiv Gandhi in the midst of the 1991 Indian Congress election campaign, or that of Robert Kennedy, in 1968, during the US presidential primaries.

Protection of campaign materials   The security of crucial campaign materials must be treated with as much seriousness as that given to their design. Just as manufacturers protect their patents, the campaign manager and main planners cannot reveal certain scheduled developments of the campaign.

The requirement of secrecy surrounding the future of the campaign is all the more imperative given the speed of radio, television, and the Internet. In countries where political commercials are legal, a costly, long prepared communication campaign using expensive spots can be completely invalidated if an opponent, having learned of their contents, hurriedly designs negatives spots to mine the terrain the campaign was to occupy. So, just as the campaign team must keep up with changes in the opponents' campaigns (while staying strictly within the law), it owes it to itself to protect its own campaign. To this end, aside from physical protection of the premises and campaign materials, the security department in certain cases can carry out preliminary personal inquiries into some of the campaign participants, especially before appointing them.

Protecting the campaign's computerized tools and its electronic communications has also become a foremost necessity:

- the whole internal communication network, Intranet, including communication with decentralized field operatives, must be secure;
- external electronic communications, including the various Internet web sites, blogs and so on have to be securely protected in order to avoid pirate actions by hackers, from "plain" freezing of the web sites to "piracy," with fake data replacing the genuine ones, and so on.[22]

OTHER OPERATIONAL PERSONNEL   A good campaign manager knows that he should hire a minimum number of professionals for operational posts, even if it means putting them on a salary, whereas, paradoxically, the volunteers, who came to help might not be. There is no point, for instance, for the campaign manager himself to have a volunteer as his private secretary if the latter cannot transcribe fast dictation or is not familiar with computers and software packages.

Secretaries, telephone operators, and even, if necessary and if the funds permit, cooks and chauffeurs, in other words a considerable number of miscellaneous operational staff can be found in the central campaign organization as in any private company, but with the drawbacks previously described due to the short duration of the contract.

The people working with the central campaign organization, whether paid or not, are thus numerous and accomplish quite diverse tasks. Nevertheless, as mentioned earlier, part of the difficulty of motivating them over some length of time lies in their being entrusted with more routine tasks than they would have expected. A good part of the most "noble" activity of the political communication campaign, that is, the planning element, partly escapes the central campaign organization because it is the province of outside professional communication consultants, although they might consider the candidate as a mere customer, not a charismatic leader.

8.4.2   Outside consultants

It is difficult for a candidate to conduct his campaign without calling on consultants outside his own party or close circle of advisors. Today, the complexity of political marketing makes their contribution necessary at some stage. So the candidate, or his communication specialists, generally enlist the aid of qualified consultants at some point or another during the campaign, either to advise them on the content of the communication itself, or simply to benefit from their technical expertise. While the alleged first "true" political campaign consultant, Edward Bernays, the well-known author of *Propaganda*, was a singular exception at the time, advising politicians and presidents from Coolidge to Eisenhower, today, the increased professionalization of political communication we have frequently pointed out needs these communication experts more than ever and thousands of them are in business.[23]

Because of their rather technical nature, many areas of political communication are almost never dealt with internally within the campaign organization, and are tacitly left to the competence of outside consultants:

- opinion polls and surveys;[24]
- designing the posters for billboards;
- planning and conducting direct mail campaigns;
- designing and producing videos and television spots;
- conceiving and airing the Internet campaign with its ever-changing new "Web 2.0" uses, and so on.

But their undeniable utility does not mean that their services come without certain major drawbacks.

8.4.2.1   *The utility of outside consultants*
The contribution of outside communication advisors can be tremendous. Just like external auditors called in by any type of commercial firm, outside campaign consultants are often in a better position to diagnose problems and offer solutions not

previously envisaged by those caught up in the campaign organization hierarchy. Furthermore, their assistance is not limited to mere expertise at the service of the political communication campaign, however considerable it is. Their contribution carries a symbolic dimension, which reinforces the technical aspect of their aid to the campaign.

8.4.2.1.1 The expertise of outside consultants   The communication campaign usually has much to gain in precision and quality thanks to the participation of these highly qualified professionals:

- Their expertise is nearly always far superior to that of the campaign organization members, since they are long-term marketing practitioners. They know all the ins and outs: how to differentiate between the qualities of the various media, what particular angles to take in a negotiation, the most recent innovations in the area of communication and advertising, and so on.
- Unlike the campaign organization, their mode of operating is tried and true. Since their existence is not bound by a short life-cycle, they have accumulated a greater body of experience. Because they have often been hired for previous political communication campaigns, they can even, in a certain way, compensate for the memory of past campaigns that campaign organizations generally lack.
- They are obviously experienced users of the media by which the campaign is to be conveyed, and know which media will best serve the various actions scheduled in the media plan.
- Finally, from a financial point of view, because they have regular connections with the individual media, given that the candidate is one customer out of many, they can usually negotiate lower advertising rates, if only because they have bought advertising space in bulk beforehand.

Therefore, a modern political communication campaign cannot afford to do without special consultants, especially when it has (inevitably) decided to use paid advertising, whatever the medium.

8.4.2.1.2 The symbolic value of the participation by outside consultants   The need to employ specialized outside consultants in political marketing has become practically mandatory in terms of internal communication within the political sphere. The fact that a candidate is supported by a well-known consultant or consulting agency, even if it is paid, lends additional credibility to the campaign and can improve and reassure staff morale: it gives them the feeling that things are well in hand. In recent years, Bill Clinton's 1992 campaign manager James Carville and George W. Bush's assistant, Karl Rove, have achieved such high symbolic status, like Jacques Séguéla for François Mitterrand in France, or Alastair Campbell for Tony Blair in the United Kingdom. This is also why many political communication advisors have become an integral part of the campaign process in many democratic countries.

This symbolic value seems to have gained importance even in relatively recent democracies whose political leaders often hire western consultants to assist them. Probably to set themselves apart from former totalitarian regimes, and to avoid being accused of using American specialists, many of these politicians now also hire well-known Western European, particularly French, communication consultants: from the former Argentine President Raúl Alfonsín, to the leaders of some formerly communist Eastern European countries. On the contrary, in other cases, well-known American consultants have been sent abroad more or less officially to help "friendly" foreign leaders, particularly in Israel, where James Carville was sent to help Ehud Barak in 1999 – while Benjamin Netanyahu was helped by Arthur Finkelstein, the "magic hand" of the US Republicans at the time.[25]

8.4.2.2   *The drawbacks of working with outside consultants*
8.4.2.2.1 Problems caused by consultants as "outsiders"   The very fact that consultants are outside the candidate's circle of usual supporters and regular collaborators is always likely to cause problems of adaptation. First, consultants might have trouble becoming quickly familiarized with the personality or the political proposals of those they are hired to help. This may simply be for lack of a genuine effort, though this is less frequent now than in the past. On the other hand, consultants do not always involve themselves in the campaign process as fully as might be hoped, just like mercenaries in the distant past were sometimes less reliable than the king's own vassals. Though the outsider factor can at first be an advantage, since it allows greater leeway with regard to possible inertia within the campaign organization, it can nevertheless become a negative facet. In attempts to counterbalance this potential drawback, candidates often prefer, if at all possible, to work with the same communication agency from one campaign to the next.

Naturally, communication consultants have learn to overcome this problem; like all external auditors, they know that their sudden arrival in an organization always carries the risk of being regarded as negative by its members. But, in political marketing, this disadvantage is probably heightened, and so, then, proportionally, are the difficulties of counteracting it, by the fact that they are hired and paid to do a job that the members of the campaign organization are mostly doing on a voluntary basis, because the latter believe in the ideas, or at least in the charisma of the candidate they support. This difference of state of mind considerably increases the psychological tensions between the two categories.

8.4.2.2.2 Dangers of the consultants' short term vision   The other drawback caused by the consultant's external situation is their short-term reasoning. They are hired temporarily for a partnership limited in time, with a view to achieving the objectives for which they are paid. Therefore, they do not feel responsible, so to speak, for the long-term consequences of their advice. Some of the apparently professional solutions they propose can thus have ambiguous consequences for the candidate:

beneficial in the short term to his immediate purpose, they can prove destructive in the long term, from a strategic point of view.

This danger is all the greater because outside communication agencies are sometimes hired for an election campaign at the last minute. The consequential obligation for them to provide immediate results can then be quite detrimental. Candidates therefore prefer to limit the risk by enlisting the aid of the same outside consultants from one campaign to the other. The latter thus become "second circle" advisors, so to speak.

Two other drawbacks, though minor, should nevertheless be pointed out. First, because their employment has become so widespread, some outside consultants end up with the impression that their candidate-client would not be elected without their help and tend to develop a condescending attitude toward their interlocutors, particularly with the regular activists and sympathizers of the political parties. This can be a demobilizing factor for the latter.

Secondly, independent or marginal candidates often have trouble finding consultants who will agree to work for them, whether for budgetary reasons, or even on ideological grounds, which puts them at a distinct disadvantage. Many agencies sometimes fear that some of their regular non-political customers might be frightened away if they participated in the campaign of a "non-conformist" politician.

This phenomenon can even become en embarrassment, as was the case in the United States in the 1950s. Most Madison Avenue advertising agencies then preferred to work for the Republicans, because the people supporting Eisenhower were also significant industrialists and capitalists who were these agencies' regular customers. At the beginning of the 1955–56 campaign, since no "established" agency wanted to work with the Democrats, Madison Avenue executives for a time seriously considered assigning one or two employees from each of the main agencies to form a special team to help the Democrats, and in this way avoid putting any particular one of them in jeopardy![26]

However useful outside consultants may be, these constraints must always be taken into account, with the risks of dysfunction they induce. We shall now examine some of the ambivalent characteristics the field staff throughout the constituency presents for the campaign organization.

8.4.3   The field organization

In today's age of mass media, the value of local networks is often underestimated. The use of marketing for modern political communication has made the participation of activists and sympathizers seem less and less necessary to the campaign: they are sometimes even regarded as "dead weight," with obsolete habits.

Activism has diminished in consequence, whereas activists and sympathizers still have an important role to play in modern political communication. Even if the field personnel might not always be a campaign's ideal relay, they are still highly useful, and modern political marketing often underutilizes its activists and volunteers.

8.4.3.1   Field personnel and their role in political communication

8.4.3.1.1 The two categories of local personnel: activists and volunteers   There are two categories of campaign field personnel:

- the activists are usually long-standing party members and constitute its back-bone on the local scale. In most countries, they are not paid for their activities, and pay their party an annual subscription;
- the volunteers are generally occasional campaign participants. who decide to involve themselves personally in a particular campaign, usually due to the effect of the candidate's charisma.

It follows that candidates who enjoy the endorsement of an established political party have a considerable advantage: they have a network of activists at their finger-tips. On the contrary, independent candidates, or those endorsed by a party with a low level of local representation, are handicapped by the fact that they will find no activists to help them, but only budding sympathizers.

There is another handicap linked to the absence of a ready network of activists. For their contribution to the campaign to be operational, volunteers need to be trained by activists. As simple as the tasks required of them might appear, these often require experience that the activists generally take upon themselves to transmit (even if the relationship between the two categories can at times be tense, due to the difference in the nature and length of their commitment). In the absence of a well-established activist network, the training and supervision of volunteers thus becomes much more difficult.

8.4.3.1.2 Value of field personnel   The campaign organization has a vital need for local activists for two main reasons:

- planning the candidate's local appearances and accompanying him;
- acting as a local relay for the communication campaign.

Welcoming the traveling politician   We have already emphasized the com-plexity of scheduling the candidate's activities on the road. Even if scouts are sent by the central organization in the field before his visit, a minimum of qualified activists are necessary to provide a local support network. It is essential that they cover the entire constituency; the support of temporary volunteers is not usually as effective, especially in countries where sympathizer training is poorly organized.

Then, we must also remember that, even in today's world, the candidate, while on the campaign trail, still requires the help of a relatively large number of activists and volun-teers in the field. A single reason can explain this: without activists and volunteers, paid operational personnel would have to be hired, which would use a considerable amount of the campaign's finances. Though the common image of activists and volunteers is one of individuals sticking posters in unauthorized spots to publicize meetings, for instance, it should not be forgotten that they perform many other functions. For example, planning and holding a public rally requires a large organizational staff to act as stewards, not only for security reasons but also to ensure the event's success. People may even be hired to applaud, as is the custom on theatrical first nights.

LOCAL RELAY FOR THE CAMPAIGN   The local relaying of the communication campaign requires the same knowledge of the field. All activities should be adapted to the local context, from the simple distribution of leaflets and literature to knowing which local media might publish petitions or carry advertising with the greatest effectiveness and visibility. Of course, especially when it comes to advertising, outside consultants hired by the candidate on the national level generally have local contacts, who ordinarily relay their commercial action. But to adapt the whole campaign to local political contingencies, local relays for the campaign organization are also a valuable, if not a preferred, means.

Furthermore, the role of activists and volunteers by themselves in the communication process, as opinion relays for the other local inhabitants, remains considerable. It alone would justify an effort to keep this capacity operational. They are an irreplaceable medium for approaching the non-politically committed acquaintances and other local residents. Political marketing professionals are obviously unable to fulfill this function. As for the technical training of activists and volunteers for direct mail campaigns or telephone or door-to-door canvassing, this should simply be planned for at the outset of the campaign.

In any case, the increasing use of direct marketing in recent years has brought to the forefront the need for a wide and well-distributed network of activists and volunteers throughout the constituency (or the country). Again, employing activists and sympathizers allows for the reduction of campaign costs, even if the lack of technical training among non-professionals sometimes creates problems.

In many countries then, the main problem for communication campaigns is rather the absence of technical training among local activists and volunteers. Today, in countries like the United States, parties have few permanent activists, and even fewer local paid officials,[27] but they traditionally swell with a large number of regular volunteers who come back to help out for each election, every two or four years. If the primaries campaign was not so long, volunteers would probably not have enough time to learn the ropes, and the two major American parties would not easily gain sufficient stamina without the aid of a true structure of permanent activists instead.

8.4.3.2   *Underutilization of field personnel in current political marketing*
The ongoing value of activists and volunteers for political communication suggests that the local personnel is probably underemployed in today's political marketing, due to a dual evolution, for which it is partly responsible:

- the expansion of the mass media has provoked a considerable drop in activism;
- the professionalism required by modern means of communication has appeared beyond the reach of activists and volunteers.

8.4.3.2.1 Expansion of the mass media and drop in activism

PARTY LOSS OF INFLUENCE OVER THE RISE OF POLITICIANS   The drop in activism can first be explained by the declining influence of political parties themselves in most western countries: weak parties mean fewer activists.

The increasing importance of mass media, particularly audiovisual mass media, in modern political communication has naturedly provoked a decline in the importance of parties. A candidate once had to claim the support of a national political party if he wanted to reach high office, on the national level at least. Without television, travel throughout his constituency was mandatory, and hence the need for the help and active support, of many activists and volunteers at each campaign halt.

Today, thanks to the electronic mass media, a politician can instantly make apparently direct contact with citizens by appearing on television, and can get a response through public opinion polls and the Internet. A politician who comes across well in front of the TV cameras no longer needs the help of a a political party to him connect with the ordinary voter, even if this link is rather somewhat weak.

In the United States today, for example, personalities of all kinds solicit nomination from one of the two main parties only at the last minute, when it can no longer be denied them. Before turning to one party or the other, industrialists or media stars first make their breakthrough thanks to their media popularity, however established. The primaries system favors this process by allowing relatively independent candidates from the party machinery to declare themselves as sympathizers, to campaign, to outshine candidates better supported by the party organization, and thus impose themselves on it during the final Convention. George McGovern's candidacy in 1972, for instance, followed this rule: the leaders of the Democratic party were well aware that he had little chance of winning against incumbent president Nixon, then at his peak, but they were unable to block his ascent because of his enormous popularity with the media.[28] The 1992 presidential elections even showed that a candidate, Ross Perot, could run independently from the two main parties thanks to his fortune and his sweeping television campaign, and even make an excellent impression, another, clearer sign of this phenomenon.

The process is not confined to the more developed and media-minded countries of the world. The same has happened recently in many other countries holding democratic elections. In 1990, for instance, a Peruvian of Japanese descent, Alberto Fujimori, unexpectedly won the presidency of Peru, without any prior political affiliation, although his main opponent, the Nobel Prize-winning author Mário Vargas Llosa, was supported by a consensus among most of the established political parties. The same process also occurred when trade unionist Lech Walesa defeated incumbent prime minister Mazowiecki, though the latter was the favorite of the Polish political class.

Of course, this loss of influence of organized parties in modern political life has had as a logical consequence the quantitative drop in activist recruitment, but the loss has also been a qualitative one, though the Internet might have been responsible for some changes in that drop, as Obama's 2008 campaign success with local activists has demonstrated.

WEAKENING BONDS AMONG PARTY MEMBERS   The rise of mass media in modern political communication also has led to a weakening of the internal links that make up party structure. Today's politician is often little concerned with devoting time to specifically internal communication among his own party's activists. Since the mass media enables him to reach them while at the same time addressing an external audience, he considers a single communication to be satisfactory and much more economical in terms of time invested.

This results in an undeniable loss of quality in the contribution of the field personnel. Activists and volunteers are aware that the politician no longer addresses them specifically as a group. They thus feel ignored, and this has a powerfully detrimental effect on their morale, and consequently their potential activities. Herein lies another explanation of the current drop in activism. Since there little satisfaction to be gained from participation in a political party, why bother to join if this satisfaction is no different from that of a sympathizer? This also confirms the importance of the campaign manager's role. For example, if the campaign manager is very efficient, he can provide cover while the candidate is campaigning.

8.4.3.2.2 Professionalization of volunteer tasks   It might seem contradictory to speak of the professionalization of volunteer tasks, since the first notion theoretically excludes the second. Yet when it comes to most traditional volunteer activities in a campaign, candidates or political parties would rather hire paid professionals than explain to long-standing local activists or new volunteers why their methods are obsolete and why they should undergo training.

This happens in most democratic countries. For example, one of the volunteers' main tasks in the past, organizing a rally and guaranteeing its security, is no longer their responsibility. Crowd control, or handling intruders, is not an improvised skill. Rather than take risks, or to go through training, major political parties are more likely to hire specialized security personnel, notably for large rallies during a national campaign. And since the rally agenda is never left to the local campaign organization, but is determined by the prior campaign plan, there is not much ileft for volunteers to do.

In countries like the United States, the extraordinary rise of televised campaign advertising has also had a similar effect. The politician feels more secure, since professionals to whom this work has been entrusted have direct control over the production of such programs.

In most cases then, volunteers in many democratic countries are always at least minimally trained. They are given detailed handbooks, sent e-mails, or, at best, videos, which explain how to organize a political meeting, how to go about canvassing, and so on. For instance, the central field co-ordinator for Barack Obama's 2008 campaign, Temo Figueroa, had training camps all around the United States, and most of his 1,500 field delegates attended sessions.[29] "How to's" are also frequently downloadable on the campaign web sites.

In any case, when a strong activist base exists, too much of its activity is often regarded with suspicion by the candidates: they fear problems in harmonizing the national campaign with its local variations, and in keeping it coherent. They also fear the difficulty of having to keep the entire team in line with the increasingly strict rules and regulations which have been introduced as a result of the numerous scandals that have broken out in so many democratic countries, themselves stemming in part from the huge financial outlay modern political communication requires.

On the whole, internal communication within political parties needs to be reconsidered in many democratic countries. Ideally, good political marketing should plan a true internal communication campaign within the campaign organization, more particularly intended for its field personnel, the local activists and volunteers. Conducted in parallel with the political campaign intended for the voters, this internal campaign should be allocated considerable funds, and not regarded as secondary. A reinforcement of the whole political communication process would result. Of course the ease of use and the low cost of the Internet should now be put to use to that effect.

Finally, we must note here that the rise of the Internet has somehow halted the decrease of volunteers we have analyzed earlier in this chapter, at least in the United States. One of the strengths of Barack Obama's 2008 presidential run was to foresee that new evolution and to understand how it would be helpful not to underestimate the need for local relays and to find many of them through the Internet. In a few indecisive states, Obama's campaign is even said to have contacted some key Democratic field personal nearly a year before the primaries to secure local help well ahead of time, to the dismay of Hillary Clinton's staff who arrived too to recruit them.

Even if they sometimes appear to be obsolescent in relation to the modern means of political marketing, political parties do retain their usefulness in assisting the political communication campaigns of the candidates they support. In the event they manage to maintain a decentralized network of activists, with geographically well-distributed offices. This structure is probably irreplaceable, since it is impossible for a single campaign to achieve such a result within a few months.

But it must be understood that the modernization of political communication has caused a considerable increase in the professionalism required of the campaign personnel. What can unskilled volunteers do when one has to juggle with election legislation, fundraising problems, cash-flow and income smoothing, along with many other specialized routine tasks, among them the physical protection of the candidates?

Organizing a modern political communication campaign has almost become a business like any other, and in some respects more difficult to run than ordinary companies, due to the problems inherent to its ephemeral nature, which further increases the need for help from all sorts of professional personnel. Even volunteers should now try to reach a minimal level of skills, a task which political marketing would do well to take as seriously as any other.

Notes

1   Throughout this book, we distinguish between regular party activists, who are permanent party members supporting the party and/or its politicians, and "volunteers" who are supporters rather than members, often brought into action on a particular campaign because they are drawn to a particular politician's personality or due to specific circumstances.

2   The rapid failure of Howard Dean during the 2004 US presidential election is such an example: after the initial success of his pre-campaign thanks to the Internet, his campaigning team was not really prepared to actually run – hence, for example, his financial trouble at the beginning of the primaries, because he had been advised not to spend all the funds raised as soon as collected, way before the start of the race!

3   These two points explain why campaign staffers are very rarely dismissed, even if their work is unsatisfactory, or if they turn out to be ill suited to the job; instead they are often sidelined or assigned a a less challenging task, while a person better suited for the job at hand is taken on. Laying off personnel would weaken the morale of the team, and prove rather pointless anyway, since the inadequate staffer is most probably an unpaid volunteer, or, at the worst, is on the payroll for a relatively short time (the exception being the United States, where radical decisions of this kind must sometimes be taken by the campaign organization, because the primaries are drawn out over a long period of time).

4   A good example of the bond and trust between the campaign manager and the presidential candidate is given by Chris Hegedus' and Arthur Pennebaker's documentary, *The War Room*, shot in Bill Clinton's campaign headquarters in Little Rock, Arkansas in 1992.

5   It was, for instance, one of the main hurdles Barack Obama had to dismantle for the fight against McCain, when he had to seek the help of former Hillary Clinton sympathizers after winning the 2008 primaries, in spite of the fact that she took so long to concede defeat, thus making the switch even harder for her supporters.

6   Here again, this is clearly shown by the aforementioned film *The War Room*; many episodes of the final year of *The West Wing*, the TV series on the US presidency and presidential campaigns which benefited from the help of genuine political communication advisors, also expose the campaign manager (Josh) as giving orders and advice hour by hour from the campaign headquarters of a candidate always on the move around the country, while hardly leaving the premises himself.

7   The successive campaigns of the two French Socialist candidates for the presidency in 2002 and 2007, Lionel Jospin and then Ségolène Royal, were hindered by such mistakes; in the former example, the speechwriters did not get on with the campaign management and had decided to remain at Socialist Party headquarters, while the campaign headquarters were in another Paris neighborhood; as for Ségolène Royal, she deliberately separated herself and her senior staff from the permanent Socialist Party members who were theoretically also campaigning for her; in both cases, this led to disastrous internal miscommunications, contributing to her defeat.

8   In Kayden 1978.

9   From the Commission web site http://www.fec.gov/ (last accessed December 2, 2010).

10   These are just a few "fringe" contributions normally tolerated in most countries, and not those that border on illegality: for instance, a campaign supplier willingly "forgets" to invoice a job and declares it in the year-end report as an "unrecoverable unpaid bills" rather than claiming direct donations for a politician; or a "generous" business patron

who negotiates a rock-bottom rate for advertising spots in favor of the campaign, with the understanding that other spots, commissioned for his own company, will be paid top dollar, sometimes at the expense of the shareholders.

11　See Tuman 2008.

12　Changing legislation explains the rapid rise in the number of Political Action Committees, from 500 in 1974, to more than 4,000 registered by the Federal Election Commission in 1986, and so on.

13　Ross Perot allegedly spent a total of US$58.7 million, all but US$1.3 million from his own pocket (*International Herald Tribune*, October 30, 1992).

14　Federal funding would have limited him to spending US$84 million, eight times less than what he ended up spending.

15　Politicians holding office are also now more and more being victims of the same phenomenon: caught unaware by any passer-by's smart phones, they see their most insignificant words or attitudes sometimes misinterpreted by nearly immediate exposure on the Web – forcing them to hire specialists to maintain Internet Watch cells, as did French President Nicolas Sarkozy a few months after being elected.

16　In 1960, John Kennedy is said to have delivered 64 speeches in the last week of his presidential campaign, while both Jimmy Carter and Gerald Ford allegedly delivered a speech on average every six hours for the 1976 campaign, etc. (see Trent and Friedenberg 2004),

17　On the contrary, personal dilemmas sometimes occur when the speechwriter does not agree with what he is asked to write, a phenomenon superbly rendered in a 1991 Italian movie, *Il Portaborse*, by Daniele Luchetti, directly inspired by local politics.

18　Pseudo-events must be carefully conceived, since their superficiality might backfire on their conceivers. Shortness of stature can thus hinder politicians in unexpected ways, such as when Michael Dukakis was shown driving a tank during the 1988 US presidential campaign, and looked too small in the huge vehicle. During the 2007 French presidential campaign, Nicolas Sarkozy was seen astride a small pony usually ridden by children, since an advisor had wanted to avoid an embarrassment similar to Dukakis and the tank. As Sarkozy was somewhat short, he might have looked too small astride a full-sized horse.

19　This allows the paper to obtain cheaper rates from the printer, as the latter can schedule more effectively the use of his machines.

20　For instance, from whom should authorization be requested to use a popular song during a meeting, and to whom are authors' royalties to be paid, etc.?

21　See for instance Michel Le Seac'h, 1981, on the henchmen hired by Richard Nixon's team.

22　Even more difficult is avoiding the counter effect of misleading spam e-mails, so-called "phishing" e-mails, pretending to raise funds for the campaign, etc.

23　See for instance Holtz-Bacha et al. 2007; Steger, Kelly and Wrighton 2006, etc.

24　At least for designing them, and usually for conducting most of the field interviews; members of the campaign organization usually only define the survey objectives, and later are involved in interpreting the results, with the help of the agencies hired for the job.

25　In Serge Halimi 1999. After his management of Bill Clinton's successful 1992 campaign, James Carville went on to be one of the most highly-demanded political consultants in the world, with equally prestigious clients.

26　One agency finally committed itself to the Democrats, and the "pooling" system was not implemented.

27 The notorious former party bosses, who, at the beginning of the twentieth century, used to "organize" immigrant voting in exchange for finding them work and shelter, as seen in the recent Tom Cruise movie *Far and Away*, are now almost an extinct breed.

28 This mechanism can also work against politicians whose media popularity is at an all-time low and no longer guarantees protection. The party can then afford to dismiss them without the fear of voter retaliation, as happened with Margaret Thatcher.

29 Their nickname was "camp Obama" – see http://www.huffingtonpost.com/zack-exley/obama-field-organizers-pl_b_61918.html (last accessed December 2, 2010).

9

The particularities of local campaigns

A politician's usual sphere of action is a local one: town halls, local and regional councils, parliamentary representation. The careers of many do not go much farther, while national elections, naturally, are hunting grounds reserved for certain prominent leaders.

When a politician effects a local communication, he can have two objectives: get elected for office, or, having been elected, maintain contact with his fellow citizens. We will not deal with the latter case, closely connected to the communication of the local administration itself. This chapter will be devoted only to political communication during local election campaigns.

Most of the components of modern political marketing we have discussed previously still apply to communication campaigns. We will not review them. But two aspects are particular to local campaigns:

- problems of coexistence with national campaigns, which often take place simultaneously;
- the emphasis of certain communication means, due to their suitability given the limited geographical scale of the campaign.

9.1   The coexistence of local and national campaigns

Candidates for local office have to conciliate two seemingly contradictory requirements, which complicate their communication campaign:

Campaign Communication and Political Marketing, First Edition. Philippe J. Maarek.
© 2011 Philippe J. Maarek. Published 2011 by Blackwell Publishing Ltd.

- whatever their personal opinion, they have to strive for the best possible synergy with the national campaigns conducted by the party to which they are affiliated;
- they nevertheless have to maintain a minimal local dimension

9.1.1 Introducing a national dimension in local campaigns

Today, in most cases, local election campaigns are conducted on two levels:

- on the one hand, a unified campaign on a national scale is carried out by the main political parties, often with significant consequences on the local level;
- on the other hand, each candidate running for local office undertakes a political campaign tailored to his constituency, which might cause co-ordination problems with the national campaign.

9.1.1.1 *Increasing preeminence of the national dimension in local elections*

Throughout the twentieth century, it has become increasingly difficult for candidates to conduct their campaign on the local level without taking into account the national campaigns conducted by the parties to which they are affiliated (the nature of interplay varying according to the country, the electoral system, and the way candidates are designated). The local "barons" who once ruled unchallenged over their constituency have been replaced in many instances by candidates unknown to the local population, selected by their party or movement and who therefore owe their office to their affiliation with that party and the success of its national campaign.

This phenomenon is the simply the result of the rise of mass media in most democratic countries. Not only has it transformed the nature of communication itself by breaking up the traditional relay networks for opinions, mass media have partially dissolved the relationship between serving politicians and their fellow citizens. Now that even the more isolated citizens own a television set, the relationship of proximity between the voter and the local candidate for office has been completely altered.

Today, ordinary citizens are more familiar, or rather, think they are more familiar, with national political leaders than the local candidate asking for their vote: they see national leaders on their television screen every day, on the evening news or the political talk shows, while local candidates do not appear in much more than occasional regional newscasts, at best. In the United States, in 2004, researchers found that while 55% of the televised newscasts of the 11 largest cities dedicated at least one item to coverage of the presidential campaign, only 8% had done so for one of the current parallel local campaigns (while elections for Congress and state governorships were being fought, and a lot of local issues, were at stake in most states).[1] It is no surprise, then, that citizens often do not even care about the candidate's name on the ballot paper, but care only about the political party to which the local candidate belongs or the national leader.

Consequently, the politician campaigning in his constituency has a considerable problem of positioning. His constituents no longer want to know what his personal stand is on one political issue or another, but his opinions on the issues discussed by the leaders of his party. Since the media expose citizens directly to a party's national communication campaign, they are much more aware of it.

The local campaign can only disregard the national one in two instances:

- when the candidate is a strong, charismatic personality with significant roots in the constituency (being an incumbent is no longer sufficient);
- when the constituency is so isolated that external considerations are not influential, which is generally the case for municipal elections in the smallest towns or villages.

In the other instances, local campaigns are now much more complex than one might think at first. Although their local nature should exclude any consideration external to the constituency where the election is held, they are much more subtle. A delicate balance between the two campaigns has to be sought, and the problem of coherence between the local and national campaigns must be solved.

Candidates for local office can thus no longer afford to campaign without liaising with the national campaign conducted by their party, and by its national leaders. Quite often, one or several members of the local campaign team are even specifically assigned to the task of co-ordination.

9.1.1.2   Co-ordinating the two kinds of campaigns

When successful, co-ordination between local and national campaigns can generate positive results. It is not only a matter of preventing local candidates affiliated to the major parties from making blunders in the eyes of their voters, because of discrepancies between the local campaigns and the national one. The goal is to achieve the best possible synergy between the two campaigns. In this case, it is even possible to seek a dual synergy: both concrete and symbolic.

9.1.1.2.1 Concrete synergy   If local politicians agree to harbor their campaigns within their party's general guidelines, they can benefit from considerable concrete support, which saves on both expenses and resources. Obviously, the national party starts by helping in formally selecting the local politician as its local representative and by facilitating contact between the candidate and campaign staff. This task is now quite easy: clicking on a map of the constituency on the party web site immediately provides the necessary information.

Party assistance can also place at the candidate's disposal:

- "regular" party activists and volunteers, because of their previous campaigning experience;
- the party's established local offices;
- existing funds or fundraising circuits;
- lists of sympathetic voters in the constituency;
- election material common to the national and local campaigns put out by the national party organization (leaflets or posters on which the name of the local candidate simply has to be added, and so on); here, the Internet has considerably facilitated the process by being quicker and virtually cost-free;
- the advice and logistic support of the party's central campaign organization, etc.

Today, considerable co-ordination efforts are generally planned by the party's campaign teams on the national level. They provide for variations of certain elements of the political communication campaign throughout the local constituencies, with minor adaptations for each case. In many countries, major parties organize "summer workshops" so as to unify to the greatest possible extent the campaigning methods of the local politicians and their most dedicated activists.

In the best possible situations, they even plan co-ordination of the local campaigns on a regional level, to harmonize better with the party's national campaign. This has happened for instance in the United States: since 1976, each state branch of the Republican Party has the services of an "organization manager" sent by the federal structure, and 15 "regional political managers" co-ordinating their actions in close conjunction with a special cell of the central campaign organization.

Naturally, concrete synergy presents some disadvantages, since it partially diminishes the autonomy of the local candidates in the light of their commitment into their party's common communication mold. They have to maintain a harmony between their own and the national campaign, since in the opposite case, they could not benefit from their party's aid. It becomes absurd to develop truly independent campaign issues, as they incur additional expenses. In such circumstances, it is no longer possible to use national campaign material and there is the risk of losing financial help if the differences become too marked. The gain obtained thanks to concrete synergy is then often counterbalanced by the loss of the candidate's autonomy with regard to their party's national campaign organization, or even its national leaders.

9.1.1.2.2 Symbolic synergy Similarly, considerable symbolic synergy can be established once the candidate running for local office appears to be in harmony with the issues adopted by his party, if its image is positive in the eyes of the voters, of course.

Due to the importance of audiovisual mass media, this symbolic synergy creates, in voters' eyes, a tacit link between the local campaign and that conducted on a national scale by the leaders of the candidate's party: clearly exposing this connection allows the candidate to accumulate two symbolic advantages connected to the preeminence of audiovisual media in contemporary society.

Therefore, local politicians more and more frequently ask their most charismatic party leaders to come and publicly support them within their constituencies (usually on the occasion of a more important meeting than the "routine" ones) in order to:

- benefit from a kind of anointing as in medieval history: the endorsement by a senior party figure approving and supporting the candidate is akin to royal anointing (the "superior" authority officially dubs the candidate in the eyes of their voters as their local representative who thus obtain public validation of this symbolic affiliation);
- receive greater media coverage, and possible access to the national media reporting the national leader's visit, a worthwhile advantage since the symbolic association then becomes explicit, even if exposure is minimal.

Furthermore, the support national political leaders give local candidates improves the morale of the local donors, activists and sympathizers and thus adds to local campaign finances.[2]

The negative side of this synergy still resides, here again, in the undeniable loss of autonomy which results. Candidates must adhere closely to the party line of the national campaign if they are to take advantage of this symbolic synergy.

The quest for the best possible synergy, symbolic as well as concrete, between the local and national campaigns is then a perilous adventure for the candidate:

- if he or she attempts to dispense with it, and does not take into account his party's national campaign, voters may be confused;
- if synergy is sought, but not properly achieved, the effectiveness of the candidate's campaign will not be significantly improved;
- on the other hand, if the synergy is too effective, it might diminish his autonomy in too obvious a way for his voters.

The candidate and his consultants must therefore make a clear assessment of the extent to which this loss of autonomy is compatible with their own communication campaign, and incorporate the results of this assessment in their actions.

9.1.2   The need to maintain a local dimension

Even if the national dimension has grown in importance, the local dimension should not be neglected (which would be paradoxical, to say the least). The candidate cannot limit himself to a quest at any cost for synergy between the local and national campaigns. Such excess can appear blatant to voters and may anger them: they might feel that the local candidate's actions are simply dictated by decisions made at the national level. This phenomenon has occurred throughout the world, and quite a few attempts to transplant a candidate from the central party organization into a local political context have failed notoriously, due to the ignorance of the transplanted candidate of the local dimension of the elections, irrespective of the candidate's and the national consequences it might have. Even in two-party systems with an advantageous election system, an election for a parliamentary seat, for instance, is in some ways a local election. The candidate must, therefore, take into account the particular features of the constituency in which he is campaigning; furthermore, he has at his disposal some well-suited analytical tools.

9.1.2.1 Precinct analysis: taking into account the particularities of the constituency in relation to the national context of the election

Especially when conducted by a transplanted candidate, local campaigns should first be based on detailed field analysis. It is impossible to campaign in Florida or Nice and neglect the large retired population, or in Detroit, Turin, or Wolfsburg, without considering the importance of the automotive industry in the local economy and its current problems, and so on. And since a local campaign obviously encompasses fewer people and a smaller area than a national one, qualitative research done by personnel sent into the field should be carried out more systematically than in the national campaigns, where quantitative data is often the only readily available.

Similarly, the campaign must respect the principle of coherence with previous local campaigns, which can prove difficult. It is possible that the latter can have taken different stands from the national party organization on certain issues. This can be due to various factors: local political issues, the personality of the previous candidate endorsed by the same party, and so on. The problem is particularly acute when a "new" politician is campaigning for the first time in a constituency, particularly when he has been parachuted by the national party (meaning that the candidate has been selected for a constituency where he or she has no previous association).

Taking into account the particular features of the constituency might oblige candidates to discard certain materials or even help put at their disposal by their party's national campaign plan, and sometimes even encourage them to distance themselves from it, to adjust better to the local mood. An example of the sort is Arnold Schwarzenegger's victory in the 2003 election for the state governorship of California, which he fought on the Republican ticket, but without any support from fellow politicians, in order to promote himself as a candidate close to the local voters.

Another irreducible particularity of local campaigning is tied to the variance between people who will not vote in local and for national elections. Voter participation can vary considerably according to the type of election, in very distinct ways from one constituency to another. Sometimes, participation is higher in some constituencies for local elections than for national ones, or the opposite can occur. In some constituencies, abstentionists always refuse to vote in all elections, while in others, they may boycott certain types of elections but vote in others. These variations might even differ throughout the different districts of the constituency. The field analysis must therefore pay particular attention to the differences in voter participation for the different categories of elections, and try to determine precisely the reasons for this. Habitual abstentionists can then be targeted according to the type of election the particular campaign is concerned with.

9.1.2.2   Specific analytical tools for local elections

In most instances, the usual survey and analytical methods apply to local elections, with only a slight adjustment for scale.

But the reduced scale of the local constituency also allows candidates access to extremely accurate information on the micro-geographical level. Some analysts go so far as to obtain sales statistics on the highest selling publications on newsstands in the various districts of the constituency. Individual voter registration, notably including political affiliation for closed primaries, also constitutes a prime tool.

More frequently, political marketing organizations use the previous election results from each polling station. This allows them to map voter tendencies in different electoral districts quite precisely and determine which ones the communication should concentrate on. This provides, for each polling station, or district, two very useful indicators for the political marketing process: a mobility index and a proximity index.

9.1.2.2.1 Mobility index of each polling station   The voter mobility index for each polling station clearly indicates in which zones of the constituency the less reliable voters are to be found. It is also possible to differentiate voter mobility by political preference. This index is obtained simply by comparing the votes obtained by the candidate (or the previous candidate) in previous elections, and can be enhanced by making the same kind of comparison for the other main political parties (since mobility might be different for them). The index score is found by calculating the difference between the highest and lowest results, and then by comparing it with the index score of the whole constituency.[3]

The mobility index is a good way to refine campaign targeting by indicating in which polling stations the swing voters are located, whose votes are crucial. It is worth remembering that the mobility index gives a more precise indication than an analysis of the variation of the differences in votes obtained by the candidates.

9.1.2.2.2 The proximity index   It is also possible to construct a "proximity index" of each polling station in relation to the candidate, using the results obtained during previous elections of the same nature. The index score of each polling station is obtained by calculating the ratio between the percentage of the previous votes in favor of the candidate at the polling station and the average percentage he obtained throughout the constituency.[4] In this way, each district can be precisely described according to its proximity to the candidate, an excellent means of refining the targeting.

In order to obtain a proximity index when a candidate is running for office for the first time in a constituency, a comparison with the previous results of the candidates of the same party or who defended similar issues is normally used, the same method as for calculating the mobility index.

Computer technology has led in some cases to a candidate's hiring special analysts of geographical particularities, whose work is known as "electoral geography." The speed of computerized data processing allows them to cross the two scores described above with the standard socio-cultural data of the constituency, to perfect the communication campaign district by district. The targeting might thus be radically

modified, with many subsequent changes for the campaign in some specific neighborhoods, from the communication means to employ to the campaign issues to
develop in particular.

9.2   The preferred communication means of local campaigns

In any case, whether the aim is to develop the best conceivable synergy with the
national campaign or, on the contrary, to adapt the communication to the local particularities as closely as possible, the candidate can use, in his constituency, most of
the political marketing methods discussed in the previous chapters, from the more
classical ones (rallies) to the more modern (phone marketing, the Internet, etc.).

But the campaign's reduction in scale encourages the use of two tools in
particular:

- modes of communication that imply direct and effective contact with the recipients can be used with much greater ease;
- a thorough knowledge of the local media can be used to good advantage.

9.2.1   Direct contact with the local population: personal campaigning

Unlike what happens in elections covering a broader geographical scale, local
campaigns make it perfectly feasible for the candidate to have frequent direct contacts with many of the "ordinary" citizens, in a high proportion to the total number
of potential communication recipients. As a rule, the smaller the constituency is,
the more direct contacts should be privileged, so-called "personal campaigning."
Of course, the candidate will not be able to see all the voters. But maintaining a
large number of direct communication contacts can remedy that: they will transform the candidate's many interlocutors into as many opinion relays who will pass
on their contact among their "customers" in the field of information – who are
often their customers in every respect, in the case of shopkeepers, craftsmen, and
professionals.

Some of the more traditional means of political communication are thus quite
operational in the case of local elections. Three in particular are well-suited to local
communication situations:

- canvassing;
- distributing locally-targeted leaflets and other printed campaign material;
- maintaining regular office hours.

9.2.1.1   Canvassing
In this case, the candidate goes out to make direct contact with as many voters as
possible, by visiting their homes, while touring the constituency.

The Americans were obliged to develop this means of direct contact to its fullest potential due to the primaries system of designating the presidential candidate of each of the two main parties. Primaries create a strange distortion: the presidential candidate must first and above all conduct a successful local communication campaign in several small states, which may not always be the most representative. For instance, if a candidate obtains a good result in the first primary election, in New Hampshire, it immediately ensures him or her favorable media coverage totally disproportionate to the habitual electoral weight of this small state of hardly 1.3 million inhabitants: an American political analyst has calculated than during the 1976 primaries, the designation of the 38 New Hampshire delegates led to 20 "long" items in the evening newscasts of the three main television networks, whereas three months later, the election of the 428 delegates of the state of New York only generated 30 items.[5] Presidential candidates are thus obliged to start a national campaign in a country of more than 300 million inhabitants by seeking favor in small states, just like a Congressional Representative must do. This explains the ongoing importance of canvassing in modern political marketing in North America.

At the local level, the practice of canvassing is highly recommended: it circumvents all mediated means of communication in favor of direct access to the recipient, however brief this contact might be. This gives voters the feeling that the candidate is truly "their" elected official, that he cares about his constituency and about its specific problems and that he is active in the field, whether or not he manages to maintain this presence once elected.

We have mentioned previously that national communication campaigns can also enlist the help of local activists and volunteers to canvass the population, on behalf of the politician.[6] But in the case of local elections, this mode should be excluded: the local politician's refraining from appearing in person could produce negative effects among a large number of his fellow citizens. So the candidate has to be seen canvassing, at least in part of the constituency (depending on its size), with activists supplementing him where and when he cannot physically go.

We must emphasize here that the physical and sociological characteristics of housing conditions in countries like the United States or the United Kingdom are generally conducive to canvassing. Streets consisting of suburban houses in these countries considerably increase the ease and visibility of the campaigning politician, but blocks of flats are a different proposition as the candidate will need to use the elevator to travel between floors and will therefore be less visible. In countries where the urban characteristics are not as favorable, or in other kinds of urban surroundings, candidates will instead mimic actual canvassing by visiting people at work, especially in shops, market stalls, and so on.

To increase its effectiveness, canvassing is often preceded by a preliminary telephone call or residents' survey announcing the politician's forthcoming visit to the neighborhood.

9.2.1.2   The distribution of locally-targeted leaflets and other printed material

Public distribution of printed material, generally pamphlets and leaflets, or copies of party newspapers, is and remains one of the traditional tools of local political communication, especially during peak hours in railway or bus stations, and so on. Today, however, this method is often considered to be a natural complement of some other communication means, rather than as a communication tool in its own right. One does not in fact expect high readership of political flyers, but instead they act as a reminder and reinforcement of a previous communication.

It should be mentioned that a well-organized street distribution of printed material should respect a certain number of guidelines. The first and foremost is obviously the adaptation of the material to the local campaign. For instance, general material sent out by the national campaign which would seem irrelevant to the concerns of local voters should perhaps not be distributed. The final guideline is the obligation to collect all leaflets that may litter the sidewalk when the job is through! Volunteers should have strict instructions to do so.

9.2.1.3   Office hours

Personal availability is more a component of day-to-day communication in local constituencies than a part of the election campaign itself. It allows local citizens to know that they can meet the politician at a precise time and place, at regular intervals (one or two hours a week seems a minimum). This direct contact is obviously an excellent means of communication, since the politician can speak directly to his constituents. But the latter must seek out this contact voluntarily as the politician no longer comes to them. They have to go to meet him, which means that they are generally motivated. For that reason, during a campaign a candidate will probably not meet the undecided voters who might be persuaded to vote for him.

Minimal office hours should nevertheless be held during the campaign, not only for the voters, but at least to give activists and sympathizers a chance to meet the candidate in person, thus reinforcing the morale of the campaign organization. Declaring that the candidate is personally available to the voters of his constituency is a political communication message by itself, assuring proximity. Even if a voter does not visit the candidate during his office hours, he knows he has had the opportunity, which gives him gratification, without the need of an actual encounter with the campaigning politician.

9.2.2   Mediated contact with the local population

Though the campaign at the local level should (and must) preferably rely on direct communication means, it should also use other media as a complement, and not overestimate their importance. With very few exceptions, the local politician, even if he sometimes obtains access to the electronic media, mostly regional ones, will not usually compare favorably with national political leaders who will be seen on the screen shortly after him.

However, adequate knowledge of the particularities of the local media is quite useful for the communication campaign. They should be carefully integrated into a detailed local media plan, according to the issues raised and to the image the candidate is trying to convey.

One of the main tasks of the persons in charge of the analysis of the constituency will then be to study the local media. This study can be much more complex than first envisaged: an apparently insignificant local radio station or a low-circulation neighborhood newspaper sometimes reaches an unexpected area and/or quality of distribution. In some places, they may dominate their competitors for a very specific reason, which merits more careful examination (characteristics of the urban structure, micro-history of a district, etc.).

It should be noted here that the diminishing number of local newspapers and magazines throughout the world, because advertising has moved to the Internet as well as the economic crisis, has currently reduced their contribution to local political campaigns. Of course, the Internet may partly remedy the situation, but not completely.

In countries where regional television channels or regional subsidiaries of national networks exist, this can be correlated with the rise of a new generation of well-established local politicians. Whenever local TV channels have developed popular local or regional newscasts, they have significantly helped many local politicians, whose standing has been elevated by the fact that they appeared on television just like major national political leaders. A TV viewer (if he or she does not watch the news regularly or look at TV schedules) may easily mistake the local newscast for the national one, which in any case will immediately follow with a similar presentation. This has been of considerable help to quite a few well trained local politicians endowed with a certain degree of telegenic presence. They have thus been able to obtain considerable local standing, which even allows them at times to have their say in national issues and debates.

This means, of course, that it is increasingly difficult for politicians of any stature to avoid the electronic media. Everywhere, the rise of local television channels and the diversification of choices offered to the viewers, due to the slow but steady development of cable networks, will soon make their presence felt in local campaigns. This is particularly true in the United States, were television broadcasting has traditionally been built around local channels which are only syndicated with national networks for a few hours during the day: here local news is prevalent, and the campaign needs to be positively visible.

***

Today, local election campaigns are therefore becoming ambiguous and paradoxical on the core issues than before.

First, while needing to respect the local dimension which is theirs by nature, they should preferably be planned in perfect co-ordination with national campaigns directly available to their potential voters, on the national audiovisual media and on the Internet, and conducted by the local politician's party and its national leaders.

As regards form, although they should not rely on excessive use of media, in favor of more traditional direct communication tools, local campaigns are also strengthened by the use of the more modern ones, such as phone marketing or the Internet. This makes the professionalization of local political communication clearly necessary, exactly as at the national level. Today, even politicians campaigning in the smallest constituencies may suddenly be confronted by TV cameras or need to address properly the most modern communication tools when they are put to use by their opponents. And obviously, this increased need to professionalize the tasks is more difficult to satisfy for local campaigns which are hindered by a much smaller and less specialized staff than national campaigns and sometimes less funding (in proportion to the size of the campaign precinct, of course).

In sum, the days when a locally prominent politician could behave as he pleased in his constituency have long since passed. Nowadays the same sort of politician will need to be endowed with an audiovisual charisma and a mastery of modern media which will allow him a freer hand, and might even help him attain nationwide stature.

Notes

1 "Local politics garners less TV coverage," in *USA Today*, February 16, 2005. The study was conducted during the month before E-Day, from October 4 to November 1, 2004, in these 11 cities on 44 local channels and totaling 2,166 hours of newscasts.

2 One drawback is that when the party thinks that a constituency may not be won, no national leader of the party will travel to help, which will obviously be a blow to an already weakening campaign. National party campaign co-ordinators usually try and keep secret the list of such "blacklisted" constituencies that will receive little support.

3 To take one example: if the candidate or a previous candidate affiliated to the same party obtained at a polling station 35%, 33%, and 40% of the votes during the three previous similar elections, the score will be 7. If the constituency score is 14, it means that the station mobility score is $7/14 = \frac{1}{2}$, meaning that the station regroups unwavering voters very committed to their choices. On the contrary, if the score had been more than 1, the result of that polling station could be considered less stable than the constituency and probably more interesting to target.

4 For example, if the candidate obtained 40% of the vote in the whole constituency in the previous election, and 50% at a particular polling station, the proximity score for this polling station for this vote would be be 1.25 (50/40).

5 In Kessel 1988.

6 See Chapter 4.

Conclusion: how to use this book ...

The growing use of political marketing is not only a fashionable trend, a mere gimmick to sell candidates as easily as bars of soap, as some used to sneer. It is just one element in the inevitable evolution of modern society, due in particular to the spread of mass media and the rise of new media, particularly the Internet.

By fragmenting the audience, by breaking with the traditional communication process, by rendering local opinion relays and existing neighborhood communication networks nearly useless or obsolete, the pervasiveness of the electronic mass media has radically transformed modern political communication. The rise of modern political marketing has been a consequence of this, but for two opposing reasons:

- it is based on an intensive and systematic use of these same mass media;
- but its spectacular development is also a result of politicians' attempts to keep their communication "operational," despite this spread of mass media which damages the effectiveness of their former means of communication.

Thus practiced, political marketing has put into question not only political communication properly speaking, but the whole political sphere. This upheaval has been fostered by the quite natural tendency of politicians to employ it without giving much thought to its long term consequences: in the case of an election communication campaign, they are always pressed to find as many effective means as possible, especially when they hope to win the race. This phenomenon has been even clearer recently when astutely led Internet communication campaigns, playing on the new Web 2.0 tools, from blogs to *YouTube*, have allowed an unexpectedly quick breakthrough for some politicians, doing away with the political party apparatus in the United States as well as in many other countries.

Campaign Communication and Political Marketing, First Edition. Philippe J. Maarek.
© 2011 Philippe J. Maarek. Published 2011 by Blackwell Publishing Ltd.

The excessive reliance on political marketing therefore gives one of the best explanations of the frequent drop in voter participation in most western democratic countries, for two reasons: one technical, the other fundamental:

- many traditional means of political communication have been discarded or semi-neglected for they are no longer considered sufficiently cost-effective, although they in turn encouraged increased political participation (local meetings organized by activists, searches for new volunteer support, direct contacts, and so on); on the contrary, "new media" such as the Internet either link only the most politically motivated citizens seeking more information, or find new audiences but without the motivation to increase their political participation to the extent of the classical "human" opinion relays.

- as for the second reason, the natural short-term pragmatism of political marketing, to the detriment of long term political concepts, has overemphasized the role of personalized modern political communication through the mass media, rather than political issues as such, meaning the very substance of politics. We must not forget that the aim of political marketing is obviously not to increase the political participation and civic-mindedness of the voters, but mainly to win an election. Politicians have, even now, have promoted their own private persona as an ingredient of their campaigns to the extent that this personalization is leading to a "peopolisation" or "tabloidization" of campaigns that is very remote from the political ideals of the Founding Fathers.

This short-term vision has weakened coherent independent political discourse, and, furthermore, the political class' capacity for action: the temptation becomes very strong to limit oneself to satisfying voters' demands, as they appear through the lens of public opinion surveys. This is undoubtedly one of the explanations for the current demise of political ideologies in many countries, where words like "communism," "liberalism," or socialism seem to have lost their political substance.

The overly short-term vision of political marketing, consciously accepted by many politicians concerned only with efficiency, has caused them to oversimplify their messages, reducing them to a banal mold, and creating a greater distance between the voter and the elected official. This is a radical departure from the strength and the traditional quality of the link which formerly bound them, when only "classical" political communication tools were employed. Consequently, it has all too often resulted in the paradox of "despecializing" the political communication process due to overspecialization of its methods.[1]

Surveys and other studies have clearly indicated that the outcome of an election is made on the fringe: a relatively small shift in voters is often enough to change the results. This has occurred several times, from the famous 1960 presidential election in the United States, when less than 1% of the votes separated Kennedy and Nixon, to the notorious 2000 and 2004 near-draws painfully gained by George Bush Jr. But this fringe is in most cases composed of the two categories of citizens who do not have strong political opinions, or who hardly express them: undecided voters and abstentionists make the difference when the gap between final candidates is narrow.

But since these two voter categories are by nature the less permeable to politics, commercial marketing specialists have transferred their methods into the political sphere without really giving it much thought. They manage to convince many of their clients that the best way to attract undecided voters or abstentionists is to stop playing politics, so as to win them over using professional methods. They have also asked politicians to increase the personalization of their campaigns in a seductive process that has little to do with traditional political discussion of the issues, with an increasingly disturbing risk of populism, never very far away when personalization is too strong, as Silvio Berlusconi's example in Italy has clearly demonstrated.[2]

Politicians have then been trapped by professional communication consultants, who give them formal and fundamental arguments to encourage them to simplify and to neutralize their communication, to the point of caricature in the following ways:

- formal arguments, because they have been warned that when using imprecise and hard-to-manage media, such as television, it is necessary to use simple language, when not reduced to the extreme;
- fundamental arguments, because they have also been convinced they should neutralize their communication in order to convince non-political voters whom they would not have been able to reach by political persuasion.

The excesses of this unrestrained hold of the instrument over those it is supposed to serve explain how the somewhat mythical entity of "public opinion" that polls and surveys construct every day has come to exercise a true dictatorship.

Of course, a certain degree of simplification of the political message can improve its impact. But the depoliticization thus required by many communication strategies has too often been understood by the politicians as an inducement not to maintain any true substance, in other words, an inducement to merely reel off in parrot fashion the people's common concerns as opinion surveys show them. In some instances, this results paradoxically in bringing to the foreground certain positions formerly considered as extreme, such as xenophobia.

Yet public opinion is only an artificial juxtaposition of particular interests, by compiling the answers of each individual polled, and cannot form the political entity that survey fanatics pretend to impose. Tautologically, reflecting the public's own image back on it, this can only diminish the necessities of collective interest, for which the individual does not feel a direct need.

Nevertheless, we must acknowledge that the page has already been turned. It is impossible to go backwards, when McLuhan's *Global Village* has become a reality. Even in most developing countries, a television set is accessible somewhere to the most destitute, not to mention the media dependence of people in the more advanced countries. The televised "decisive" debate generally held between two main candidates for high political office has for instance become a fixture in the electoral ritual of most democratic countries, even the poorest ones, although their high rating is not always met with an equally high satisfaction level. Even if its penetration is still low on some continents, the Internet is also a tool of this twenty-first-century "globalization" and now allows any fringe political movement or previously unknown politician to be only a click away from the whole world, so to speak. Events in Tunisia and Egypt in 2011 have even demonstrated that the Internet and cell phones may now be a significant tool of political change. This considerably increases the need for politicians to always be able keep up to date properly with changes in modern media. As modern political marketing is inextricably linked to the global evolution of society, particularly to the prevalence of mass media, it has become impossible to really challenge it.

This explains why the frequent imitation by many countries of modern political communication tools initiated in the United States has sometimes misled people to believe that the world is under the influence of an "Americanization" of campaigns. In fact, among other factors we have mentioned, the forerunning development of modern media in the United States, from television to the Internet, the particular electoral system of this country, with the primaries doubling the actual voting, have enabled that country to develop sophisticated political marketing tools and methods more quickly, which are later imitated elsewhere without any other pretense than merely a similar "professionalization" of their local political communication.[3] In fact, professionalization is the key word there, linked to political marketing: professionalization of the means, and professionalization of the actors themselves.[4]

But modern political marketing has probably not yet fully managed to accommodate the use, however excessive, of the instruments put at its disposal by the newly developing media, with the older instruments of political communication, beginning with activist networks and political parties. Their mode of operation needs to be rethought in order to draw the most benefit from the potential synergy between the two spheres. They must find a way to play their part again in the mediation between citizen and politician, which has been put aside by the short circuit provoked by the surge of the mass media first and the Internet later. In any event, politicians have still not yet mastered political marketing methods fully enough to use them to enhance their communication. Paradoxically, the fringe political parties and lobbies have apparently encompassed the new media more quickly and have even sometimes overtaken the more established political parties, as in the European referendums in France and Ireland in 2005 or the referendum on mosques in Switzerland in 2009. Green parties all around the world also clearly benefit from this, and in some countries, like France or Germany, they are now playing on equal terms with older, more "established" parties.

In fact, the use of political marketing is probably not yet systematic enough and adequately understood to make it both sufficiently effective with respect to the voter and more useful to the common cause. Politicians still too often tend to use it only as a last-minute remedy, instead of practicing political marketing throughout their term in office. This would be much more useful for the political actions they undertake, and would allow them the benefit of previous experience, even before the start of the campaign. This would also provide a clear indication to voters that politicians are not only capable of getting elected once every four, five, or seven years. Naturally, we have in mind here true "political" communication, on the core political issues, and not a personal image-building safety net for incumbent politicians wishing to be re-elected. Such systematic implementation would also help compensate the perils of a political communication campaign too closely connected with election deadlines. In spite of its relative technical sophistication, political marketing cannot be a miracle cure, only a stimulant whose effectiveness is variable.

In a way, mastery of modern political communication is probably the least of evils one could wish on the political sphere, to prevent it from one day losing all touch with the representational processes that are at the core of democracy.

Politicians must therefore adapt to the modern practice of political communication and make sure the odds are in their favor by learning its methods even before they are needed, and with as much care, devotion, and keenness as Demosthenes putting pebbles into his mouth.

Notes

1   See Maarek 2004b.
2   See for instance Mazzoleni 2009.
3   The scholarly dispute on whether or not the dissemination of modern political marketing around the world is the result of an "Americanization" of politics or simply of the modernization and professionalization of politicians' communication strategies has mostly come to an end, most abscribing now to the "modernization" point of view (see Blumler and Gurevitch, in W. Lance Bennett and Robert M. Entmann 2001, Lilleker 2006, Holtz-Bacha et al. 2007, Strömbäck 2009, etc.).
4   Some scholars have even built up a professionalization "index," taking into consideration the 11 communication tools to be used in order to qualify a campaign as "professionalized" (see Strömbäck 2009). But this empirical model, which sums up what were the most modern communication methods only a few years ago, is too dependent on temporary variables to be effective. New media, or new uses of media, have in fact already rendered the model obsolete (today, we could, for instance, add to the index compulsory use of Internet social networks, etc.). Also, this kind of model dealing only with communication "techniques" does not take into account the "human factor," so to speak. So plainly looking for the presence of a global political marketing approach, as much as in communication means, as in the campaigning politician's personal behavior, seems a sufficient criterion of professionalization for our purpose.

Appendix 1: Memorandum of Understanding between the Bush and Kerry Campaigns for the 2004 Televised Debates (extract)

Memorandum of understanding

This Memorandum of Understanding constitutes an agreement between Kerry-Edwards, '04, Inc. and Bush-Cheney, 04, Inc. (the "campaigns") regarding the rules that will govern debates in which the campaigns participate in 2004. This agreement shall be binding upon the Bush-Cheney and Kerry-Edwards Campaigns and, provided it agrees to sponsor the debates by executing this agreement on or before September 22, 2004, upon the Commission on Presidential Debates (the "Commission").

(...)

5. Rules Applicable to All Debates

The following rules shall apply to each of the four debates:

(a) Each debate shall last for ninety (90) minutes.
(b) For each debate there shall be no opening statements, but each candidate may make a two (2) minute closing statement.
(c) No props, notes, charts, diagrams, or other writings or other tangible things may be brought into the debate by any candidate. Neither candidate may reference or cite any specific individual sitting in a debate audience at any time during a

Campaign Communication and Political Marketing, First Edition. Philippe J. Maarek.
© 2011 Philippe J. Maarek. Published 2011 by Blackwell Publishing Ltd.

debate. If a candidate references or cites any specific individual(s) in a debate audience, or if a candidate uses a prop, note, or other writing or other tangible thing during a debate, the moderator must interrupt and explain that reference or citation to the specific individual(s) or the use of the prop, note, or other writing or thing violates the debate rules agreed to by that candidate.

(d) Notwithstanding subparagraph 5(c), the candidates may take notes during the debate on the size, color, and type of paper each prefers and using the type of pen or pencil that each prefers. Each candidate must submit to the staff of the Commission prior to the debate all such paper and any pens or pencils with which a candidate may wish to take notes during the debate, and the staff of the Commission will place such paper, pens, and pencils on the podium, table, or other structure to be used by the candidate in that debate.

(e) Neither film footage nor video footage nor any audio excerpts from the debates may be used publicly by either candidate's campaign through any means, including but not limited to, radio, television, internet, or videotapes, whether broadcast or distributed in any other manner.

(f) The candidates may not ask each other direct questions, but may ask rhetorical questions.

(g) The order of questioning and closing statements shall be determined as follows:

   (i) The Commission will conduct a coin toss at least seventy-two (72) hours before the first presidential debate. At that time the winner of the coin toss shall have the option of choosing for the September 30 debate, either (a) whether to take the first or second question, or (b) whether to give the first or second closing statement. At that time, the loser of the coin toss will have the choice of question order or closing statement order not exercised by the winner of the coin toss. For the October 8 debate, the loser of the coin toss shall have the option of choosing either (a) whether to take the first or second question, or (b) whether to give the first or second closing statement, with the winner of the coin toss having the choice of question order or closing statement not exercised by the loser of the coin toss. The Commission shall set a time at least seventy-two (72) hours before the October 8 debate at which the candidates shall make their choices for that debate.

   (ii) For the October 13 debate, the order of questioning and closing statements shall be determined by a separate coin toss in the same manner as the September 30 debate, to take place at least seventy-two (72) hours before the debate.

   (iii) The order of questioning and closing statements for the October 5 vice presidential debate shall be determined by a separate coin toss in the same manner as for the September 30. debate, to take place at least seventy-two (72) hours before the debate.

(h) Each candidate shall determine the manner by which he prefers to be addressed by the moderator and shall communicate this to the Commission, at least forty eight (48) hours before the September 30 debate.

(i)   Whether or not a debate runs beyond the planned ending time, each candidate shall be entitled to make a closing statement in accordance with subparagraph (b). The Commission shall use its best efforts to ensure that the TV networks carry the entire debate even if it runs past the specified ending time.

(j)   No question shall be asked of a candidate by the moderator if less than six (6) minutes remain in the scheduled time of the debate.

(k)   The candidates shall not address each other with proposed pledges. (I) In each debate, the moderator shall:

  (i)   open and close the debate and enforce all time limits. In each instance where a candidate exceeds the permitted time for comment, the moderators shall interrupt and remind both the candidate and the audience of the expiration of the time limit and call upon such candidate to observe the strict time limits which have been agreed upon herein by stating, "I am sorry… [Senator Kerry or President Bush as the case may be].., your time is Up";

  (ii) use his or her best efforts to ensure that the questions are reasonably well balanced in all debates and within the designated subject matter areas of the September 30 and October 13 debates in terms of addressing a wide range of issues of major public interest facing the United States and the world;

  (iii) vary the topics on which he or she questions the candidates and ensure that the topics of the questions are fairly apportioned between the candidates;

  (iv) use best efforts to ensure that the two candidates speak for approximately equal amounts of time during the course of each debate, and;

  (v)   use any reasonable method to ensure that the agreed-upon format is followed by the candidates and the audience.

6.   Additional Rules Applicable to September 30 and October 13 Debates

For the September 30 and October 13 debates, the candidates will appear at podiums. The September 30 and October 13 debates shall be governed by the rules set forth in section 5 and the following additional rules:

(a)   There shall be no audience participation in the September 30 and October 13 debates. After the start of each debate and in the event of and in each instance whereby an audience member(s) attempts to participate in the debate by any means thereafter, the moderator shall instruct the audience to refrain from any participation in the debates as described in section 9(a) (viii) below. The moderator shall direct the first question to the candidate determined by the procedure set forth in subparagraph 5(g). The candidate receiving the question shall be entitled to give an opening response not to exceed two (2) minutes, and thereafter the other candidate shall be permitted to comment on the question and/or the first candidate's answer for up to one and one-half (1~) minutes. Thereafter the moderator in his discretion may extend the discussion for a period of time not to exceed sixty (60) seconds, but the moderator shall begin each such discussion by calling upon the candidate who first received the question. To the extent that the moderator opens extended discussion, the moderator shall use best efforts to ensure that each candidate has a maximum of approximately thirty (30) seconds to comment in the extended discussion period.

(b) The moderator shall then ask a question of the other candidate, and the answer, comments by the other candidate, and extension of discussion by the moderator shall be conducted as set out in paragraph 6(a) above for the first question. Thereafter the moderator shall follow the procedure in paragraph 6(a) above by asking a question of the first candidate and shall continue with questions of the candidates in rotation until the time for closing statements occurs.

(c) During the extended discussion of a question, no candidate may speak for more than thirty (30) seconds.

(d) The moderator shall manage the debate so that the candidates address at least sixteen (16) questions.

(e) At no time during these debates shall either candidate move from their designated area behind their respective podiums.

(...)

9.   Staging

(a) The following rules apply to each of the four debates:

   (i)   All staging arrangements for the debates not specifically addressed in this agreement shall be jointly addressed by representatives of the two campaigns.

   (ii) The Commission will conduct a coin toss at least seventy-two hours before the September 30 debate. At that time, the winner of the coin toss shall have the option of choosing stage position for the September 30 debate. The loser of the coin toss will have first choice of stage position for the October 8 debate. The loser of the coin toss or his representative shall communicate his choice by written facsimile to the Commission and to the other campaign at least seventy-two (72) hours before the October 8 debate. The stage position for the October 13 debate will be determined by a coin toss to take place at least seventy-two (72) hours before the debate. The stage position for the October 5 vice presidential debate will be determined by a separate coin toss to take place at least seventy-two (72) hours before the debate.

(iii) For the September 30, October 8, and October 13 debates, the candidates shall enter the stage upon a verbal cue by the moderator after the program goes on the air, proceed to center stage, shake hands, and proceed directly to their positions behind their podiums or their stools in the case of the October 8 debate. For the October 5 vice presidential debate, the candidates shall be pre-positioned before the program goes on the air, and immediately after the program goes on the air the candidates shall shake hands.

(iv) Except as provided in subparagraph (d) (viii) of this paragraph 9, TV cameras will be locked into place during all debates. They may, however, tilt or rotate as needed.

(v) Except as provided in subparagraph (d) (viii), TV coverage during the question and answer period shall be limited to shots of the candidates or moderator and in no case shall any television shots be taken of any member of the audience (including candidates' family members) from the time the first question is asked until the conclusion of the closing statements. When a candidate is speaking, either in answering a question or making his closing statement, TV coverage will be limited to the candidate speaking. There will be no TV cut-aways to any candidate who is not responding to a question while another candidate is answering a question or to a candidate who is not giving a closing statement while another candidate is doing so.

(vi) The camera located at the rear of the stage shall be used only to take shots of the moderator.

(vii) For each debate each candidate shall have camera mounted, timing lights corresponding to the timing system described in section 9(b) (vi) below positioned in his line of sight. For each debate additional timing lights, corresponding to the timing system described in section 9(b) (vi) below, shall be placed such that they are visible to the debate audiences and television viewers.

(viii) All members of the debate audiences will be instructed by the moderator before the debate goes on the air and by the moderator after the debate goes on the air not to applaud, speak, or otherwise participate in the debate by any means other than by silent observation, except as provided by the agreed upon rules of the October 8 town hall debate. In the event of and in each instance whereby an audience member (s) attempts to participate in a debate by any means, the moderator shall instruct the audience to refrain from any participation. The moderator shall use his or her best efforts to enforce this provision.

(ix) The Commission shall use best efforts to maintain an appropriate temperature according to industry standards for the entire debate.

(x) Each candidate shall be permitted to have a complete, private production and technical briefing and walk-through ("Briefing") at the location of the debate on the day of the debate. The order of the Briefing shall be determined by agreement or, failing candidate agreement, a coin flip. Each candidate will have a maximum of one (I) hour for this Briefing. Production lock-down will not occur for any candidate unless that candidate has had his Briefing. There will be no filming, taping, photography, or recording of any kind (except by that candidate's personal photographer) allowed during the candidates' Briefing. No media will be allowed into the auditorium where the debate will take place during a candidate's Briefing. All persons, including but not limited to the media, other 18 candidates and their representatives, and the employees or other agents of the Commission, other than those necessary to conduct the Briefing, shall vacate the debate site while a candidate has his Briefing. The Commission will provide to each candidate's representatives a written statement and plan which describes the measures to be taken by the Commission to ensure the complete privacy of all Briefings.

(xi) The color and style of the backdrop will be recommended by the Commission and mutually determined by representatives of the campaigns. The Commission shall make its recommendation known to the campaigns at least seventy-two (72) hours before each debate. The backdrops behind each candidate shall be identical.

(xii) The set will be completed and lit no later than 3 p.m. at the debate site on the day before the debate will occur.

(xiii) Each candidate may use his own makeup person, and adequate facilities shall be provided at the debate site for makeup.

(xiv) In addition to Secret Service personnel, the President's military aide, and the President's physician and the Vice President's military aide

(xv) and the Vice President's physician, each candidate will be permitted to have one (I) pre designated staff member in the wings or in the immediate backstage area during the debate at a location to be mutually agreed upon by representatives of the campaigns at each site. All other staff must vacate the wings or immediate backstage areas no later than five (5) minutes before the debate commences. A PL phone line will be provided between each candidate's staff work area and the producer. Other than security personnel not more than two (2) aides will accompany each candidate on the stage before the program begins.

(xvi) Each candidate shall be allowed to have one (I) professional still photographer present on the stage before the debate begins and in the wings during the debate as desired and on the stage immediately upon the conclusion of the debate. No photos shall be taken from the wings by these photographers during the debate. Photos taken by these photographers may be distributed to the press as determined by each candidate.

(…)

(d) In addition to the rules in subparagraph (a), the following rules apply to the October 8 debate:

   (i) The candidates shall be seated on stools before the audience, which shall be seated in approximately a horseshoe arrangement as symmetrically as possible around the candidates. The precise staging arrangement will be determined by the Commission's producer subject to the approval of representatives of both campaigns.

   (ii) The stools shall be identical and have backs and a footrest and shall be approved by the candidates' representatives.

   (iii) Each candidate shall have a place to put a glass of water and paper and pens or pencils for taking notes (in accordance with subparagraph 5(d)) of sufficient height to allow note taking while sitting on the stool, and which shall be designed by the Commission, subject to the approval of representatives of both campaigns.

   (iv) Each candidate may move about in a predesignated area, as proposed by the Commission in consultation with each campaign, and may not leave that area while the debate is underway. The pre-designated areas of the candidates may not overlap.

   (v) Each candidate shall have a choice of either wireless hand held microphone or wireless lapel microphone to allow him to move about as provided for in subparagraph (iv) above and to face different directions while responding to questions from the audience.

   (vi) As soon as possible, the Commission shall submit for joint consultation by the campaigns a diagram for camera placement.

   (vii) At least seven (7) days before the October 8 debate the Commission shall recommend a system of time cues subject to approval by both campaigns, and consistent with the visual and audible cues described in sections 9(b) (vi).

   (viii) Notwithstanding sections 9(a) (iv) and 9(a) (v) a roving camera may be used for shots of an audience member only during the time that audience member is asking a question.

   (ix) Prior to the start of the debate neither the moderator nor any other person shall engage in a "warm up" session with the audience by engaging in a question or answer session or by delivering preliminary remarks.

(...)

Appendix 2: Internet "Final Rules" decided by the Federal Elections Commission, March 27, 2006[1]

Internet Final Rules

The Commission has approved regulations that narrowly expand the definition of "public communication" to include certain types of paid Internet content. This change complies with the district court's determination in *Shays v. FEC* that the Commission could not exclude all Internet communications from its "public communication" definition.

As detailed below and in the accompanying 800-line article, the revised rules also modify the Com- mission's disclaimer requirements, add an exception for uncompensated individual Internet activities, revise the "media exemption" to make clear that it covers qualified online publications and add new language regarding individuals' use of corporate and labor organization computers and other equipment for campaign-related Internet activities.

Background

The Bipartisan Campaign Re- form Act of 2002 (BCRA) requires that state, district and local political party committees and state and local candidates use federal funds to pay for any "public communication" that promotes, attacks, supports or opposes (PASOs) a clearly identified federal candidate. Congress defined "public communication" as a communication by means of any broadcast, cable or satellite communication, newspaper, magazine, outdoor advertising facility, mass mailing, or telephone bank to the general public, or any other form of general public political advertising." 2 USC. §421(22). Based on that definition, the Commission

Campaign Communication and Political Marketing, First Edition. Philippe J. Maarek.
© 2011 Philippe J. Maarek. Published 2011 by Blackwell Publishing Ltd.

expressly excluded all Internet communications from its regulatory definition of the term. In its other BCRA rulemakings, the Commission incorporated the term "public communication" into provisions on generic campaign activity, coordinated communications and disclaimer requirement. By excluding Internet content from the definition of public communication, the Commission effectively exempted most Internet activity from those regulations. The term was also used in the definition of an "agent" of a state or local candidate and in certain allocation rules governing spending by SSFs and non connected committees. 11 CFR 300.2(b) and 106.6(f)

On October 21, 2005, the US District Court for the District of Columbia in Shays rejected the Commission's decision to exclude all Internet communications from the definition of "public communication." 337 F.Supp. 28 (D.D.C. 2004), aff'd, 414 F.3d 76 (D.C. Cir. 2005). The court concluded that some Internet communications do fall with in the scope of "any other form of general public political advertising" and, therefore, required the Com- mission to determine which Internet communications were encompassed by that term.

The Commission issued a Notice of Proposed Rulemaking (NPRM) on March 24, 2005, seeking comment on possible rule changes and held public hearings on June 28 and 29, 2005. For more information, see the May 2005 Record, page 1 and August 2005

Final Rules

Public Communication. While the new regulations continue to exempt most Internet communications, those placed on another person's web site for a fee are now considered "general public political advertising" and, therefore, qualify as "public communications." By contrast, unpaid Internet communications, including blogs, e-mail and a person's web site, are not.

Coordination. Content that a person places on one's own web site is not included in the definition of "public communication," even if it includes republished campaign material. Therefore, their republication of a candidate's campaign materials on their own web site, blog or e-mail does not constitute a "coordinated communication." However, when a person pays a fee to republish campaign materials on another person's web site, the republication would qualify as a "public communication."

Disclaimer Requirements. Under the new rules, political committees must include disclaimers on their web sites and their widely- distributed e-mail, i.e., more than 500 substantially similar messages, regardless of whether the e-mail messages are solicited or unsolicited. Others are not required to include a disclaimer on their own web site or e-mail messages. Persons other than political committees need only include disclaimers on paid Internet advertising that qualifies as a "public communication" and then only if the communication includes certain content such as a message expressly advocating the election or defeat of a clearly identified federal candidate. 11 CFR 110.11.

Uncompensated Individual Internet Activities. Online campaign activity by uncompensated individuals or groups of individuals is exempt from the definitions of contribution and expenditure. 11 CFR 100.94. This exemption applies whether the individual acts independently or in coordination with a candidate, authorized committee or political party committee.

Exempt Internet activities include:

- Sending or forwarding election-related e-mail messages;
- Providing a hyperlink to a campaign or committee's web site;
- Engaging in campaign-related blogging;
- Creating, maintaining or hosting an election-related web site; and
- Paying a nominal fee for a web site or other forms of communication distributed over the Internet.

Media Exemption. In general, a media entity's costs for carrying bona fide news stories, commentary and editorials are not considered "contributions" or "expenditures," unless the media facility is owned or controlled by a federal candidate, political party or federally registered political committee. See 2 U.S.C. §431(9)(B)(i) and 11 CFR 100.73 and 100.132. The new regulations clarify that the exemption, commonly known as the "news story exemption" or the "media exemption," extends to media entities that cover or carry news stories, commentary and editorials on the Internet, including web sites or any other Internet or electronic publication. See also AOs 2005-16, 2004-7 and 2000-13.

The media exemption applies to the same extent to entities with only an online presence as those media outlets that maintain both an offline and an online presence. See the E&J for revised regulations. 11 CFR 100.73 and 100.32.

Corporate and Labor Internet Activities. Commission regulations have long permitted stockholders and employees of a corporation and members of a union to make occasional, isolated or incidental use of the organization's facilities for voluntary political activity. The new regulations clarify that employees may use their work computers at the workplace and elsewhere to engage in political Internet activity, as long as that use does not prevent them from completing their normal work or increase the overhead or operate expenses for the corporation or labor organization. The organization may not condition the availability of its space or computers on their being used for political activity or to support or oppose any candidate or political party. 11 CFR 114.9.1

State and Local Party Activities. If a party committee pays to produce content that would qualify as federal election activity (FEA)—e.g., a video that PASOs a federal candidate—and pays to post that content on another person's web site, then the entire costs of production and publication of the content must be paid for with federal funds. 11 CFR 100.24. The costs of placing content on the party committee's own web site, however, are not restricted to federal funds. See the E&J for revised 11 CFR 100.26.

The final rules were published in the April 12, 2006 Federal Register (71 FR 18589) and will go into effect on May 12, 2006. The final rules are available on the FEC web site at http://www.fec.gov/law/ law_rulemakings.shtml and from the FEC Faxline 202/501-3413. — Carlin E. Bunch

Note

1   *Record*, the *FEC* journal, Vol 32, Number 5, May 2006; see also www.fec.gov

Bibliography

Alexander, H.E. and Bauer, M., 1991, *Financing the 1988 Election*, Westview Press, Boulder, San Francisco, Oxford.

Alger, Dean E., 1989 *The Media and Politics*, Prentice Hall, New Jersey.

Allen, Craig, 1993, *Eisenhower and the Mass Media, Peace, Prosperity and Prime Time TV*, University of North Carolina Press, Chapel Hill and London.

Ansolabehere, S., Behr, Roy, and Iyengar, S.,1993, *The Media Game, American Politics in The Television Age*, Macmillan, New York.

Ansolabehere, Stephen and Iyengar, Shanto, 1994, Of horseshoes and horse races: experimental studies of the impact of poll results on electoral behaviour, *Political Communication*, 11, (4), 413–430.

Ansolabehere, S., Behr, Roy, and Iyengar, S., 1995, *Going Negative: How Political Advertisements Shrink and Polarize the Electorate*. Free Press, New York.

Asher, Herbert, 1992, *Polling and the Public, What Every Citizen Should Know*, Congressional Quarterly Press, Washington, DC.

Balle, Francis, 1990/2005, *Médias et Société*, Montchrestien, Paris, twelfth edition.

Barwise, P. and Ehrenberg, A. 1988 *Television and its Audience*, Sage, London.

Baudrillard, Jean, 1968, *Le système des objets*, Gallimard, Paris.

Baudrillard, Jean, 1970, *La société de consommation*, 1979, Paris.

Baudrillard, Jean, 1972, *Pour une critique de l'économie politique du signe*, Denoël, reprinted by Gallimard, Paris.

Beaudry, Ann and Schaeffer, Bob, 1986, *Winning Local and State Elections, The Guide to Organising Your Campaign*, Macmillan, The Free Press, New York.

Benoit, William L., 2007, *Communication in Political Campaigns*, Peter Lang, Oxford/New York.

Benoît, Jean-Marc, Benoît, Philippe, and Lech, Jean-Marc, 1986, *La Politique à l'affiche, Affiches électorales et publicités politiques 1965–1986*, Editions du May, Paris.

Berelson, Bernard R., Lazarsfeld, Paul F. and Mc Phee, William N.,1954, *Voting, a Study of Opinion Formation in a Presidential Campaign*, University of Chicago Press, Chicago, reprinted in 1986.

Campaign Communication and Political Marketing, First Edition. Philippe J. Maarek.
2011 Philippe J. Maarek. Published 2011 by Blackwell Publishing Ltd.

Berkman, Ronald and Kitch, Laura W., 1986, *Politics in the Media Age*, McGraw-Hill Book Company, New York.

Bernays, Edward, 1928, *Propaganda*, reprinted by IG Publishing, New York, 2005.

Blondiaux, Loïc, 1998, *La fabrique de l'opinion, une histoire sociale des sondages*, Éditions du Seuil, Paris.

Blumler, Jay, 1984, *Communicating to Voters, Television in the First European Parliamentary Elections*, 1984, Sage, Beverly Hills and London.

Blumler, Jay, Cayrol, Roland, et al., 1978, *La télévision fait-elle l'élection?*, Presses de la Fondation nationale des sciences politiques, Paris.

Boller, Paul F. 1984/2004, *Presidential Campaigns, From George Washington to George W. Bush*, Oxford University Press, Oxford.

Bon, Frédéric, 1974, *Les sondages peuvent-ils se tromper?*, Calmann-Lévy, Paris.

Bourdieu, Pierre, 1979, *La distinction, critique sociale du jugement*, Éditions de Minuit, Paris.

Bourdieu, Pierre,1973, L'opinion publique n'existe pas, in *Les Temps Modernes*, 318, 1292–1309.

Brader, Ted, 2006, *Campaigning for Hearts and Minds*, University of Chicago Press, Chicago.

Brock, David, 2004, *The Republican Noise Machine*, Random House, New York.

Bruce, Brendan, 1992, *Images of Power, How the Image Makers Shape Our Leaders*, Kogan Page, London.

Calbris, Geneviève, 2003, *L'Expression gestuelle de la pensée d'un homme politique*, CNRS Editions, Paris.

Carville, Jeames and Begala, Paul, 2002, *Buck Up, Suck Up,… and Come Back When you Foul Up, 12 Winning Secrets from the War Room*, Simon and Schuster, New York.

Champagne, Patrick, 1990, *Faire l'opinion (le nouveau jeu politique)*, Éditions de Minuit, Paris.

Charaudeau, Patrick, 2005, *Le discours politique (les masques du pouvoir)*, Vuibert, Paris.

Cornfield, Michael, 2004, *Politics Moves Online, Campaigning and the Internet*, The Century Foundation Press, New York, 2004.

Crewe, Ivor and Harrop, Martin, 1986, *Political Communications: the General Election Campaign of 1983*, Cambridge University Press, Cambridge.

Crewe, Ivor and Harrop, Martin, 1989, *Political Communications: The General Election Campaign of 1987*, Cambridge University Press, Cambridge.

Crewe, Ivor, Gosschalk, Biran, and Bartle, John, 1998, *Why Labour Won the General Election of 1997*, Frank Cass, London and Portland.

Davis, Richard, *The Web of Politics*, 1999, *The Internet's Impact on the American Political System*, Oxford University Press, New York and Oxford.

Davis, Richard and Owen, Diana, 1998, *New Media and American Politics*, Oxford University Press, New York and Oxford,

Delporte, Christian, 2006, *Images et politique en France au XX° siècle*, Nouveau Monde, Paris.

Denton, Robert E. Jr. (ed.), 2002, *The 2000 Presidential Campaign, A Communication Perspective*, Praeger, New York.

Denton, Robert E. Jr. (ed.), 2009, *The 2008 Presidential Campaign, A Communication Perspective*, Rowman and Littlefield Publishers, New York.

Diamond, E. and Bates, S., 1984, *The Spot, The Rise of Political Advertising on Television*, MIT Press, Cambridge, MA, . new edition 1992.

Druckman, James N., Kifer, Martin J. and Parkin, Michael, 2009, Campaign communications in US congressional elections, *American Political Science Review* 103 (3), 343–366.

Edelman, Murray, 1988, *Constructing the Political Spectacle*, University of Chicago Press, Chicago.

Entman, Robert, 1991, *Democracy Without Citizens: Media and the Decay of American Politics*, Oxford University Press, New York.

Esser, Frank and Pfetsch, Barbara, 2004, *Comparing Political Communication*, Cambridge University Press, Cambridge.

Feldman, Lauren, and Goldwaithe Young, Dannagal, 2008, Late-night comedy as a gateway to traditional news: an analysis of time trends in news attention among late-night comedy viewers during the 2004 presidential primaries, *Political Communication*, 25, (4), 401–442.

Ferdinand, Peter, 2000, *The Internet, Democracy and Democratization*, Frank Cass, London and Portland.

Foot, Kirsten A. and Schneider, Steven M., 2006, *Web Campaigning*, MIT Press, Cambridge, MA.

Franklin, Bob, 2005, *Packaging Politics, Political Communication in Britain's Media Democracy*, Bloomsbury Academic, London, second edition.

Geer, John G., 2006, *In Defense of Negativity, Attack Ads in Presidential Campaigns*, University of Chicago Press, Chicago.

Gerstlé, Jacques, 1996, L'information et la sensibilité des électeurs à la conjoncture, *Revue française de science politique*, 46 (6), 731–752.

Giasson, Thierry, 2006, Les politiciens maîtrisent-ils leur image?, *Communication*, 25, (1), 95–107.

Godwin, R. Kenneth, 1988, *One Billion Dollars of Influence, The Direct Marketing of Politics*, Chatham House Publishers, Chatham, NJ.

Goldenberg, Edie N. and Traugott, Michael W., 1984, *Campaigning for Congress*, Congressional Quarterly Press, Washington, DC.

Golding, P., Murdock, G. and Schlesinger, P., 1986, *Communicating Politics, Mass Communications and the Political Process*, Holmes and Meier, New York.

Gores, Stan, 1988, *Presidential and Campaign Memorabilia*, Wallace-Homestead Book Company, Greensboro, NC.

Graber, Doris A., 1993, *Media Power in Politics*, Congressional Quarterly Press, Washington, DC, third edition.

Graber, Doris, A., 1993, *Mass Media and American Politics*, Congressional Quarterly Press, Washington DC, fourth edition.

Grabe, Maria Elizabeth and Page Bucy, 2009, Erik, *Image Bite Politics, News and the Visual Framing of Elections*, Oxford University Press, Oxford.

Grunberg, Gérard, 1995, Des candidats aux aguets. Le Sondage tue-t-il le vote?, *Le Monde des débats* 28,

Gunlicks, Arthur B., 1993, *Campaign and Party Finance in North America and Western Europe*, Westview Press, Boulder, CO, San Francisco, and Oxford.

Habermas, Jürgen, 2006, Political communication in media society: does democracy still enjoy an epistemic dimension? The impact of normative theory on empirical research, *Communication Theory*, 16 (4), 411–426.

Hadden, Jeffrey K. and Shupe, Anson, 1988, *Televangelism, Power and Politics on God's Frontier*, Henry Holt, New York,

Halimi, Serges, 1999, Faiseurs d'élections made in USA, *Le Monde Diplomatique*, August issue.

Hallin, Daniel C. and Mancini, Paolo, 2004, *Comparing Media Systems*, Cambridge, Cambridge University Press.

Hart, Roderick, P., 1987, *The Sound of Leadership, Presidential Communication in the Modern Age*, University of Chicago Press, Chicago.

Hershey, Marjorie Randin, 1984, *Running for Office (The Political Education of Campaigners)*, Chatham House Publishers, Chatham, NJ.

Holz-Bacha, Christina, Mancini, Paolo, Papathanasopoulos, Stylianos, and Negrine, Ralph, 2007, *The Professionalisation of Political Communication*, 2007, Intellect, Bristol/ Chicago.

Iyengar, Shanto and Kinder, Donald R., 1987, *News that Matters, Television and Public Opinion*, University of Chicago Press, Chicago.

Iyengar, Shanto, 1994, *Is Anyone Responsible? How Television Frames Political Issues*, 1994 University of Chicago Press, Chicago.

Iyengar, Shanto and McGrady, Jennifer A., 2007, *Media Politics, A Citizen's Guide*, W.W. Norton and Co., New York.

Jamieson, Kathleen H., 1993, *Dirty Politics, Deception, Distraction and Democracy*, Oxford University Press, New York and Oxford.

Jamieson, Kathleen H., 1996, *Packaging the Presidency, A History and Criticism of Presidential Campaign Advertising*, Oxford University Press, New York and Oxford.

Jamieson, Kathleen H., Auletta, K., and Patterson, T.E., 1993, *1-800-PRESIDENT*, The Twentieth Century Fund Press, New York.

Johnson, Dennis W., (ed.), 2009, *Campaigning for President 2008*, Routledge, London.

Jones, Jeffrey P., 2005, *Entertaining Politics*, Rowman & Littlefield, Maryland, USA

Jones, Nicholas, 1995, *Soundbites and Spin Doctors, How Politicians Manipulate the Media and Vice Versa*, Cassell, London.

Jones, Nicholas, 1997, *Campaign 1997, How the General Election Was Won and Lost*, Cassell, London.

Kaid, Lynda Lee (ed.), 2004, *Handbook of Political Communication Research*, Lawrence Erlbaum and Associates, Hillsdale, NJ.

Kaid, Lynda Lee and Holtz-Bacha, Christina, 1995, *Political Advertising in Western democracies*, Sage, London.

Kaid, Lynda Lee and Ann Johnston, 2001, *Videostyle in Election Campaigns*, Praeger, New York.

Kaid, Lynda Lee, Nimmo, Dan, and Sanders, Keith. R., 1986, *New Perspectives on Political Advertising*, Illinois University Press, Carbondale, IL.

Kaid, Lynda Lee and Holtz-Bacha (ed.), 2008, *Encyclopedia of Political Communication*, Sage, London, 2 volumes.

Katz, Elihu, 1950, The two-step flow of communication, in B. Berelson and M. Janowitz, *Reader in Public Opinion and Communication*, Glencoe Free Press, Glencoe, IL

Katz, E., 1957, The two-step flow of communication: an up-to-date report on a hypothesis, *The Public Opinion Quarterly*, 21 (1), 61–78/

Katz, E. and Lazarsfeld, P., 1964, *Personal Influence, The Part Played by People in Mass Communications*, Glencoe Free Press, Glencoe, IL.

Kavanagh, Dennis, 1995, *Election Campaigning, The New Marketing of Politics*, Blackwell, Oxford and Cambridge, MA.

Kayden, Xandra, 1978, *Campaign Organization*, DC Heath and Company, Lexington, MA and Toronto.

Kellner, Douglas, 1990, *Television and the Crisis of Democracy*, Westview Press, Boulder, CO, San Francisco, and Oxford.

Kessel, John H., 1988, *Presidential Campaign Politics*, The Dorsey Press, Chicago, IL, third edition.

Klapper, Joseph, 1960, *The Effect of Mass Communication*, New York, Free Press, first published by Glencoe, original edition, 1949.

Kluver, R., Jankowski, N.W., Foot, K.A. and Schneider, S.M., (eds), 2007, *The Internet and National Elections*, Routledge, London.

Kuhn, Raymond, 2007, *Politics and the Media in Britain*, Palgrave Macmillan, Basingstoke.

Lance Bennett W., 1992 *The Governing Crisis, Media, Money and Marketing in American Elections*, St. Martins Press, New York.

Lance Bennett W. and Entman, Robert M., 2001, *Mediated Politics, Communication in the Future of Democracy*, Cambridge University Press, Cambridge.

Lavrakas, Paul J. and Holley, Jack K., 1991, *Polling and Presidential Election Coverage*, Sage London and New York.

Lazarsfeld, P. et al.,1948, *The people's choice (How the Voter Makes Up His Mind in a Presidential Campaign)*, Columbia University Press, New York, reprinted in 1968.

Lazarsfeld, P. et al.,1955, *Voting, a study of opinion formation in a presidential campaign*, Chicago University Press, Chicago.

Lendrevie, J. Lévy, and Lindon, D., 2006, *Mercator, théorie et pratique du marketing*, Dunod/ Masson, Paris, eighth edition.

Levine, Myron A., 1995, *Presidential Campaigns and Elections, Issues and Images in the Media Age*, Peacock Publishers, Itasca, IL.

Le Seac'h, Michel,1981, *L'État marketing*, Alain Moreau, Paris.

Lilleker, Darren G., 2006, *Key Concepts in Political Communication*, Sage, London.

Lilleker, Darren G., Jackson, Nigel A. and Scullion, Richard, 2006, *The Marketing of Political Parties, Political Marketing at the 2005 British General Election*, Manchester University Press, Manchester.

Lunz, Frank I., 1988, *Candidates, Consultants and Campaigns: The Style and Substance of American Electioneering*, Blackwell, New York.

Maarek, Philippe, J., 1986, *Média et Malentendus (cinéma et communication politique)*, mai 1986, Edilig, collection "Médiathèque", Paris.

Maarek, Philippe J., 1989, Le message télévisé a-t-il besoin du discours politique?, *Mots 20*, 23–42.

Maarek, Philippe J., 1995, *Communication and Political Marketing*, J. Libbey, London.

Maarek, Philippe J., 1997, New trends in French political communication: the 1995 presidential elections, *Media, Culture and Society*, 19 (3), 357–368.

Maarek, Philippe J., 2002, Les mauvais choix de communication de Lionel Jospin, *Quaderni*, 48, 5–12.

Maarek, Philippe J., 2003, Political communication and the unexpected outcome of the 2002 French presidential elections, *Journal of Political Marketing*, 2 (2), 5–12

Maarek, Philippe J. (ed.), 2004a, *La communication politique française après le tournant de 2002*, L'Harmattan, Paris.

Maarek, Philippe J., 2004b, Professionalization of political communication: a necessity or a danger?, in Juliana Raupp and Joachim Klewes, *Quo Vadis Public Relations? (Festschriff für Barbara Baerns)*, VS Verlag für Sozialwissenschaften, Wiesbaden.

Maarek, Philippe J., (ed.), 2007a, *La Communication politique et l'Europe: de juin 2004 à mai 2005, chronique d'un «non» annoncé*, L'Harmattan, Paris.

Maarek, Philippe J., 2007b, *Communication et marketing de l'homme politique*, LITEC/ LexisNexis, Paris, third edition.

Maarek, Philippe J., (ed.), 2009, *La Communication des élections présidentielles de 2007, participation ou représentation?*, L'Harmattan, Paris.

Maarek, Philippe J. and Wolfsfeld, Gadi, 2003, *Political Communication in a New Era*, Routledge, London.

Maisel, Louis Sandy, 1986, *From Obscurity to Oblivion, Running in the Congressional Primary*, The University of Tennessee Press, Knoxville, second revised edition.

Margolis, Michael and Resnick, David, 2000, *Politics as Usual, The Cyberspace Re-volution*, Sage, Thousand Oaks CA, London, and New Delhi.

Matalin, Mary and Carville, James, with Knobler, Peter, 1994, *All's Fair, Love, War, and Running for President*, Random House, New York.

Mattelart, Armand, 2004, *Histoire des theories de la communication*, La Découverte, coll. *Repères*, Paris, third edition.

Mazzoleni, Gianpietro and Sfardini, Anna, 2009, *Politica Pop*, Il Mulino, Italy.

McCombs, M.E. and Shaw, D.E., 1972, The agenda setting function of the press, *Public Opinion Quarterly*, 36, 176–187.

McMahon, Tom, 2000, The impact of the internet on Canadian Elections, *Electoral Insight*, Elections Canada, 2 (1). Available at http://www.elections.ca/res/eim/article_search/ article.asp?id=94&lang=e&frmPageSize= (last accessed January 25, 2011).

McNair, Brian, 1995, *An Introduction to Political Communication*, Routledge, London, New York.

Medvic, Stephen K., 2010, *Campaigns and Elections, Players and Processes*, Wadsworth, London.

Melder, Keith, 1992, *Hail to the Candidate, Presidential Campaigns from Banners to Broadcasts*, Smithsonian Institution Press, Washington, DC and London.

Memmi, Dominique, 1986, *L'affiche électorale italienne*, Presses de la FNSP, Paris.

Minow, Newton N. and Lamay, Craig L., 2008, *Inside the Presidential Debates, Their Improbable Past and Promising Future*, University of Chicago Press, Chicago.

Negrine, Ralph, 1989, *Politics and the Mass Media in Britain*, Routledge, London.

Negrine, Ralph, 1996, *The Communication of Politics*, Sage, Thousand Oaks, CA, London, and New Delhi.

Negrine, Ralph and Papathanassopoulos, Stylianos, 1996, The Americanization of political communication, *The Harvard International Journal of Press/Politics*, 1 (2), 45–62.

Nelson, Michaerl (ed.), 2010, *The Elections of 2008*, CQ Press, Washington, DC.

Nesbit, D.D., 1988, *Videostyle in Senate Campaigns*, University of Tennessee Press, Knoxville, TN.

Neuman, Russell W., Just, Marion R., and Crigler, Ann N., 1992, *Common Knowledge,News and The Construction of Political Meaning*, The University of Chicago Press, Chicago.

Newman, Bruce I., 1994, *The Marketing of the President, Political Marketing as Campaign Strategy*, Sage, Sage, Thousand Oaks, CA,London, and New Delhi.

Newman, Bruce I., 1999, *The Mass Marketing of Politics, Democracy in an Age of Manufactured Images*, Sage, Thousand Oaks, CA, London, and New Delhi.

Newman, Bruce I., 1999, *Handbook of Political Marketing*, Sage, Thousand Oaks, CA, London, and New Delhi.

Nimmo, Dan D. and Sanders, Keith R., 1981, *Handbook of Political Communication*, Sage Publications, London and New York.

Nimmo, Dan D. and Swanson, David. L, 1990, *New Directions in Political Communication*, Sage, London and New York.

Noelle-Neumann, Elizabeth, 1993, *The Spiral of Silence: Public Opinion – Our Social Skin*, University of Chicago Press, Chicago.

O'Shaughnessy, N., 1990, *The Phenomenon of Political Marketing*, Macmillan, London.

Paletz, David. L. and Entman, Robert M., 1981, *Media Powers Politics*, The Free Press, New York.

Paletz, David. L., 1999, *The Media in American Politics, Contents and Consequences*, Longman, New York and Harlow.

Patterson, Thomas E., 1980, *The Mass Media Election: How Americans Choose Their President*, Praeger, New York.

Patterson, Thomas E., 2003, *The Vanishing Voter: Public Involvement in An Age of Uncertainty*, Vintage, New York.

Perloff, Richard M., 1998, *Political Communication: Politics, Press and Public in America*, Lawrence Erlbaum, London and Hillsdale, NJ.

Plasser, Fritz, with Plasser, Gunda, 2002, *Global Political Campaigning, A Worldwide Analysis of campaign Professionals and Their Practices*, Praeger, New York.

Prisby, Charles, 2008, Perception of candidate character traits and the presidential vote in 2004, *Political Science and Politics*, XLI (1), 115–122.

Ramirez, Francis, and Rolot, Christian, 1988, *Choisir un président, vérités et mensonges d'une image télévisuelle*, Ramsay, Paris.

Ridout, Travis N. and Rottinghaus, Brandon, 2008, The importance of being early: presidential primary front-loading and the impact of the proposed western regional primary, *Political Science and Politics*, XLI, (1), 123–128.

Sabato, Larry J., 1981, *The Rise of Political Consultants: New Ways of Winning Elections*, Basic Books, New York.

Sabato, Larry J., 1989, *Campaigns and Elections*, Scott, Foresman and Company, Glenview IL, Boston and London.

Salmon, Christian, 2007, *Storytelling, la machine à fabriquer des histoires et à formatter les esprits*, La Découverte, Paris.

Salmore, Barbara G. and Salmore Stephen A., 1989, *Candidates, Parties and Campaigns. Electoral Politics in America*, CQ Press, Washington, DC, second edition.

Sanders, Karen, 2009, *Communicating Politics in The Twenty-First Century*, Palgrave Macmillan, Basingstoke.

Scammell, Margaret, 1995, *Designer Politics, How Elections are Won*, St. Martin's Press, London.

Schroeder, Alan, 2000, *Presidential Debates, Forty Years of High-Risk TV*, Columbia University Press, New York.

Semiatin, Richard J. (ed.), 2008, *Campaigns on the Cutting Edge*, CQ Press, Washington, DC.

Seymour-Ure, C., 1974, *The Political Impact of Mass Media*, Constable, London.

Seymour-Ure, C., 1968, *The Press, Politics and the Public*, Methuen, London.

Sfez, Lucien, 1993, *Dictionnaire critique de la Communication*, PUF, Paris.

Shaw, Catherine, 2004, *The Campaign Manager*, Westview Press, Boulder, CO, third edition.

Sheckels, Theodore F. (ed.), 2009, *Cracked but Not Shattered, Hillary Rodham Clinton's Unsuccessful Campaign for the Presidency*, Lexington Books, Lanham, MD.

Shea, Daniel M. and Burton, Michael John, 2006, *Campaign Craft (The Strategies, Tactics, and Art of Political Campaign Management*, Praeger, New York, third edition.

Steger, W.P., Kelly, S.Q., and Wrighton, J.M., 2006, *Campaigns and Political Marketing*, Haworth Press, Philadelphia.

Strömbäck, Jesper, 2009, Selective professionalisation of political campaigning: a test of the party-centred theory of professionalised campaigning in the context of the 2006 Swedish election, *Political Studies*, 57 (1), 95–116.

Torre, Carlos, de la and Conaghan, Catherine, The hybrid campaign tradition and modernity in Ecuador's 2006 presidential election, *The International Journal of Press/Politics*, 14, 335–352.

Trent, Judith S. and Friedenberg, Robert V., 2008, *Political Campaign Communication, Principles and Practises*, Rowman and Littlefield Publishers, Lanham, MD, sixth edition.

Tuman, Joseph, S., 2008, *Political Communication in American Campaigns*, Sage, London.

Vavrek, Lynn, 2009, *The Message Matters, The Economy and Presidential Campaigns*, Princeton University Press, Princeton, NJ.

Walch, James, 1999, *In the Net (An Internet guide for Activists)*, Zed Bodes, London and New York.

Waller, Robert,1988, *Moulding Political Opinion*, Croom Helm, London.

Wayne, Stephen J., 2008, *The Road to the White House, 2008*, Wadsworth Publishing, Belmont, CA, eighth edition.

West, Darrell M., 2010, *Air Wars: Television Advertising in Election Campaigns, 1952–1992*, Congressional Quarterly Press, Washington, DC, fifth edition.

Williams, Andrew Paul and Tedesco, John. C., 2006, *The Internet Election: Perspectives on The Web in Campaign 2004*, Rowman and Littlefield Publishers, Lanham, MD.

Worcester, R. and Harrop, M.,1982, *Political Communications: The General Election Campaign of 1979*, George Allen and Unwin, London.

Wring, Dominic, 2005, *The Politics of Marketing the Labour Party*, Palgrave, London.

Wring, Dominic, Green, Jane, Mortimore, Roger and Atkinson, Simon, 2007, *Political Communications, The General Election Campaign of 2005*, Palgrave, London.

Index

abstentionists, voting 46, 77, 148, 225, 233

activists, political 9, 28n, 69n–70n, 83, 85, 88, 105, 150, 157n, 168, 179, 184, 185, 186, 187, 212, 217n
  campaign material 63, 106, 107, 108, 112n
  and canvassing 95, 106, 108, 150–1, 154
  and central campaign organization 162, 183
  demotivation of 129, 211
  and direct marketing 149, 150, 154
  and fundraising 147
  and mass media 63, 162, 166, 168, 169, 170, 213, 214
  impact of professionalism 213, 215
  at local level 40, 41, 95, 129, 146, 166, 213, 214, 216, 224, 228, 233
  mobilization of 59, 63, 110, 162
  networks of 40, 41, 95, 150, 153, 212, 213, 216, 225
  politicians and 57, 85, 88, 99, 105, 135, 181, 183, 196, 215, 216, 225, 228, 229
  training of 95, 149, 213
  see also sympathizers, volunteers

advertising and political marketing 2, 35–7, 38, 65, 67, 99, 110, 183, 190, 193, 194, 196, 197, 209, 216
  billboard advertising 107–10, 245
  commercial and political compared 10, 13, 35–6, 199
  Internet marketing 63, 230
  in the press 62, 64, 102, 103
  on TV 13, 15, 16, 20, 58, 59, 63, 64, 123, 130, 199, 215
  see also negative commercials, political commercials, political marketing

advertising manager 200, 202–3

agenda setting 62, 65, 66, 102, 115–16, 123, 130, 140, 199

Agnew, Spiro 16–17

Ailes, Roger 15

Alfonsín, Raúl 210

America Coming Together 25

American Political Consultants Association 10

analysis of information see under tools

Anderson, John B 19

Araujo, Angelica 173

Arias, President Oscar 49

Campaign Communication and Political Marketing, First Edition. Philippe J. Maarek.
© 2011 Philippe J. Maarek. Published 2011 by Blackwell Publishing Ltd.

Aubry, Martine 120
Audacity of Hope, The 105
audiovisual media and tools 91, 113,
    114ff, 230
    and decline of political parties 134–5
    delayed impact 115–16
    and direct marketing 91, 152ff
    and Internet 169
    media training 118–23
    presentation 119
    problems of access to 124–5
    and political communication 123ff,
        135
Aznar, José María 68n

Bachelet, President Michelle 49
ballots 8, 73, 77, 79, 81, 113, 222
bandwagon, political 84, 85
Barak, Ehud 210
barometers, political 78–9
Bentsen, Lloyd 19
Berlusconi, Silvio 1, 119, 234
Bernays, Edward 208
Biden, Joe 18, 19, 49
bidirectionality of political
        communication 61, 141
    Internet and 160, 162, 169
    re-establishing 148ff
    voters and 150, 151
Bin Laden, Osama 20
Bipartisan Campaign Reform Act (BCRA)
        (2002) 23, 190
    Article 527 21, 23–5
Blair, Tony 68n, 71n, 209
blogging 64, 158, 160, 162–3, 164, 165, 169,
        170, 171, 179, 197, 207, 232, 245
    activists 168, 170
    "blogosphere" 72
    Howard Dean 25–6, 192
    party 25–6, 159, 166, 167, 168, 169,
        170–2
Bloomberg, Michael 20–1
Blum, Leon 47
Brazil 110, 114, 125
Brock, Senator Bill 145
Brown, Gordon 114
Bruni-Sarkozy, Carla 103, 134

"Buckley v Valeo" (Supreme Court
    ruling) 20, 190
Bush, President George H.W. 18, 19, 21, 22,
    38, 59, 89n, 118, 126
Bush, President George W. 21, 38, 48, 59,
    99, 112n, 138n, 139n, 163, 209,
    Appendix 1
    campaign style 18, 25, 69n, 126, 167
    elections 9, 19, 28n, 80, 114, 127, 161,
        195, 233
    527 Group and 22, 23, 131

Cahill, Mary Beth 183
Cameron, David 114
campaign: 3, 64, 190
    and activists/volunteers 215–16
    administration 203–8
    aggressiveness of campaigns 21–2
    audiovisual media 124ff7
    campaign costs 1, 20–1, 67, 84, 85, 94,
        130, 148–9
    campaign headquarters 55, 110, 155, 168,
        179, 186–9, 205, 206
    campaign organization 56, 59, 106, 142,
        146, 147, 162, 169, 179, 182, 183,
        185, 188, 189, 196, 198, 205–6,
        208, 223
    campaign design and set-up 41, 47, 72,
        181–4
    campaign plan and objectives 3, 55–6,
        75–6
    coherence and continuity 37, 198–9
    communications 144, 146
    conquest campaign 55, 133, 172
    contact with voters 94ff
    co-ordinating local and national
        campaigns 222
    effective communication 37–8, 59
    effects of failure 35
    e-Marketing 170
    field and context analysis 40–2
    field organization of campaign 211ff
    finance 190ff, 194–5
    goals 57, 74, 233
    grassroots campaigning 94–5
    images and themes 47ff
    internal communication 169, 188, 216

campaign: (*cont'd*)
  and the Internet 20, 25–6, 63, 158ff, 166ff
  late starts 57, 58, 59, 69
  legal aspects 21–2, 195–6, 204–5
  literature 88, 106–10, 168, 198–9, 207
  local campaigning 94, 95, 199, 206, 213, 220ff
  "low blows" 22
  management style 184–7
  and the media 27, 55, 59, 60ff, 64, 66–7, 99, 100, 101ff, 113ff, 123ff, 141, 149ff, 155, 158, 168, 171, 200ff, 229, 244
  need for specific advantage 38, 41
  negative messages 165, 202
  and opposition campaigns 52, 72, 198, 207
  and past campaigns 37–8, 76–7
  psycho-sociological handicaps 180
  public relations officer 200, 201
  reaction to campaigns 60–1
  "road crew" 205–6
  security of candidates 206–7
  speeches 199
  staff and officers 180, 181, 183, 188, 196ff, 203, 205, 207, 212ff, 217n
  storytelling and campaigns 26–6
  strategies 37, 38–9, 40ff, 102, 103
  structure of a campaign 181ff
  style of campaign 21–2, 54–5, 184–6, 200, 201–2
  synergies 22
  targeting audiences 46, 63, 64, 65, 75, 78, 79, 88, 94
  task division types 184–6
  themes and issues 17–18, 51–2, 53–4, 63, 87, 233
    simplification of themes 17–18, 131, 135
    determining themes 51ff, 73
  timetable 55–7, 58–9, 74
  tone of the campaign 54–5
  trial campaign 55–8, 74
  types of campaign 58–9
  see also activists, audiovisual media, Bipartisan Campaign Reform Act, canvassing, consultants, direct mail, funding, local campaigns, opinion polls, political commercials, political communication, political marketing, primaries, elections – presidential, televised debates, television, tools, volunteers
campaign manager 180, 181–3, 185, 186, functions of 182, 207
campaign treasurer 145, 181, 192, 193, 194, 195, 196, 203–4
Campbell, Alistair 71n, 209
candidates 88, 93
  benefits of party support 212, 222–3
  "cabinet" 52, 181–2
  canvassing 95–6, 227
  incumbents and new candidates compared 88, 180, 188
  independent 49, 124, 125, 193, 195, 211, 212, 214
    see also Ross Perot
  marginal 125, 165, 211
  meeting voters 95, 96, 227, 228
  physical appearance 12, 13, 116–17, 119, 120, 122, 127
  transplanted 225
  see also campaigns, local campaigns, media, televised debates, televised newscasts, television
canvassing 94–6, 227–8
Carter, Amy 19
Carter, President Jimmy 16, 19, 20, 30n, 58, 132, 137n, 218n
Carville, James 29n, 132, 209, 210
Castellanos, Alex 29n
caucuses 8, 9
CBS 15, 123
Celebrity (campaign ad) 23
cell phones 163, 164, 171, 173
charisma, political 69, 117, 135, 181, 208, 210, 212, 222, 224, 231
Chatel, Luc 138n
Chávez, Hugo 70n
"Checkers Speech" 12–13, 26
Cheney, Dick 19
Chile 49, 110
Chinchilla, President Laura 49
Chirac, President Jacques 66, 68n, 70n, 111n, 112n, 136n, 171
Citizens United v Federal Election Commission (Supreme Court ruling, Jan 2010) 21, 25, 130, 190, 195

Clark, General Wesley 51
Clegg, Nick 114
Clinton, Hillary 29n, 79, 89n, 111n, 120,
    132, 134, 137n, 217n
    campaign 21, 23, 30n, 57, 117, 139n,
        183, 216
Clinton, President Bill 20, 21, 22, 29n, 37,
    38, 54, 69n, 89n, 123, 124, 132, 133,
    134, 139n, 209, 218
    campaign 9, 17–18, 19, 28n, 46, 58, 68n,
        118, 127, 137n, 145, 153, 190, 217n
Cohn-Bendit, Daniel 41
Collor, Fernando 114
commercial and political marketing
    compared 33ff
Commission on Presidential Debates
    124, 125
Communication Act 1934 124
    Section 315 21, 29n, 130, 132
    impact upon campaigning 22–3
Conseil Supérieur de l'Audiovisuel
    (CSA) 67, 124, 196
consultants 38, 40, 52, 77, 95, 180,
    218n, 233
    and campaigning 25, 50, 53, 58–9, 63, 65,
        67, 75, 85, 89, 118, 120, 121–2, 130,
        135, 174n, 185–7, 208–11, 224
    drawbacks of using 180, 210–11, 234
    expertise 189, 196, 209, 213
    symbolic value of 209–10
    utility of 208
Coolidge, Calvin 9, 208
Costa Rica 49
Couric, Katie 129
Cronkite, Walter 137n

"Daisy Spot" 14–15, 22, 29n
DailyMotion 163
Davies, John W. 9
Davis, Rick 183
de Gaulle, President Charles 41, 68n
Dean, Howard 25, 26, 51, 69n, 158
    Internet campaign 169, 174n, 183, 190,
        217n
DeGeneres, Ellen 124, 133, 134
Democratic Party 10, 12, 25, 26, 190, 211
"Democrats for Reagan" political campaign
    ad 132

Désirs d'Avenir (French political
    blog) 26, 169
Dewey, Thomas E 28n, 79, 84
direct contact see under meetings
direct mail 11, 56, 141ff, 190
direct marketing 94, 148ff
    bidirectionality of 141ff
    and campaign 144
    disadvantages of 145–8
    and fundraising 145, 146
    and political communication 143,
        144, 156
    traditional media 141, 158, 171
"Disclose Act" (June 2010) 21
Dole, Bob 17, 18, 20, 68n, 118
donations 21, 23, 63, 85, 95, 144,
    145, 152, 167, 169, 173, 192,
    195, 204
Doyle, Patti Solis 188
Dukakis, Michael 19, 22, 218n
Duke, David 119

Edwards, John 19, 30n
"Eisenhower answers America" 12
Eisenhower, Mamie 26
Eisenhower, President Dwight D.
    1952 campaign of 2, 11, 12, 28n, 114,
        142, 157n
    and development of political
        marketing 11, 118, 208
elections: 28, 35, 39, 40, 41, 42, 47, 50, 55,
    58, 59, 60, 72, 75, 109, 110, 113–14,
    143, 153, 155
    history 9–10
    and the Internet 166ff
    and opinion polls 84
    Presidential elections 11, 14, 20, 21,
        22, 27
    1948 14, 28n, 79, 84, 85
    1952 2, 11–13, 26, 118, 144
    1956 13
    1960 13–14, 15, 19, 26, 28, 82, 113, 118,
        125, 199, 233
    1964 14–15, 22, 145, 146, 193
    1968 15, 68n, 207
    1972 15, 16, 214
    1976 16–17, 18, 19, 22, 41, 58,
        139n, 228

elections: (*cont'd*)
  1980 18, 19, 54, 87, 99, 128
  1984 19, 20, 51, 123
  1988 19, 22, 38, 218n
  1992 19, 20, 21, 22, 28n, 38, 41, 49, 54,
    58, 59, 89n, 118, 124, 133, 137n,
    138n, 190, 195, 209, 214
  1996 11, 19, 25, 41, 68n, 118, 145, 153
  2000 19, 22, 25, 37, 53, 99, 112n,
    161, 233
  2004 19, 21, 23, 25, 26, 48, 59, 69n, 84,
    114, 127, 131, 138n, 163, 169, 217n,
    221, 233
  2008 19, 20, 21, 23, 25, 26–7, 46, 57, 105,
    11n, 117, 120, 129, 130, 132, 133,
    145, 158, 163, 165, 170, 173, 190,
    195, 197, 214, 215
  see also campaigns, local campaigns,
    rallies, individual candidates
electoral geography 226–7
electorate 52, 76, 81, 82
  female candidates 82
  influencing 18, 42, 84, 105
  local campaigns 95
  and minority candidates 82
  non-receipt of messages 60
  and political marketing 42, 87
  political affinities 45, 96
  targeting 42–7, 226–7
  see also image, opinion polls
electronic media *see* Internet
Ellen DeGeneres Show 20, 124, 133, 134
e-Marketing 170
"end of ideology" 54
environmentalist parties 69n, 80, 125
"Equal Time Rule" 67, 124, 125
Estrosi, Christian 173
extremists 80, 82, 155

Facebook 25, 26, 72, 163
Fabius, Laurent 136n
Faith of My Fathers (McCain) 112n
Fäldin, Thorbjörn 51
Falwell, Jerry 152–3
far right parties, support for 80, 82, 89n
Federal Communication Commission
    (FCC) 25, 67, 124, 130, 190, 196

Federal Elections Commission 21, 25, 166,
    190, 218n, Appendix 2
  *see also Citizens United v Federal Election
    Commission*
Federal Election Campaign Act (FECA)
    1971 29n
feedback and communication process 161
Ferraro, Geraldine 19, 120
Fey, Tina 134, 172
field analysis 39, 40–1, 42, 73, 144, 225
field co-ordinator, campaign 181, 183–4,
    185, 186, 187, 196, 215
Figueroa, Temo 215
financing of campaigns *see* under
    campaigns
Finkelstein, Arthur 210
"527 Groups" 23, 25, 30n, 131
flyers, as political marketing tool 106, 229
Ford, President Gerald 16–17, 19, 41, 139n,
    218n
forums, Internet 162, 163, 166
Fox, Michael J. 134
France 79, 80, 81, 107, 111n, 113, 134, 138n,
    171, 173n, 174n, 194, 195, 209, 235
  media in 10, 27, 30n, 64, 65, 66, 67, 136n,
    101, 102, 105, 112, 120, 124, 136n,
    196
  political campaigning in 30n, 37, 54, 67,
    68n, 70n, 109, 111n, 112n, 113, 124,
    125, 137n, 157n, 183
  surveys in 83, 84, 85, 89n, 90, 148
  2007 Presidential election 30n, 49, 53,
    129, 158, 169, 193, 197
  see also Sarkozy
fringe parties 217n–18n, 233, 235
Fujimori, President Alberto 114, 135,
    139n, 214
fundraising 20–1, 62, 96–7, 172, 190, 192–3,
    194, 195ff, 203–4

Gandhi, Rajiv 207
gender and political message 45, 49, 82
geodemographics 40
Germany, Federal Republic of 68n, 80, 193
Giscard d'Estaing, President Valéry 51, 69n,
    137n
Glenn, John 51

Global Village 233
Godard, Jean-Luc and text as message 16
Godwin, R. Kenneth 156
Going Rogue (Palin) 105
Goldwater, Senator Barry 14, 15, 145, 193
Gorbachev, Michael 119
Gore, Al 19, 22, 37 53, 99
grassroots campaigning 95–6, 111n
Guaino, Henri 199

Hall, Arsenio 133, 134
Hilton, Paris 23
"horse race" story 86, 125, 132
"How's that General?" 13
Hughes, Chris 26

"iconomorphology" 117
Iliescu, Ion 114
"image making" by politician 2, 3, 16, 39,
    40, 41, 48, 49, 53, 55, 56, 62, 63, 115,
    118, 173, 230
  image building 26, 27, 47, 54, 64, 89,
    134, 236
  incompatible images 50, 51, 131
  maintaining image 11, 50, 58
  negative image 14, 15, 22, 23, 127, 128–9
  perception of image 48, 50, 119, 120,
    122, 189
industrialists and political campaigning
    211, 214
Information Watch (by campaign staff) 39,
    41, 172, 218n
Internet 158ff, 166, 171, 173n, 208, 216,
    230, 231
  access to Internet 24, 165, 233
  bidirectionality of 162
  and campaigning 25, 63, 72, 131, 155,
    166ff, 197
  feedback from 161
  and fundraising 172, 190–1
  growth of 10–11, 131, 140
  interactivity 161–3
  and internal campaign
    communication 169
  Internet forums 162, 163
  maintaining "buzz" 170
  multiple aspects 159–61

as rumor mill 25, 120, 159, 171, 172, 198
  shift from "pull" to "push" media 141,
    158, 165, 172, 173
  and targeting 161
  2004 Presidential campaign and 169
  as "virtual conduit" 164–5
  web broadcasting 163
  see also blogs, opinion polls and surveys,
    social networks
interviews 20, 43, 66, 78, 79, 103, 123, 133,
    201, 203
  of voters 80, 82, 83, 89n–90n, 148, 167
Intranet 63, 169, 188, 189, 206, 207
Iowa Caucus 9, 22, 58
iPhone 71n, 103, 164, 173
Iraq 1

Jaurès, Jean 47
"Jennifer's Ear" campaign ad (UK) 132,
    139n
Johnson, President Lyndon B. 14–15
Jordan, Jim 183
Jospin, Lionel 37, 68n, 70n, 112n, 120, 217n
journalists 158
  influence of 43
  and politicians 97, 103–4, 111n, 112n,
    126, 129, 132, 203
  and press attaché 201–2
  reinterpreting televised debates 135
  and theatricalization of politics 129

Kayden, Xandra 188
Kemp, Jack 19
Kennedy, Jackie 26
Kennedy, John Fitzgerald 28n, 115, 116,
    118, 199
  election campaign 13–14, 19, 82, 122,
    131, 137n, 218n, 233
  see also Nixon-Kennedy debate
Kennedy, Robert F. 207
Kennedy, Senator Edward 22, 30n, 132
Kerry, John 19, 21, 23, 48, 59, 114, 127, 131,
    138n, 183, Appendix 1
Ketchum, Carlton 193
King, Larry 123
Klapper, Joseph 43
Kohl, Helmut 68n, 113

Lazarfeld, Paul 61
leaflet distribution 56, 64, 95, 120, 106, 168,
      179, 189, 198, 213, 223, 227, 229
leftist parties 80
Lehman Brothers 38
Lehrman, Lewis 20
Leno, Jay 20, 65, 133
Leotard, François 118–19
Letterman, David 132, 133
Lieberman, Joe 19
LinkedIn 163
lobbies 52, 140, 153, 170–2, 235
local campaigns and politics 8, 11, 35, 73,
      94, 95, 199, 206, 213, 220ff, 231n
   analytical tools 72ff, 225–6
   area analysis 225
   canvassing 227–8
   communication methods 227ff
   contact with local population 227,
      229–30, 231
   elections 18, 20, 35, 53, 73, 116–17
   impact of mass media 221–2
   loss of local autonomy 146, 223, 224
   and national dimension 221ff
   office hours and campaigning 229
   polling stations 226–7
   printed materials 229
   replacement of "political barons" 221
   synergy 222, 223–4, 233
   and voters 95
   see also Press
local relays 57, 111n, 146, 212, 216
Long, Senator Huey 10
Louis XIV of France 2
Lucey, Patrick Joseph 19
Lula, Inácio 114

Machiavelli, Niccolò 2
Madison Avenue and political
      campaigns 210
marginal parties 80, 211
   on the Internet 170–2
marketing and publicity 33–5
   marketing tools 91, 93ff, 101, 213,
      233, 140
   political and commercial compared
      33ff, 70n
Mazowiecki, Tadeusz 214

McCain, John 20, 114, 167, 217n
   Presidential campaigns 9, 161
   2008 campaign 19, 21, 23, 28n, 38, 65–6,
      68n, 112n, 130, 132, 133, 139n,
      183, 190
   choice of Sarah Palin 18, 37, 46, 49,
      120, 129
McGovern, Senator George 16, 214
McLuhan, Marshall 60, 233
media 1, 27, 93ff, 115, 136n, 233
   agenda setting of mass media 70n,
      115–16, 136n, 199
   choice of media 63–4
   impact on activists 213–15
   media and message 62–3
   media priority 62
   media training of candidates 118–23,
      135, 136n
   media, publicity and special contacts 100
   politicians and 52
   and quest for speed 63
   selection of appropriate media 62
   and selectivity of perception 60
   significance of local media 200, 213,
      227, 230
   and simplification of message 12,
      121, 234
   synergy seeking among channels 65–6
   target types and distribution 12, 45, 63,
      64, 65, 66–7, 105, 106, 107, 109, 131,
      133, 227, 229
   types of 63
   see also activists, audiovisual media,
      Internet, radio, television
media manager 202–3
media stars and political campaigning 214
meetings 8, 14, 18, 44, 60, 63, 64, 99, 100,
      104, 128, 133, 144, 151, 152, 154,
      190, 199, 203, 207, 213
   closed meetings 94, 97, 154, 191, 226
   going through crowds 99, 100
   group meetings 96
   impact of mass media on political
      parties 214
   and local campaigns 222, 224, 230, 233
   meetings and targeting 98
   open meetings 87, 97–8, 110, 122, 167
   publicizing of special contacts 100

substitutes for 96ff
and targeting 98
see also Internet
Meetup.com 25, 169
Merkel, Chancellor Angela 47, 103, 113, 120
Mitterrand, President François 41, 54, 69n,
    70n, 137n, 139n, 157n, 208
mobility index 226
Mondale, Walter 17, 19, 124
Moral Majority 140, 153
morphopsychology of politicians 60
Morris, Dick 46–7
MoveOn.org 163
MySpace 25, 26, 72, 163

Nader, Ralph 41
Napolitan, Joe 67
negative commercials 12, 22, 131–2
Nelson, Terry 183
Netanyahu, Benjamin 210
Netherlands 83
New Hampshire primary 8, 9, 22, 58, 228
Nixon, President Richard M. 11, 198
    Presidential election campaigns 12–14,
       15, 19, 115, 116, 122, 214, 233
    Checkers Speech 12–13, 26
Nixon-Kennedy debates 13–14, 16, 18, 28,
    28n, 113, 114, 122, 125

Obama, Barack 1, 19, 20, 21, 23, 25–6, 79,
    82, 103, 111n, 120, 132, 139n, 174n
    campaign strategy 18
    fundraising 192
    Internet campaign 25–6, 165, 170, 173
    pre-election campaigns 57
    presidential campaign 26–7, 29n, 30n,
       49, 71n, 111n, 114, 130, 133, 134,
       138n, 139n, 145, 158, 163, 183, 190,
       214, 215, 217n
    writings 26, 27, 105, 112n
Obama's Baby 165
Obama girl (parody) 165, 170, 174n
Obama, Michelle 20, 103, 134
opinion polls and surveys 12, 45, 56, 70n,
    73, 77ff, 89n, 90n
    costs 83–4
    determining issues 12, 52
    dictatorship of the survey 86–7

different types of poll 42, 74, 78–9
impact of 84, 85–7
interviews 79, 81–1
non-directive focus groups 79
and objective setting 75–6
as part of the media 86
political and consumer compared 77
representativeness of 80
structural lack of reliability 79, 81, 82,
    83, 87
target audiences 42
and targeting 42ff
opinion relays 43, 83
opposition research 72, 198
Ottinger, Richard 50
"Ottinger Syndrome" 50, 51, 131

Palin, Sarah 105, 120, 134, 136n, 172, 197
    selection as McCain's running mate 18,
       37, 46, 49, 129
    debates 18, 19
Palme, Prime Minister Olof 51
party politics 231
    marginal parties 80, 165, 170, 171
    usefulness of 216
    weakening of bonds 28n, 134–5, 155, 215
    and the web 166
Passed Over (campaign ad) 23, 30n
Pecrese, Valerie 173
"peoplolisation" 136, 233
Perot, Ross 19, 20, 21, 41, 49, 84, 118, 137n,
    138n, 195, 214, 218n
Peru 114, 214
petition campaigns 25, 26, 96, 97, 140, 169,
    201, 213
    see also Communication Act 1934
phone marketing as political campaign
    tool 84, 87, 141, 160, 173, 191,
    213, 231
    effectiveness of 80, 88, 149
    personalizing communication 148–9
    and re-establishing bi-directionality
       148–52
podcasts 163–4, 174n
political advertising:
    commercials 12–13, 14, 15, 16, 18, 19–20,
       21, 27, 28n, 36, 67n, 109, 129, 130–2,
       194, 196, 199, 207

political advertising: (*cont'd*)
  internet 165
  negative 13n, 22, 23, 25, 132
  spots 10, 11, 12, 13, 16, 19, 20, 28n, 29n,
    58, 59, 63, 64, 99, 109, 123, 124, 130,
    132, 137n, 163, 174n, 190n, 192, 193,
    194, 196, 207, 209, 218n
  vapor ads 139n
  see also Daisy spot, Passed Over spot,
    Willie Horton spot
Political Broadcast Committee UK 196
political communication 35ff
  and audiovisual media 123ff
  conquest communication 45, 46, 63,
    95, 102
  effectiveness of various formats 172
  government regulation of 27
  information 35, 74ff
  infrastructure 179
  and Internet 165ff, 231
  loss of effectiveness 60
  maintenance communication 45, 46,
    47, 95
  propaganda 35, 68n
  segmenting the population 43–7
  selectivity of perception 60–1
  and targeting 42ff
  ways of improving communication 61–2
  see also campaigns, local campaigns,
    media, phone marketing, political
    marketing
"political correctness" 82
political debate 1–2, 16
political information provision 2
"Political Information System", US 87
political marketing 1–2, 26, 33, 35, 38, 94ff,
    232ff
  audiovisual marketing 91
  benefits of 53–4
  and campaign themes 52
  coherence 37, 225
  and commoditization of politicians 34
  cost of 67
  distrust of 2–3
  foundations 2, 11–27
  fragmentation of market 232
  main stages of 39

marketing and voter participation 233
and means of communication 91
methods adopted 35
negative marketing 18–19, 23
originality of 33
and past campaigns 76–7
and political discourse 1, 2, 118, 135, 233
and primaries 8
re-examination of earlier campaigns
    37–8, 181
researching targets 42ff
rules of conduct 37–8
targets 46
short-termism 233
strategies 2, 42
unidirectional tools 101
and voter participation 155, 227
see also advertising, blogs, campaigning,
    direct marketing, 527 Groups,
    Internet, media, opinion polls,
    opinion relays, political
    communication, politicians
politicians
  and acquiring information 35, 73, 77–8,
    87–8
  and activists 150, 215
  and advisors 52, 53, 85, 86, 122, 124, 127,
    179, 180, 181, 182, 208, 211
  autonomy of 51, 52, 108, 191, 223, 224
  billboard advertising 107–8, 112n
  campaign strategies 41, 58, 59, 179ff
  campaign themes 51ff, 76, 79, 144ff
  candidacy statements 65
  charisma 134–5
  coherence of campaign 37–8
  and communication advisor 1, 2, 50, 103,
    118, 119, 120, 121, 132, 208, 209
  creating and maintaining image 47–8,
    51, 55
  differentiation from other candidates
    38, 57
  and electoral system 58
  engaging with voters 94ff, 99, 100, 141,
    147, 151, 152, 153, 154, 160, 162,
    165, 166, 171, 199, 221
  feedback 59, 95
  framework 49ff

and fundraising 21, 145, 146, 155, 172, 191–6, 204
gender 82, 120
gestures, effect of 117
image 2, 27, 39, 41, 48, 49, 50, 51, 55, 62, 63, 64, 115, 120
incoming candidates 88, 180, 225
incumbents 37, 38, 88, 121, 143, 180–1, 201, 236
and indirect political broadcasts 132, 133
and the Internet 163, 164ff, 173, 231, 232, 235
and journalists 43, 97, 102, 103, 104, 129
marketing advisers 65, 72, 75
and media 52, 60, 61, 65, 66, 67, 86, 97, 103, 115, 118, 123ff, 130, 132, 134, 135, 135, 200, 214, 221, 231
local politics 222–31
 see also local politics
media training 118–23, 135, 137n
modifying objectives 76
non-verbal communication 115, 116–18, 120, 122, 127, 136n
and opinion polls 81, 83, 84, 85, 87
and parties 214
personalizing effect 26–7, 134, 206ff, 233, 234
physical appearance 116, 119, 120, 230
playing to camera 121–2
and political advisors 49, 50, 53, 83
political commercials 19–20
"political outsiders" 9, 10, 41, 125, 210, 211
and the press 101ff
prestigious supporters 94
private life of 22, 103, 129, 132, 133–4, 136
professionalization 67
relations with adversaries 52, 109, 116, 131
security considerations 38, 100
spheres of activity 220
and surveys 52
and telephone chains 150
and television 11, 13, 18, 20, 28, 99, 118–23, 125ff
traveling 212–13

USP 48, 49
and voters 35, 45–6, 60, 63, 81, 93, 94–7, 98, 108, 105, 114, 132, 190, 199–200, 218n, 222, 227, 235
vocal attributes 117
wealthy donors 94
see also audiovisual media, campaign manager, candidates, consultants, direct mail, Internet, meetings, opinion polls, Ottinger Syndrome, political marketing, primaries, rallies, televised debates
polling station 80, 226
posters and billboard advertising 36, 60, 69n, 107–10, 212
 and Internet 25
 voluntary/unauthorized posters 109–10, 111n, 212
press attaché 198, 200, 201–2, 203
Press, printed matter and political communication: 115
 free newspapers 101, 105
 internal printed matter 106–7
 mass-market magazines 103
 non-partisan 101, 103–4
 and other media 102
 partisan 102, 104–5
 and political commitment 212, 223
 quality of communication 101–2
 tracts 102, 105, 141
 see also Internet
primaries 8, 9, 28n, 228
 as unidirectional tool 101ff
proximity index 226
pseudo-event 128, 201
public opinion polls *see* opinion polls
public relations, politicians and 3, 8, 9, 13, 14, 63, 64, 104, 196, 200
public relations officer 15, 16, 104, 200, 201

Quayle, Dan 19

Radio Act 1927 124
radio and political campaigning 10, 27, 62, 63, 64, 114, 117, 124, 152, 163, 164
 direct marketing 153, 199, 202, 207, 230
 political commercials 130

rallies 98–9, 110
  manipulation of media 99
  volunteers and 215
Rather, Dan 123, 137n
Reagan, President Ronald 41, 119, 124
  Presidential election 17, 19, 29n, 30n, 54,
      68n, 87, 114, 124, 137n
  and use of TV 16, 99, 116, 124, 128, 132
Reeves Jr, Thomas Rosser 11–12
Reinsch, Leonard 13
reporters *see* journalists
Republican Party, US 9, 12, 26, 41, 47, 129,
      145, 191, 193, 211
  and co-ordination of local
      campaigns 223
Robbins, Tim 134
Robertson, Pat 153
Rockefeller, Nelson 20
Romania 1, 114
Roosevelt, President Franklin D. 10
Rospars, Joe 26
Ross Perot Reform Party 168
Rove, Karl 209
Royal, Ségolène 120–1
  electoral campaign 26, 49, 53, 69n, 129,
      138n, 158–9, 169, 183, 197, 217

Salinger, Pierre 13
Sarkozy, President Nicolas 1, 103
  and triangulation 47
  2007 election 26, 27, 30n, 69n, 99, 128–9,
      199, 218n
  use of Internet 26, 99, 164, 174n, 218n
Schroeder, Gerhard 113
Schwartz, Tony 15
Schwarzenegger, Arnold 20, 65, 133, 225
scout (political) 206
Séguéla, Jacques 209
700 Club 153
Shays v FEC 244, 245
simplification of political themes 17–18,
      48, 49, 53–4, 234
Skype 160, 164, 180
SMS 163, 173
social networks on Internet and political
      campaigns 158, 168, 170
social non-participants 155
Sorensen, Theodore (Ted) 28n, 199

soundbites, use of 123, 163
South Korea 173
Spain 68n, 101, 171
spam, political 166, 173, 174n, 218n
Spiral of silence theory 90n
Stassen, Harold 28n
steering issues, handling 129–30
Stephanopoulos, George 29n
Stevenson, Adlai 12
Stirn, Olivier 138n
Stockdale, James 19
Stoiber, Edmund 113
storytelling and campaigns 26–7
support committees 97
Switzerland 85
sympathizers, political 69n–70n, 110, 147,
      168, 185, 190, 211, 212, 213, 215,
      217n, 223, 224
  campaigning among 8, 41, 45, 46, 87,
      105, 193, 229
  communicating with and maintaining
      links 96, 98, 106, 153, 162, 166, 169,
      183–4
  exposure 60, 181
  and finance 41, 63, 85, 145, 192, 193
  local networks 41, 183–4, 189
  making use of 99, 104, 149, 151, 154, 179,
      196, 212
  and primaries 9, 214
  see also activists, volunteers

"tabloidization" 233
talk shows 20, 133
targets:
  abstentionists 225
  campaign targets 36, 40, 47, 65, 73, 75,
      96, 226
  communicating with 97, 98, 100, 105,
      106, 107, 109–10, 154, 191
  identifying 73, 74, 75
  Internet and 161–2, 170
  local targets 228, 229
  and marketing 155
  and the media 141ff
  objectives 75
  priority targets 56, 62
  researching 42ff, 65, 74, 75, 76
  segmenting population 44

TV broadcasts 12, 65–6, 131, 133, 134, 140
triangulation 47
types of target 42–3, 45, 46, 63, 184–5
voters 45, 46, 107, 154
Telecommunications Act 1996 140
"telephone chains" 150
telethon 152, 153, 157n, 170
"televangelists" 152–3, 157n
television 1, 10, 44, 60, 63, 64, 65, 78, 99, 100, 102, 11n, 113, 115, 230
domination of political marketing 18, 172, 214
impact of cable TV 131, 133, 233
indirect political programs 132–4
influence on politicians 116ff, 128–31
and media training of candidates 118–23, 135
and opinion polls 86
significance of close-ups 15, 117, 122
see also campaign, candidates, direct marketing, Internet, Nixon-Kennedy debate, political commercials, televised debate
televised debates 11–12, 14, 15, 18–19, 27–8, 113, 114, 124, 125–8, 130, 135, 137n, 138n
broadcast control 127–8
dealing with interruptions 126
decor 126
filming 126–7
editing techniques used 127
history of 13ff
negative impact 18–19
negotiating technical details 125–6
see also Nixon-Kennedy debate, political commercials
televised newscasts 12, 65, 86, 99, 115, 123, 124, 128–30, 132, 135, 158, 221, 228, 230
Thatcher, Prime Minister Margaret 54
Toledo, Alejandro 114
tools, informational and analytical 72ff
demands of activists and volunteers 88
different types of 76
direct mailing 88
feedback from rallies 87
general principles 73ff

and local campaigns 226
mail and phone calls 88
need for careful analysis 88
political debates 135
unidirectional 101
see also opinion polls
tracts, as political marketing tool 141
"triangulation" (political cross-targeting) 47
trinkets as campaigning material 110
Truman, President Harry S. 14, 84, 85
Truman-Dewey election opinion poll 79, 84
Twitter 25, 71n, 163, 173, 174n
Tyminski, Stanislaw 135

underdogs, political 84, 90n
unidirectional tools 101
Unique Selling Proposition (USP) 12, 17–18
and politician's image 48–9
and simplification of message 17, 53–4, 233
United Kingdom 27, 54, 65, 67, 79, 80, 89n, 101, 105, 113, 131–2, 138n, 139n, 156n, 228
United States: 3, 65, 67, 89n, 113, 125, 145, 146, 193, 195, 196, 228
development of political marketing 7, 10ff, 110

Vargas Llosa, Mário 214
Ventura, Jesse 168, 174n
Videos/DVDs and political marketing 63, 64, 114, 141, 152, 153–4, 163, 208
internal 153
external 153–4
and election meetings and rallies 87, 154
journalists and 135
online 163–4, 165, 167, 171, 197
Vietnam War 14, 22, 23
Viguerie, Richard A. 191
volunteers, political 69n–70n, 85, 88, 95, 146, 157n, 185, 186, 187, 207, 211, 212, 216, 232
and fly-posting political posters 109–10, 111n, 212
impact of professionalization 213, 215, 216, 233

volunteers, political (*cont'd*)
  in local campaigns 228
  training of 213
  see also activists, campaign, sympathizers
"Vote Different" political campaign ad 132
voters 8, 11, 13, 54, 69n, 76, 77, 80, 121, 145,
      155, 166, 233, 233, 235
  alienation of voters 233
  analysis of 39, 40
  and candidates' gender 49, 82
  direct contact with politicians 94–101
  floating or swing 45, 46, 54, 84, 85, 133, 134
  fringe votes 231–2, 233
  influencing 172
  Internet 63, 166, 170, 216
  and local campaigns 221, 226, 229, 230
  mapping of voter tendencies 58, 59,
      226–7
  and media exposure 60, 105–6, 113, 117,
      131, 132
  and opinion polls 45, 74, 80, 86, 87, 106
  political preference 226
  and politicians 9–10, 14, 28, 47, 52, 55,
      100, 101, 214, 221, 225, 227, 223
  reaction to politicians 18, 25, 35, 37, 38,
      49, 129, 222, 224, 228, 233
  segmentation 44–7
  shift in voting patterns 84, 233
  steadfast voters 45, 46
  undecided voters 83, 103, 107, 136, 173,
      229, 234

voter participation 225, 233
vulnerable voters 45, 46, 84
  see also abstentionists, electorate, Ottinger
      Syndrome, political communication,
      political marketing

Walesa, Lech 119, 139n, 214
Wallop, Malcolm 16
Watergate 29n, 72, 103, 198
Web 1.0 161–2, 166
Web 2.0 158, 162–5, 166, 197, 208, 232
  web broadcasting 163–4
web sites, use of 159, 174n, 207, 232
  campaign web sites 166–8
  political ads 170
  political web sites 165ff
  as provider of information 160, 161
web surfers 26, 131, 159, 163, 166,
      167, 170, 172
Williams, Maggie 183
"Willie Horton" spot 22
Winfrey, Oprah 111n, 124, 133
Wirthlin, Richard 87
Wright, Jeremiah 139n

"Yes we Can" campaign slogan
      49, 170
YouTube 25, 72, 163, 165, 170, 172, 174n,
      197, 232

Zapatero, José Luis 68n, 134